Application Service Providers (ASPs)

Addison-Wesley Information Technology Series
Capers Jones and David S. Linthicum, Consulting Editors

The information technology (IT) industry is in the public eye now more than ever before because of a number of major issues in which software technology and national policies are closely related. As the use of software expands, there is a continuing need for business and software professionals to stay current with the state of the art in software methodologies and technologies. The goal of the Addison-Wesley Information Technology Series is to cover any and all topics that affect the IT community: These books illustrate and explore how information technology can be aligned with business practices to achieve business goals and support business imperatives. Addison-Wesley has created this innovative series to empower you with the benefits of the industry experts' experience.

For more information point your browser to http://www.awl.com/cseng/series/it/

Sid Adelman, Larissa Terpeluk Moss, *Data Warehouse Project Management.* ISBN: 0-201-61635-1

Wayne Applehans, Alden Globe, and Greg Laugero, *Managing Knowledge: A Practical Web-Based Approach.* ISBN: 0-201-43315-X

Michael H. Brackett, *Data Resource Quality: Turning Bad Habits into Good Practices.* ISBN: 0-201-71306-3

Frank Coyle, *Wireless Web: A Manager's Guide.* ISBN: 0-201-72217-8

James Craig and Dawn Jutla, *e-Business Readiness: A Customer-Focused Framework.* ISBN: 0-201-71006-4

Gregory C. Dennis and James R. Rubin, *Mission-Critical Java™ Project Management: Business Strategies, Applications, and Development.* ISBN: 0-201-32573-X

Kevin Dick, *XML: A Manager's Guide.* ISBN: 0-201-43335-4

Jill Dyché, *e-Data: Turning Data into Information with Data Warehousing.* ISBN: 0-201-65780-5

Jill Dyché, *The CRM Handbook: A Business Guide to Customer Relationship Management.* ISBN: 0-201-73062-6

Patricia L. Ferdinandi, *A Requirements Pattern: Succeeding in the Internet Economy.* ISBN: 0-201-73826-0

Dr. Nick V. Flor, *Web Business Engineering: Using Offline Activites to Drive Internet Strategies.* ISBN: 0-201-60468-X

David Garmus and David Herron, *Function Point Analysis: Measurement Practices for Successful Software Projects.* ISBN: 0-201-69944-3

John Harney, *Application Service Providers (ASPs): A Manager's Guide.* ISBN: 0-201-72659-9

Capers Jones, *Software Assessments, Benchmarks, and Best Practices.* ISBN: 0-201-48542-7

Capers Jones, *The Year 2000 Software Problem: Quantifying the Costs and Assessing the Consequences.* ISBN: 0-201-30964-5

Ravi Kalakota and Marcia Robinson, *e-Business 2.0: Roadmap for Success.* ISBN: 0-201-72165-1

David S. Linthicum, *B2B Application Integration: e-Business-Enable Your Enterprise.* ISBN: 0-201-70936-8

Sergio Lozinsky, *Enterprise-Wide Software Solutions: Integration Strategies and Practices.* ISBN: 0-201-30971-8

Joanne Neidorf and Robin Neidorf, *e-Merchant: Retail Strategies for e-Commerce.* ISBN: 0-201-72169-4

Patrick O'Beirne, *Managing the Euro in Information Systems: Strategies for Successful Changeover.* ISBN: 0-201-60482-5

Bud Porter-Roth, *Request for Proposal: A Guide to Effective RFP Development,* ISBN: 0-201-77575-1

Mai-lan Tomsen, *Killer Content: Strategies for Web Content and E-Commerce.* ISBN: 0-201-65786-4

Karl E. Wiegers, *Peer Reviews in Software: A Practical Guide.* ISBN: 0-201-73485-0

Bill Wiley, *Essential System Requirements: A Practical Guide to Event-Driven Methods.* ISBN: 0-201-61606-8

Ralph R. Young, *Effective Requirements Practices.* ISBN: 0-201-70912-0

Bill Zoellick, *CyberRegs: A Business Guide to Web Property, Privacy, and Patents.* ISBN: 0-201-72230-5

Bill Zoellick, *Web Engagement: Connecting to Customers in e-Business.* ISBN: 0-201-65766-X

Application Service Providers (ASPs)

A Manager's Guide

John Harney

✦✦Addison-Wesley

Boston • San Francisco • New York • Toronto • Montreal
London • Munich • Paris • Madrid
Capetown • Sydney • Tokyo • Singapore • Mexico City

Many of the designations used by manufacturers and sellers to distinguish their products are claimed as trademarks. Where those designations appear in this book, and Addison-Wesley was aware of a trademark claim, the designations have been printed with initial capital letters or in all capitals.

The author and publisher have taken care in the preparation of this book, but make no expressed or implied warranty of any kind and assume no responsibility for errors or omissions. No liability is assumed for incidental or consequential damages in connection with or arising out of the use of the information or programs contained herein.

The publisher offers discounts on this book when ordered in quantity for special sales. For more information, please contact:

Pearson Education Corporate Sales Division
One Lake Street
Upper Saddle River, NJ 07458
(800) 382-3419
corpsales@pearsontechgroup.com

Visit AW on the Web: www.aw.com/cseng/

Library of Congress Cataloging-in-Publication Data

Harney, John (John Michael)
    Application service providers (ASPs) : a manager's guide / John Harney.
        p. cm. — (Addison-Wesley information technology series)
    Includes bibliographical references and index.
    ISBN 0-201-72659-9 (alk. paper)
    1. Application service providers. 2. Electronic commerce. 3. Business enterprises—Computer networks. I. Title. II. Series.

HF5548.32 .H369 2001
658.8'4—dc21   2001043110

ISBN 0-201-72659-9
Text printed on recycled paper
1 2 3 4 5 6 7 8 9 10—MA—0504030201
First printing, November 2001

In memory of my parents and for my brothers—Steve, Kevin, and Chris—with love

Contents

Chapter 6   VARIETIES OF ASP   79

Chapter 7   SECURITY ISSUES FOR ASPS   103

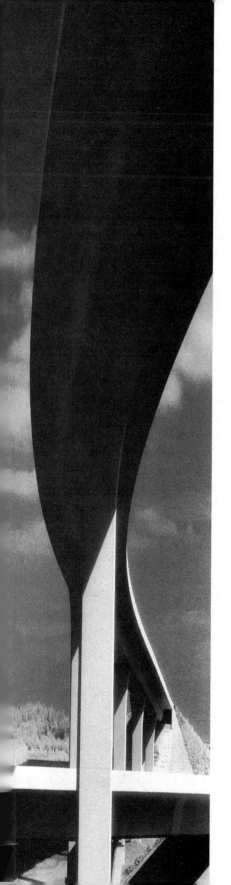

Preface

I first heard about application service providers (ASPs) about three years ago from Marty Gruhn at Summit Strategies. I think I was doing an article on e-business, and she suggested I look into the value proposition of what she called Internet application hosting. She was hot on IAH—one of the few people who really were—and thought it would dramatically change the face of corporate computing. I followed her advice, and found ASPs so compelling that I started researching and writing compulsively about any ASP-related operations. Then ASPs and ASP-wannabes started seeing my articles and, of all things, began calling *me* for advice. This was a wonderful thing because I actually got to visit some data centers and talk shop with the people in the trenches.

When I was an editor of several computing magazines, software companies would bring their new programs to the magazine offices and demonstrate them for me. That was a great part of the job because we would often actually brainstorm problems they were having like pricing strategies, the right target customer, competition, and so on. With ASP hosted applications, I could actually access the application right over my Internet connection—the "techies" just needed to give me a user ID. Later I could go out to the data center and see the "back end" of the operation—data center, network, security, storage, and so on. Very impressive. Like going to the Air and Space Museum at the Smithsonian.

At the time there were only about 50 ASPs out there, the press had not become obsessed with covering the phenomenon, and there were no formal organizations whatever devoted to ASPs. Indeed, many ASPs were glad for any kind of validation, guidance, and marketing exposure.

By my own informal estimate, there are now between 1,000 and 1,500 ASP-related businesses (called *xSPs* in the argot of the industry) out there, and it seems several new ones turn up every week. By any measure, the overnight explosion of the ASP industry is unprecedented. But what is unusual about it is that the numerical proliferation of ASPs is also complemented by their prolific diversification. ASPs already serve most vertical markets like finance, manufacturing, and health care with most major enterprise applications like e-commerce, enterprise resource planning (ERP), customer relationship management (CRM), sales automation, and collaboration. They also offer a full spectrum of information technology (IT) platforms and networks. This broad penetration is atypical—usually a new technology approach penetrates one or two vertical markets and, once established, then migrates to other markets that are most similar to those already conquered. ASPs, like other generically horizontal "consumer-oriented" technologies such as personal computers and mobile phones, are inherently more democratic.

The more democratic approach of ASPs—the diversity of market focus and the freedom of opportunity in the industry—may be its greatest strength. As yet, there is no 800-pound gorilla that can scoop up any promising new ASP and incorporate its winning tools and methods into *its* competitive arsenal. The industry is still pretty wide open—a good idea that is executed well can go far. But this democratic approach may also be the industry's greatest weakness. *Anyone* with an idea and some money can launch an ASP. The upside of such a situation is that it fosters a boom in all manner of providers. So customer organizations of all sizes in different markets can now take advantage of a truly virtual computing paradigm that cuts their costs and risks, and lets them exploit powerful applications that many could not afford as installed solutions. The downside is that, because anyone can play in this game, some amateurs stumble into the fray, try to get rich quick, fail, and disappoint their customers.

Because ASPs received the unavoidable hype attendant on such accelerated growth, some entrepreneurs looking for quick profits launched ASPs with business plans that proved—or will prove—untenable. By my own informal count, perhaps 10 to 20 ASPs have gone under for various reasons like poor business plans, dried-up funding, a bad economy, and increased competition. In the wake of 2000's dotcom flameouts on NASDAQ, any new virtual e-business plan is receiving exasperatingly close scrutiny by venture capitalists. The same goes for new e-business ventures looking for stockholders at Initial Public Offering (IPO) time. Computing analysts and press tend, sometimes, to focus on the dramatic disaster (because it makes for a good story) rather than the relatively unexciting success—even though it makes for happy customers. The result is that the same media overexposure and vendor hype that unrealistically inflated customer and investor expectations for ASPs may now have unrealistically deflated them.

I have followed IT segments like imaging/workflow, document management, knowledge management, wireless Internet access, video conferencing, personal digital assistants, asynchronous transfer mode, and others where the major players have not shown a profit for five years or more and whose stock performance has been dismal. But, when the market caught up with them, they could hardly handle all the business coming their way.

I cannot emphasize this enough: Such is the nature of a new IT market. Experts have documented that markets go through phases as they mature. They are born, proliferate, consolidate, and stratify into leaders and laggards. *The ASP market is not even three years old. It has not even finished the proliferation phase.* It will inevitably consolidate and stratify into established, major players and many other niche ones. In the meantime, do the math. Of 1,000 to 1,500 existing ASPs, fewer than 20 have had problems. In my view, *that's an incredible success rate.* Indeed, compared with the average recent success rate of small businesses in the United States—about half fail—it's phenomenal.

Keep your eye on the long-term perspective. Gartner Group estimates that worldwide revenues of ASPs will be $25.3 billion in 2004. Meanwhile, IDC predicts worldwide revenues for the xSP market (ASPs, management services providers, managed security providers, and so forth) will quadruple from $106 billion in 2000 to more than $460 billion in 2005.

The mainstreaming of virtual computing is inevitable. As the ASP industry matures, market caps will boom, major players will buy smaller niche players, financially unstable players will go out of business or get acquired, and the industry will settle into the approximate form it will maintain for many years after. In the meantime, the challenging "pull" for you, the customer, is finding a solid ASP that will give you a good deal now and be around in five years. The competitive "push" for you is choosing a viable ASP before your competition does and undercuts your value proposition by doing things like saving lots of money on hosted IT services and getting to market faster. This is particularly true for small- to-medium-size businesses, many of which until now could not afford any expensive installed enterprise systems like ERP and therefore competed at a disadvantage with Global 2000 firms that could.

As with any new product, customers must perform due diligence when engaging an unknown vendor. I wrote this book to guide you through the process for ASPs. I have purposely skirted granular current events like the stock performance of individual ASPs. I believe increased competition, the Darwinistic thinning of the ASP herd, and the inevitable merger and acquisition activity of major information technology and telecommunications vendors like Microsoft with cash-strapped ASPs will strengthen the ASP brand. If the big boys are smart, they'll let their new partners do what they do best—innovate. If individual ASPs are smart, they won't be unrealistically stubborn idealists and risk their customers' and stockholders' financial welfare by remaining independents with unstable cash flow. That said, I think your best buying strategy now is diligently educating yourself about ASP business strategies and technology infrastructures, and intelligently and exhaustively evaluating ASP candidates so you engage an ASP with services that best match your requirements and offers strong prospects for long-term success.

If I had to choose fundamental criteria for an ASP's success, they would be solid management, mastery of the technology, and a respectable client base. At this early stage of the industry, profitability—although key—is of secondary importance to a number of clients. If an ASP has oversold itself to win clients, then its references will tell the story, whereas numerous satisfied clients translate to cash flow *now*—the number one preoccupation of any new business—and profitability and solid stock valuation later.

With this in mind, I wrote this book for C-level executives and managers who are considering leasing hosted services from an ASP. It introduces you to the telecommunications and computing climate and players that spawned the ASP movement, explains the ASP business model, and tells you in pretty fine detail what technology, security, service-level conditions, and customer service and technical support you should require of an ASP. I also define and provide examples of different types of ASPs (like pure-play ASPs and full service providers) as well as xSPs (like infrastructure service providers and management service providers), whose services may best suit you. I also explain the various pricing models of ASPs and suggest which ones are best for certain types of organizations according to the activities they perform. And I discuss the ramifications of ASPs on the traditional IT reseller channel as well as explain the new channel that ASPs offer as an alternative. I also make some educated guesses about winning and losing ASP strategies, and about business and IT trends that will affect the ASP industry during the next few years. Here and there—such as in Chapter 5 about the ASP network—I've purposefully included a bit more background than most IT professionals need and clarified any terms and concepts that might otherwise confuse nontechnical managers. In my own research, I encountered inconsistencies such as contradictory definitions of identical concepts and vague, arcane, or otherwise confusing explanations of technology. I wanted to save the reader from similar frustration by providing a solid, consistent, and unambiguous conceptual foundation in this book. If you encounter information that strikes you as "computing 101," remember the lay readers—I've included it for their benefit.

That's what the chapters themselves cover. The appendices list selected ASPs that I've organized by type of xSP, vertical markets served, and applications hosted. I've also included a list of ASP organizations and publications that host exhaustive, Internet-based ASP directories and offer current news and analysis as well as invaluable information about standards and the ASP state-of-the-art.

I would also implore you to address the pertinent questions in Appendix E, Defining Your ASP Requirements. I created these questions as a checklist you can review with your ASP candidates to guarantee that the ASP-hosted applications you lease—as well as things like value-added services—are exactly what you need at the price you want to pay. These questions are also designed to get the ASP to open up about its business partners, market strategy, channel development, and other factors that will ensure its long-term success.

In fact, if I were consulting for a client who wanted to hire an ASP, I would suggest the decision makers use the book in the following way. First, read Chapters 1 through 13 to make sure you understand your ASP candidates' market positioning, ASP or xSP type, price model, and so on. Once you understand the industry terms, baseline features and functions, and competition, you can intelligently assess each ASP's value proposition and comparatively shop among various candidates. Next, peruse the appendices of ASPs by type, application, and market. I selected these ASPs because they had a certain visibility and geographical diversity, but that is my only bias. This appendix gives you a few vendors to call to get your feet wet. Then I'd suggest you look through the ASP directories at the various organizations and portals I list in the appendix on ASP organizations and publications. These offer an array of ASPs of every stripe that you can research to your heart's content. I have a similar database of ASPs culled from numerous sources, so contact me if you like. Finally, go through the pertinent questions in Appendix E with your top ASP candidates. This is the most important step in your selection process because at least 95% of anything you need to know about a potential ASP partner will be elicited from them by asking these questions. What you don't know you don't know usually comes back to haunt you later—which is why I've been so comprehensive in creating this checklist.

It's been my experience that when a buying team uses such a methodology, it becomes very clear very quickly which candidates are untenable. Your only problem then will be how to choose the best of the best. I think you'll agree that getting to face that dilemma is worth the price of the book. I wish you the best of luck.

Acknowledgments

I wish to thank all the ASP consultants at Summit Strategies, but especially Marty Gruhn and Laurie McCabe, for their generosity in sharing their opinions and research with me. For my money, Summit is the best large consultancy on ASPs in the business.

I also am grateful to the editors at the following magazines and Web portals for publishing excerpts of this book while it was in progress: Bob Yehling at SVP 4.00, *The Executive's Guide,* Claudia Willen at *Intelligent Enterprise,* Bryant Duhon at *eDoc;* and Don Ajlouni at *WebHarbor—The ASP Industry Portal.*

I also owe thanks to the various executives at the ASP Industry Consortium who shared early studies by their committees on subjects such as security that were indispensable to me in composing certain chapters of the book.

Finally, I am indebted to all the people at Addison-Wesley whose patience, persistence, professionalism—and uncommon kindness—transformed my initial attempts into a useful book: my editor, Mary O'Brien, the production staff, the reviewers, and Jacqui Doucette—who I have no doubt had more than a little to do with giving me this opportunity.

CHAPTER ONE

The Tangled Roots of the ASP Phenomenon

This chapter discusses

- Technology developments that prepared the way for ASPs
- Repeatable solutions
- The enterprise application advantage
- Innovation by acquisition
- Concentric outsourcing
- The ASP value proposition

It was no accident that the application service provider (ASP) movement coincided with the emergence of the Internet-based "new economy." In the history of computing, "disruptive" technology breakthroughs often require the convergence of preexisting information technology (IT), business, and cultural developments into combustible environments from which, when a final element or two is added, new technologies spontaneously catch fire. The late 1990s was a period characterized by such developments. Previously separate technologies were converging, small businesses discovered that they had to compete on a global basis with multinational corporations, and IT entrepreneurs—abetted by unprecedented venture capital—embraced a risk-it-all attitude about launching dotcom operations. As critical, though, was this: Customers had accepted the feasibility of Internet-based commerce. They had one major question, however. How could they deploy it quickly, easily, affordably, and on an enterprise scale? There were no easy answers.

If we step back a few years, we need not extrapolate too much from the prevailing trends of the time to fathom the sudden birth and wild proliferation of rentable virtual enterprise applications.

New Technology

In the general IT environment, it was no secret to vendors and users alike that computing and networking were converging. The Internet served as the medium for linking the two realms, but the catalyst for doing business on the Internet had been the Web browser. Prior to the browser, the Internet had been the playground for research students, scientists, "techies," and the military. After the browser, subscribers to the Internet exploded. By 1999 and 2000, its number of users were doubling every four to six months. Overnight, there materialized a huge potential customer base for Internet-based computing.

Software companies jumped on this opportunity by developing various flavors of Sun Microsystem's Java, the predominant Internet-based programming language. Once IBM, Oracle, and others committed to Java application development environments and Java-based middleware for linking legacy platforms to Web-enabled front ends, the corporate customer saw the viability of building and using applications over the Internet.

However, two limitations still stood in the way of launching global e-commerce—Internet security and bandwidth. No one would buy anything over a network that wasn't secure, and merchants couldn't handle mass virtual transactions over a narrowband network like the Internet. Then a few ingenious telecommunications (telecom) companies invented what are called *virtual private networks* (VPNs) that essentially increased the throughput and security of Internet-based connections. Although only the largest corporations could afford to build them, network service providers expanded the market by leasing VPNs they owned to existing or new customers at more affordable rates.

As these developments came to pass, customers also began to realize that they would need powerful, high-capacity storage devices to accommodate all the data they downloaded from the Internet. Storage vendors responded not only with more robust conventional storage on media like tape and optical disk, but also with networked storage, what they called *storage area networks* (SANs) that could store, virtually manage, and transfer vast quantities of data.

"Thin" client browsers, Internet-based Java, broadband VPNs, and networked storage laid the IT foundation for ASPs.

New Network

Although these enabling technology advances were important, the changed nature of the new network infrastructure catalyzed all other technology changes leading to the advent of ASPs. The Internet started the ball rolling, but the convergence of voice, video, and data networks got it up to speed—unprecedented speed.

However, the capabilities of divergent media did not constitute the extent of the change. Data start-ups like Internet service providers (ISPs) and competitive local exchange carriers (CLECs) were putting new competitive pressure on traditional phone players like regional bell operating carriers (RBOCs) and international exchange carriers (IXCs). Experts predicted that wireline data traffic would eclipse wireline voice traffic in 2003. The traditional voice players had to learn the new data game fast or risk getting landlocked in a sunset market. What's more, software players were getting into the network game. For years Sun Microsystems had been saying that "the network was the computer." The value-added Internet had proved it true. Any software not optimized for Internet playability was destined to maroon its user on his own local area network (LAN). As well, the popularity of CD-ROM and other audio/video media stoked consumer and corporate hunger for hardware that could present a multimedia experience with "as-if-you-were-there" fidelity. This meant enhancements like more powerful chips, monitors with high-definition resolution, and hard drives with the capacity to accommodate dense multimedia files downloaded from the Internet.

The need to accommodate all of this new form and content on a global network infrastructure motivated network specialists to attack the bandwidth shortage on many fronts. Telecom companies of all sizes raced to install broadband-capable fiber-optic cable in their regions. Network equipment vendors created dense wave division multiplexing (DWDM), a method that would compound the innate capacity of fiber optics many times over, as well as digital subscriber line (xDSL), a local loop technology that let customers run voice and data on the same phone line using the legacy copper wire phone infrastructure. They also enhanced routers for traditional network protocols like Frame Relay to be more powerful, flexible, and easily provisioned. And they jumped with both feet into asynchronous transfer mode (ATM), a new network protocol capable of massive bandwidth that could accommodate voice, data, and multimedia as well as customizable levels of service for different customers. Wireless vendors also seized the day. If data traffic was exploding, then wireless vendors wanted a piece of the market. They accelerated research and development (R&D) on problems like anemic wireless capacity and range, and optimized wireless devices like cell phones, laptops, and personal digital assistants (PDAs) to accommodate data downloaded from the Internet.

The eventual goal was global coverage and unlimited bandwidth for all modes of communication.

New Implementation Model

While small-to-medium-size businesses (SMBs) were embracing new technologies to compete better with the Global 2000 (G2000) multinationals, smaller systems integrators (SIs) and their software, hardware, and networking partners were developing new implementation methodologies to compete better with the Big Five and other large integrators. They found that if they specialized in certain markets and offered fixed price/time contracts, they could adequately address SMBs'—and even some larger companies'—functional requirements, as well as underbid the big integrators. The key was keeping price down with speedier deployment and less staff. The prerequisite, though, was that the customer had to accept an 80% complete solution—meaning the final system would only be customized to map to 80% of the customer's business processes.

As it turned out, SMBs really appreciated a speedier, cheaper solution. They could live with a more "generic" system that was generally tailored for the dominant applications in their market. Indeed, software vendors had been refining "verticalized" application templates for several years so their value-added resellers (VARs) could more easily use their software in vertical markets. But mid-size integrators, many of which were VARs, discovered over time that as they installed more similar applications in the same market, they did so even faster and cheaper.

A few formalized their new approach on that premise and called the result of their work *repeatable solutions.* Some even set up regional "solution centers," where they would create solutions for several regional clients at once using the same staff. With the huge business in year 2000 (Y2K) conversion in the late 1990s, they were installing testing platforms in their solution centers where they could confirm that an application was Y2K-compliant. It was a small step to use such testing environments to determine if repeatable enterprise solutions were bulletproof before they were installed on-site. Some mid-size integrators even created "help desks" in their solution centers, so the same staff that built applications could support customers as they used them. A real visionary vendor or two conceived of their solution centers as something like functionality depots where application developers could download required functionality from various partner vendors right over the Internet. In general, these integrators discovered that the further upstream they moved basic configuration, sizing, integration, and other tasks, the quicker these tasks could be accomplished. So, unlike the traditional installed implementation model, where the integrator was on the customer site from provisioning and configuration for long periods until the system went live, repeatable solution integrators often went on-site merely to install an already tested system and take it live. Regardless of whether they spent appreciable time on-site, the point was they were doing what clients wanted—accelerating deployment and cutting costs.

Repeatable solutions, therefore, were neither traditionally installed nor outsourced—they were "near sourced." Unlike installed solutions, they were built largely off-site. Unlike outsourced solutions, they were created slightly differently for each client, although often for different clients simultaneously.

New Network Outsourcing Model

Meanwhile, since deregulation, the way network services were sold and resold had gradually changed. Although having been forced to compete in long-distance voice and all forms of data services, the largest and oldest network players like RBOCs and IXCs had taken to reselling network bandwidth and egress to smaller players like CLECs and ISPs, who in turn resold it to their corporate and consumer customers. This arrangement let the newer players get into business faster by using established networks instead of building their own from scratch. It also guaranteed the older players steady revenues that could only increase if the smaller players—their supposed competition—succeeded.

To visualize this dynamic, imagine a bull's-eye target with two rings around it (Figure 1–1). Now place the RBOCs and IXCs in the center of the bull's-eye, the

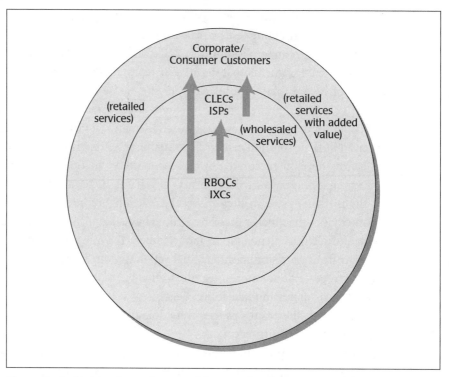

Figure 1–1   Network service providers evolve from competition to coopetition via "concentric outsourcing"

CLECS and ISPs in the first ring, and the corporate and consumer customers in the outer ring. The big players in the bull's-eye controlled most of the legacy telecom infrastructure and revenues from their long dominance in the voice markets. They had always sold their services retail to consumers and corporations in the outer circle—and still could. But, they now could also resell their services to a second wholesale market—the CLECS and ISPs in the middle ring. Indeed, to offset their lost potential data revenues, they had to. So the big players wholesaled infrastructure and bandwidth primarily, and the smaller players added value to it by doing things like tailoring their services to vertical industry customers like banks or to geographical regions within which they controlled a local network that they could link, say, to a large player's international network.

Because customers leased value-added telecom services from CLECS and ISPs, which leased their infrastructure from RBOCs and IXCs, you might call this phenomenon *concentric outsourcing*. On one level, all these telecom players were competing for customers' business. Each specialized in its core competencies and dominated the markets that they best served. An IXC could give a multinational corporation better international services because it had largely paid for its legacy network and could offer better economies of scale than a regional CLEC. By the same token, a regional CLEC serving a metropolitan area in New England might have optimized its services for insurance companies, so it could offer better value-added data services for that customer base than any other provider. While competing, though, big and small telecom players also cooperated in their wholesaling arrangements. They had to.

Although most industries have reseller channels, the telecom industry's "concentric outsourcing" channel would most notably prefigure ASP *partner coalitions*. As you'll see, ASPs are typically coalitions of players with network, software, hardware, and vertical industry expertise. While the partners cooperate on their ASP operation, they often compete in other areas. And because certain players like infrastructure service providers and network service providers control an existing state-of-the-art data center or network, many competing ASPs partner with them to leverage that general infrastructure and to differentiate themselves, also offer a unique blend of software applications and value-added services for particular markets. This "coopetition" among various players with overlapping mandates, as well as a network-centric mode of outsourcing, distinctly characterizes the new ASP "functionality utilities."

New Competition

In addition to their intrinsic merits, repeatable solutions found an increasingly receptive SMB customer base because new competitive factors were influencing those companies' markets. The international reach of the value-added Internet served as a global communications infrastructure that helped G2000 companies do business "virtually," independent of space and time. This meant they could compete 24/7, operate on thinner margins because of greater economies of scale, and enter regional markets that were previously unreachable or too costly to pursue.

At the same time, new enterprise applications like e-commerce, enterprise resource planning (ERP), and customer relationship management (CRM) were helping them, via e-commerce Web sites, to proliferate their brand and simplify the purchasing process. ERP automated their supply chains and eliminate warehousing and other costs, and CRM enhanced their customer service and enabled marketing and business intelligence gathering that generated new sales in locations like call centers that were previously cost centers.

SMBs saw the writing on the wall. Big companies were going downmarket as well as global. So, to compete with them, SMBs would have to go global in turn, as well as adopt the same new high-power enterprise applications. Going global with a Web site for branding purposes was relatively easy. Integrating that Web-enabled front end with back-end legacy data like inventory and business processes like order management was not. Harder still was installing the new enterprise applications that could link an SMB's legacy databases with its Internet storefront and streamline its overall interrelated business processes. These were million-dollar systems that often took six months to one year to install. To proliferate them globally over many offices was an almost endless operation. Even the G2000s complained that, by the time they got an installed ERP system up and going companywide, its functionality was outmoded. However, this vicious cycle of protracted deployment, upgrades, and training on the new functionality seemed the ante companies had to pay to play in the high-stakes game of global, virtual business. Many SMBs simply could not afford it.

Because they lacked the ready cash and economies of scale of G2000s, it was a matter of simply getting not enough bang for too much buck. A large company with $1 billion in revenues, for instance, could easily spend $10 million, or 0.1% of annual revenues, on a global ERP/CRM solution if it would cut costs by 20% in the first year of operation. After all, it's spending $10 million to save $200 million for virtually immediate payback on the system and for a 20-fold return on investment (ROI)—*and that's just in the first year.* An SMB with $50 million in annual revenues could spend only $5 million on a comparable solution for its smaller global operation, cut costs by 20%, and save $10 million in year one of operation. That's a twofold ROI, which is not bad, but the problem is the SMB must sacrifice *10% of its annual revenues* to earn that return. This kind of expense puts an untenable strain on the cash flow of an SMB.

Although, on the one hand, G2000s could outspend SMBs; on the other hand, new dotcom companies with low brick-and-mortar (BAM) overhead could outsave them. For example, say an entrepreneur started selling golf clubs over the Internet and kept it simple. He did not make the clubs, warehoused only what he could sell in a week, took orders and payments via credit card virtually over his Web site, packaged and shipped only small quantities of clubs at a time via FedEx, and shipped direct, not through other resellers. In short, he buys name-brand clubs wholesale from major manufacturers and, by keeping costs down, sells them for much less than the manufacturers can through their high-overhead channels of pro shops and other resellers.

If the SMB manufacturers want to compete with him, they must overhaul their business model and learn virtual business. This is not easy because they must restructure the old business organized around selling clubs business-to-business (B2B) and in bulk, cut their shipping cycles from weeks or months to days, renegotiate supplier contracts, launch just-in-time warehousing, sell custom orders of a few clubs (not thousands), and sell them business-to-consumer (B2C) to an entirely new type of customer—not pro shops, but direct to weekend golfers in their homes. Most important, the manufacturer has to restructure (re-intermediate) or eliminate (disintermediate) his reseller channel to reduce his costly overhead. What's more, he has to do all this *before* he can even think about installing ERP, e-commerce, or CRM to streamline his new processes and go virtual.

The great irony of the situation is that SMBs' success in their old BAM business model hamstrung their success in the new virtual one. Dotcoms could go from *zero to virtual* almost overnight. To compete with dotcoms, BAM SMBs needed a way to go from *backward to virtual* just as fast.

New Mergers and Acquisitions

Further compounding the competitive dilemma of SMBs was the furious merger and acquisition mentality of business in the late 1990s. To thwart hostile take-overs, create better economies of scale, and increase market share, many G2000s were merging with other G2000s—as well as implementing new enterprise applications. In reaction, many SMBs merged also—or agreed to be acquired by G2000s—to strengthen their market positions or sometimes merely to survive or cash out of the game altogether. In the high-tech sector especially, the dominant mantra became, "If you can't build it better and faster, buy the company that can." *Innovation through acquisition* essentially became a major component of many companies' R&D strategies. As a result, entire industries looked like they might consolidate to a few monolithic conglomerates controlling 80% of their markets, while a handful of SMBs divvied up the remaining 20%.

Although merger and acquisition immediately gained companies of all sizes greater scale, the downside was that they also created greater debt and more restricted cash flow. This was exacerbated by needed Y2K expenditures. IT projects that would have gotten the green light in the mid-1990s now got lower priority in large companies and simply were eliminated indefinitely at many SMBs. The dominant IT imperative at most newly merged conglomerates was integrating the legacy IT systems of the component corporations. But, frankly, most companies had no idea how long their prosperity would depend on having to merge with new partners, so few could realistically budget for, or design, an IT platform that would be homogenous throughout the conglomerate for many years.

For all of these reasons, companies of all sizes started rethinking the concept of outsourcing. They were too busy competing on many fronts to create and maintain state-of-the-art IT platforms as well.

New Alliances

What materialized from this convergence of media and cultures was another merger-and-acquisition dance. To get up to speed on data technologies and business strategies, the huge (and in the RBOCs' case, monopolistic) voice players began buying up the smaller data players. Like the G2000s, RBOCs and IXCs had deep pockets and no time, so their innovation came mostly through acquisition. Meanwhile, in hot pursuit of data services opportunities, ISPs and CLECs had proliferated wildly after telecom deregulation in the 1980s. As big as the potential worldwide data market was, there were too many vendors for all of them to prosper. Those on the bubble needed cash, and they were more than happy to have a voice player buy them (Figure 1–2).

Because of the convergence of voice and data, integrators, old-economy voice vendors, and new-economy data entrepreneurs now had at their disposal both the new Internet-based telecom tools and all the legacy voice physical infrastructure—most important, combined networks of unprecedented scope and density of penetration as well as the telcos' and ISPs' data centers from which they had been providing Web hosting. Lacking the value-added security, storage, and other enhancements that ASPs would later provide, these centers nonetheless would allow pioneers to get application hosting operations up fast in the early going. Indeed, it wasn't long before a few visionaries saw the synergies that could result if they served single iterations of enterprise software on hardware housed in data centers to multiple customers over broadband networks.

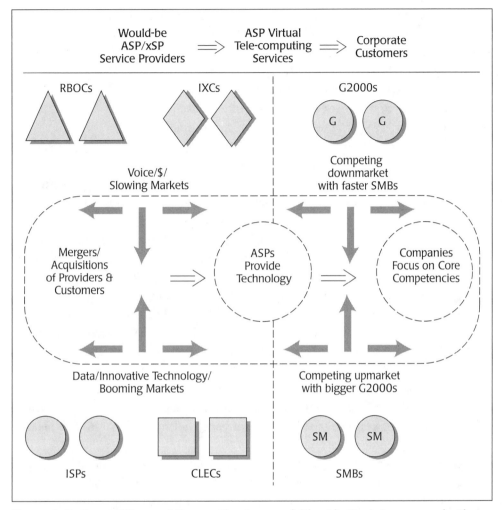

Figure 1–2 Coopetition and "innovation by acquisition" in the telecommunications and other industries helped form ASP business models and hybrid services

New Value Proposition

To recap briefly, SMB BAMs were facing strong high-end competition from G2000s and low-end competition from dotcoms. Innovation through acquisition fomented furious merger activity that left many companies with tight cash flow, heterogeneous IT platforms, and the need to integrate these diverse systems before installing new ones. Then technology advances in areas like VPNs as well as accelerated deployment strategies like "repeatable solutions" offered SMBs the chance to level the playing field. What's more, the dotcoms that had merged with older telcos now had access to data centers and a global broadband infrastructure. The competitive pressure to get into e-business fast motivated many SMBs to consider new IT options. ASPs offered compelling benefits.

Once the first ASPs made enterprise applications virtual and rentable, customers discovered the competitive viability of their new-economy value proposition. Here were virtual operations that hosted enterprise applications from secure data centers over broadband networks to multiple customers for a simple leasing fee. Unlike previous outsourcing models, the ASP "e-sourcing" one offered a largely self-contained, but also holistic, solution. Customers, for instance, were not simply porting their nonmission-critical data via expensive leased lines to out-of-house mainframes in some large system integrator's data center. They were leasing an application *plus* a complete computing platform of servers, operating systems, middleware, storage, and network. And because most ASPs leveraged existing Internet links and resold the same platform to many customers, their costs were much lower than if they offered installed systems. So they could lease systems for less and offer lease-to-buy options. In previous outsourcing models, when the lease was up the customer got his data back. In the ASP model, after 36 months or so the customer could have purchased a system, and for less per month than he might have paid simply to outsource his data management in the old model.

What's more, hosted applications were simpler to implement. In many cases, customers just turned on service almost like they would service from any utility. This offered customers better speed-to-market, but hosted applications were also affordable. Customers did not have to lay out huge capital expenditures up front. Instead, they paid for the service in monthly increments over the leasing period. Hosted applications were also less risky than installed applications. The ASP took care of upgrades, so there was no installed software to get outmoded. This made service providers more accountable. One ASP provided service and support, so there were no multiple vendors on a job to blame each other for problems. In many cases, hosted applications did not have to be integrated with numerous legacy applications—and if they did, integration was easier. If they were deployed alone, the ASP provided all hardware, software, and network, so the customer avoided having to integrate heterogeneous systems of companies they had acquired. What's more, hosted applications offered the customer one-stop shopping: The same provider performed all services, and all costs were presented on one bill.

New Industry

The formula proved more attractive than most anticipated. The ASP movement is about three years old, and worldwide there are more than 1,000 ASPs hosting applications of almost every kind. Most IT players—from integrators and VARs to software companies and telcos—are involved in some kind of ASP effort. An entirely new environment of attendant players like infrastructure service providers and ASP application aggregators (AAA) have sprung up to support ASPs.

However, these are merely the near-term phenomena. Most consulting firms predict that the total market for ASP-related services will be worth in the neighborhood of $15 to $25 billion by 2003. Some even go so far as to predict that more than 80% of all new applications will be hosted by 2010.

Hyperbole is par for the course when it comes to writing about IT. Market projections mean next to nothing if they look too far ahead—the technology simply changes too fast these days. So let's take the middle course and say that during the next 10 years (barring catastrophic setbacks like a crippling recession) ASPs could do for enterprise applications what the Web browser did for the Internet in the last 10 years—make them available to any business bold enough to flip the virtual switch.

Key Concepts

- Technology that prepared the way for ASPs—thin clients, Java, VPNs, networked storage, multimode global broadband networks
- Repeatable solutions—installed solutions tailored for one market or application that can be easily duplicated for similar clients to save them installation time and money
- The enterprise application advantage—before hosted solutions, G2000s outcompeting SMBs because they could afford installed enterprise applications and SMBs could not
- Concentric outsourcing—RBOCs and IXCs wholesaling network bandwidth and infrastructure to CLECs and ISPs that in turn retailed it to end customers

- Innovation by acquisition—marriage of ISP and CLEC data expertise/technology with RBOCs and IXC voice technology/deep pockets
- The ASP value proposition—customers getting cheaper applications faster and easier by leasing them virtually over broadband networks from an ASP instead of installing them onsite

CHAPTER TWO

The ASP Coalition—No Single Vendor Can Do It All

This chapter discusses

- An ASP
- Characteristics of the ASP hardware platform
- Players that can provide the ASP hardware platform
- Characteristics of ASP networks
- Players that can provide the ASP network
- Hosted software applications
- Trusted business advisors (TBAs)
- Infrastructure service providers
- ASP-enabling software
- Value-added ASP services

It should be apparent by now that it takes multiple, complementary vendors to create and maintain an ASP operation. In general, an ASP is always the result of a partnership among role players with core competence in one or more of the following areas: hardware, networking, software platform, hosted applications, and niche market expertise (Figure 2–1).

The ASP Hardware

The Hardware Platform Components

The hardware platform is typically comprised of the computers (mainframes, minicomputers, workstations, and personal computers [PCs]), on which the enabling software platform (operating system, database, and middleware) function. The hosted applications sit on top of the enabling

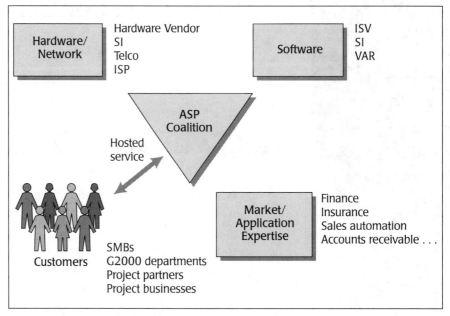

Figure 2–1 In the ASP business model, no single vendor can do it all

software platform. The hardware usually is also housed in a highly secure and climate-controlled physical data center.

Depending on the hosted services offered, a typical ASP hardware platform might be comprised of several types of servers residing, for the most part, in the ASP's data center. The server hardware, of course, is defined by the function of the software residing on it. Application servers store the hosted application operations and let that software interpret data in the databases. Database servers store and process the customer's data. Web servers deliver Web pages and let the hosted software transmit data to standard Web browsers. The servers should also be backed up with actual, identical, duplicate servers or with what's known as a *logical functionality* which duplicates that of the original server but may not be housed in a dedicated computer for just that task. Backups prevent system failure in the event a single server malfunctions (Figure 2–2).

The Key Characteristics of ASP Hardware

To support multiple hosted applications and complementary services like out-sourced storage, the hardware components should be inherently robust and scalable. Large installed hardware solutions generally support a software platform and several enterprise applications like ERP, CRM, or e-commerce. This can be a taxing load. For ASPs, the load is even heavier. After all, they host hardware *and* software platforms *plus* multiple enterprise applications for many customers. The most ambitious ASPs may even run multiple operating systems and brands of enterprise applications to address a broader customer base with different legacy computing platforms. And, although hardware for an installed solution must support scaling as users, data, and applications are added to the system, most ASP hardware must support *massive* scaling as users, data, and applications for multiple customers are added. Such a model, therefore, demands correspondingly massive computing power.

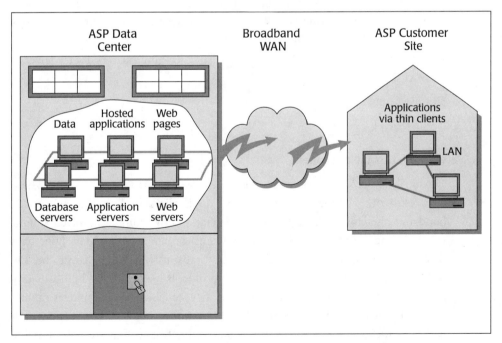

Figure 2–2 The ASP hardware platform consists of servers and enabling software

Types of ASP Hardware Providers

The following types of vendors specialize in hardware and can play the hardware partner role in an ASP operation: hardware vendors like IBM and Hewlett-Packard, international long-distance voice and data carriers (interexchange carriers or IXCs) like AT&T, regional Baby Bell voice, and data carriers (RBOCs) like Verizon, competitive local exchange carriers (CLECs) like GTE MobilNet of California that also offer data and voice services, and ISPs like Digex that historically have offered data, but are increasingly getting into voice over Internet Protocol (VOIP) services.

Many of these vendors also offer services like networking, integration, and software applications, but they are valuable as hardware partners because they design and manufacture hardware or own data centers that house hardware. IBM, for instance, can manufacture and integrate the whole gamut of hardware—System 390 mainframes, AS/400 minis, and IBM PCs. Hewlett-Packard manufactures hardware and also affordably outsources entire hardware/software platforms to promising start-ups for a minority stake in the companies. On the other hand, data/voice carriers like RBOCs, CLECs, and ISPs own or lease data centers where they traditionally housed central office telecommunications equipment. By partnering with carriers and upgrading data center infrastructures with appropriate hardware and software—instead of building them from scratch—ASPs get to market faster while also leveraging carriers' legacy telecom networks.

The ASP Network

The Network Platform Components

Obviously, voice/data carriers can also be network partners for an ASP. These networks work well for hosting enterprise applications because they are broadband and, therefore, robust. Because broadband networking has evolved at light speed during the last decade, networks like these can accommodate huge data throughput while maintaining high-quality transmission. Later we examine the technological complexities of networking protocols like ATM and high-capacity infrastructures like fiber-optic cores that have enabled such rapid advances. Here, the focus is on the general ASP-to-customer network connection path as well as the general capabilities of broadband networks that are indispensable to ASPs.

The network connection from the ASP to a corporate end user of a hosted application is typically comprised of several components provided by the ASP, the network service provider (partnered with the ASP), and the customer. In the data center, the ASP's various servers reside on its own high-speed LAN or storage network. The LAN links to the network service provider's WAN, which in turn may span other carriers' WAN connections to reach distant customers. Near the customer location, the WAN links to what's called the customer's *local loop*— a network infrastructure provided by the customer's local exchange carrier for its customers in that vicinity. The local loop links to the LAN on the customer's site. Here, workers access hosted applications from LAN-linked desktops. The customer's mobile employees may also access data and various ranges of application functionality from the ASP via wireless devices like laptops, palmtops, and cell phones (Figure 2–3).

The Key Characteristics of an ASP Network

The primary characteristic of any hosted network must be reliability. Imagine that a PC manufacturer leases an e-commerce solution from an ASP. During the first month of operation, the manufacturer misses the delivery date to a new customer, Company A, for an order for 5,000 PCs because of some failure in the ASP's network. As a result, the manufacturer loses Company A's business forever.

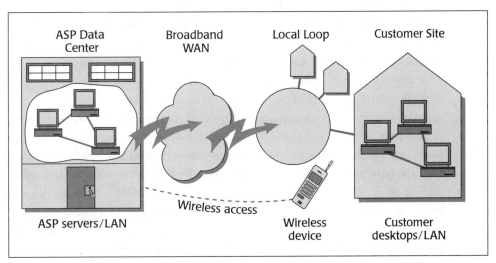

Figure 2–3   The ASP network links the data center via a broadband WAN to the customer site

There is no easy way for the manufacturer to resolve the situation through a suit or in trade in which the ASP reimburses the manufacturer with discounted service for a certain period. The damage has been done, and the amount of business lost is probably incalculable.

So network reliability is not optional. But, depending on the type of broadband network—leased lines, Frame Relay, ATM, and so forth—numerous factors can affect reliability. To begin with, you should always confirm that an ASP can at least provide basic network availability. In other words, the network will never have unscheduled downtimes long enough to jeopardize your business. Availability usually requires redundant physical access facilities at key network sites like a company's headquarters and major branch offices, as well as alternate traffic routing so transmissions can be directed around inevitable points of failure resulting from factors like bad weather and equipment malfunctions. Most ASPs offer 99.5% or better availability—and many offer better levels, depending on their network service provider. By comparison, almost "bulletproof" availability is 99.9% or better and is typically offered by extremely service-sensitive operations like telephone companies. Availability also refers to scheduled downtime that the ASP controls. Most ASPs have set hours of service with scheduled down periods for maintenance and other activities. Specifics of availability are usually determined by each customer's service-level agreement (SLA).

Depending on the ASP's target customers and long-term business plan, the following network characteristics are also desirable.

An ASP can rarely have too much network capacity. Most ASPs host multiple applications to multiple customers for each application. And each customer expects a certain level of service, even at peak-use times for all customers. So an ASP network must have the kind of throughput able to accommodate hundreds, if not thousands, of users of multiple enterprise applications.

Certain networking technologies like ATM have inherently greater capacity than others like Frame Relay and leased lines—but they also cost more. You, therefore, should stipulate a network that can accommodate your peak bandwidth requirements without breaking your budget. Also, routing and other equipment is designed for different levels of performance. Network service providers implement more or less robust routers according to traffic demands in different sections of their networks. For instance, standard e-mail traffic between two local offices from 9 AM to 5 PM would probably justify a less powerful router than would traffic between two manufacturing plants trading dense engineering drawings around-the-clock. Network service providers also use human and automated network management methods to ensure that traffic allowed onto the network does not exceed its capacity, and that traffic is appropriately rerouted when bottlenecks do occur.

The ASP, of course, can provide needed capacity in any number of ways. It may, for example, lease an ATM-based VPN with a fiber-optic core to leverage both its great optical bandwidth and its sophisticated routing intelligence that automatically chooses the "best route" for data to avoid bottlenecks. This way, even during peak-use periods, your transmissions access the network promptly and get elegantly routed to maintain adequate performance. It may also run high-bandwidth, dedicated leased lines directly to each customer's site.

An ASP's long-term operations tend to be more cost-efficient, and its customer service more responsive, if its network is scalable. As the ASP adds customers to each hosted application, it should have enough network capacity to accommodate the increased load. Ideally, the ASP should either already have the needed bonus bandwidth or be able to request it from its network service provider so it's available in reasonable time. With older networking technologies like leased lines, the ASP may have to pay for the fixed bandwidth of the new line as well as wait weeks or months for the network service provider to install it. As a result, you may pay for surplus bandwidth and delay deployment of new users until the line is installed. With more advanced networks like ATM-based VPNs, the ASP can request that the network service provider "dynamically allocate" the bandwidth it needs on the fly to accommodate a new customer.

According to many factors—number of users, intensity of use, periods of use, and so forth—different customers require different qualities of service. To address a broader initial customer base and to service it over time as customer requirements grow, an ASP should be able to charge different customers different fees for different levels of service.

A call center leasing a CRM application may have 1,000 sales "reps" using it intensely around-the-clock, and may be willing to pay its ASP a premium fee for 24/7 production-level network service. On the other hand, an in-house sales department for a different company may have 500 sales reps that need to use a hosted CRM system just as intensely, but only from 9 AM to 5 PM, Monday through Friday.

If the ASP can't offer two levels of service at different and appropriate fees to accommodate both customers, it will forfeit the business of one of them. To offer levels of service affordably, it needs a network advanced and flexible enough to switch to different throughput rates for different customers at different times. It could, of course, create custom service levels around the capacity of different leased lines that are always on—for instance, use a T3 for the 24/7 customer and use a T1 for the 9-to-5 one. But the 9-to-5 customer must still pay for bandwidth it never uses at off-peak times, and the ASP may lose that customer to another ASP that can offer cheaper usage-based pricing.

Certain ASPs, of course, have defined their target customer base so narrowly that they don't need to offer different qualities of service. An ASP leasing 24/7 e-mail services to companies with 50 to 150 customers has probably determined the range of use that its network must support. So it can provide one fixed, affordable network rate, still be profitable, and never deliver inadequate throughput.

Types of ASP Network Providers

Vendors with networking expertise are typically international voice/data carriers, RBOCs, CLECs, ISPs, and systems integrators (SIs). Any of these network players can partner with an ASP to provide network services. In general, though, the larger the ASP the more likely it will partner with large, "world-class" partners—an international carrier like AT&T, an RBOC like Verizon, a CLEC like GTE MobilNet of California, an ISP like UUNET, or an integrator like EDS.

A large ASP hosting multiple applications to numerous users and offering different qualities of service needs a reliable, proven, well-financed carrier with a robust and sophisticated network. What's more, large ASPs often have multiple data centers in different geographical regions that only a provider with broad reach can service. These large network players also often own data centers that the ASP can "repurpose" for its hosted services. And the brand name visibility of well-known providers contributes to the ASP's credibility: A network provider with a reputation for quality services lends its ASP partner market stature by association.

In keeping with the trend of "concentric outsourcing" explained in Chapter 1, mid-range ASPs more typically partner with mid-range network service providers like regional CLECs and ISPs. A mid-size ASP is more likely to have a strictly regional market focus and moderately sized target customers that won't tax smaller providers' infrastructures. And smaller providers with less overhead can lease services for lower rates to smaller ASPs, who can then pass on less costly services to their customers. Smaller providers also tend to focus on corporate customers like manufacturing plants with common usage characteristics. By specializing in these niche requirements, they can keep prices down by evolving better efficiencies in them than larger providers. Of course, an ASP pursuing defined niche customers for its own hosted services would be well served by partnering with a CLEC or an ISP that has a large, installed base of them.

SIs often manage VPNs that link a certain customer type in which they specialize. For instance, a long-time Department of Defense contractor for military vehicle parts might have a VPN that spans cities comprising the major hubs of its supply chain like Cleveland, OH, Baltimore, MD, and Washington, DC. An ASP with similar target customers in those cities might benefit by using such an integrator as a network provider.

Often, too, complementary vendors simply leverage legacy relationships to gain networking partners. For instance, if AT&T is IBM's preferred data services provider for international e-business installs, it's a small step to extend the partnership to include IBM-hosted e-business services.

The ASP Software

The ASP Software Components

As mentioned earlier, ASPs typically use one or more operating systems (like UNIX or Windows NT) and databases (like Oracle or Sybase) as well as various types of middleware to support their actual hosted applications. Middleware links applications either to one another or more elegantly to the base software platform of operating system and database. With the proliferation of Internet-based computing has come an explosion of new middleware designed to "Internet-enable" legacy software environments like client/server and mainframe. New application servers and Web servers, for instance, permit legacy data, applications, and Web pages to be accessed by users over the Internet via Web browsers.

The actual hosted applications are often called *80%* or *generic* application services because the hosted application maps to only 80% of the customer's business processes to expedite implementation. The ASP usually provides up to 20% of the remaining functionality and/or customization when you sign up for the hosted service. This strategy is dramatically faster and cheaper than traditional installed applications that require extensive customization.

Remote management of some hosted software also requires that certain client management and other software be installed on your desktops.

The Key Characteristics of ASP Software

Whatever the vendor's channel strategy, any software it hosts should have the following general characteristics. Because the hosted application will be eventually downloaded over an Internet-enabled link, in most cases it should have a Web browser interface. However, most software deployed in extended enterprises is Web-enabled, so this is almost a given. It should also be capable of being scaled across the enterprise. After all, a key element of the ASP value proposition is that hosted services let smaller companies lease enterprise software that they otherwise couldn't afford. As customers add users over time, the software must easily scale to accommodate them. The application should also be easily simplified to a portion of its original functionality. Such a "generic" version can be more easily deployed across a broad range of customers without having to be further customized. However, some vendors may also evolve generic versions to address focused niche applications. The ASP will choose a broad or narrow approach, depending on how it wants to differentiate itself from competitive hosted services. If the software is modular like most ERP packages, then simplifying it is less of a challenge: The ASP can offer select, usually commonly required, modules in the hosted version and avoid extensive customization.

Types of ASP Software Providers

Players with software application expertise are typically software vendors, SIs, and resellers. Software ASP players typically offer hosted solutions for several reasons. They might use them to sell downmarket to new customers who can't afford their installed applications or to keep from losing existing customers for their installed applications to ASPs that offer cheaper hosted software with similar functionality. They might also use them to introduce an affordable first step in a migration path to a more expensive installed application or to provide a convenient way of demonstrating the representative functionality of an installed application.

Software vendors make good ASP software partners because they excel in fast and complicated software development. By upgrading their enterprise software, they keep the ASP functionally competitive. Integrators and resellers, of course, are experienced at customization and often understand customer requirements in specific markets, or actually have customers that can be converted to hosted solutions (Figure 2–4).

ASP Market and Application Expertise

In a traditional business model, vendors typically partner with integrators and resellers to customize and resell their software to vertical markets like finance, manufacturing, and government. To host their software, software vendors use VARs, integrators, or outside ASP partners for vertical market and application expertise. For instance, the vendor might partner with one of its peak-performing VARs to simplify and host its software package as an ASP. The agreement may entail helping the VAR partner with network and other players as well as partially funding the VAR's ASP marketing and branding efforts.

If the software vendor partners with new players outside its traditional channel, it would be wise to manage existing channel relationships diplomatically so as not to alienate those channel players. After all, they can still earn revenues for the vendor by performing other activities for installed or hosted solutions like integration and technical support.

It may even opt to partner with a company like a bank chain or accounting firm that, although such a company may lack advanced IT expertise, intimately understands a particular market or application for which the vendor wants to offer a hosted service. Known as *trusted business advisors* (TBAs), these players usually help the new ASP coalition penetrate the target market, often by promoting sales of the ASP's hosted services into their existing customer bases. With this strategy, the software vendor needs to negotiate less with the traditional channel for the opportunity to offer hosted services. The TBA, in effect, becomes the brand of the ASP's hosted service in a given market. In many cases, the customer need not even know that the TBA has ASP partners.

Often, in exchange for market savvy and access to captive customers, the TBA may get to control the customer/ASP relationship: The hosted service is marketed as just another value-added service in the TBA's portfolio. For instance, Arthur Anderson might offer a hosted version of its accounting software to its customers, and use AT&T and PricewaterhouseCoopers for data center, network, and technical support "under the covers." In scenarios like this, the TBA can grow and redirect its franchise with more autonomy as long as it ensures its ASP partners their fixed share of the hosting revenues.

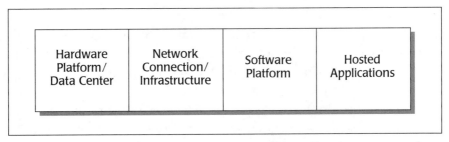

Figure 2–4 The ASP IT infrastructure is comprised of hardware, network, enabling software, and hosted applications

SUCCESS STORY

Pure-play ASP: Corio
Customer: Vertical Networks, Inc.
Key elements of the solution: Multiple hosted applications, accelerated deployment

Vertical Networks, Inc. is a "virtual corporation" comprised of multiple, independent actual corporations working together virtually to develop integrated communications platforms for SMBs. Vertical's supply chain, for instance, includes manufacturing partner, Flextronics, marketing partners, AT&T, and Telecom Italia, and global distribution partners NCR and Setta. Although virtual in concept when it began, Vertical nonetheless depended on many manual and fragmented business processes to do business with its partners and depended on legacy applications for financials, inventory control, and order management with limited scalability and compatibility. Vertical's success, and its phenomenal growth, forced it to face its IT problem. It needed a new IT platform that would seamlessly automate and integrate in-house processes with the interenterprise processes of its partners, but it also had to be affordable, support rapid growth, and entail little support from in-house staff. So would Vertical opt for upgrading its legacy platform, installing a new one, or leasing appropriate hosted applications from an ASP? With a good price, rapid deployment, and the right applications, pure-play ASP, Corio, convinced Vertical to marry its visionary business structure to a comparably virtual ASP IT infrastructure.

Corio quickly realized that, without extensive customization, no standalone application could adequately address the complexities of automating Vertical's interenterprise processes. At the minimum, Vertical's VARs needed a new e-sales application to submit orders, Vertical itself required an order management system to confirm the order, and a financial application to track receivables and payables, and its manufacturing partner needed a manufacturing application to manufacture orders. And they all had to be compatible and deployed quickly.

Knowing that long-term payback would be significant, Corio convinced Vertical to lease multiple applications consisting of CRM, financials, and

continued

order management, as well as its partner Flextronics' manufacturing application. It integrated these on the Corio Orion hardware/software integration platform. Using its FastLane accelerated deployment methodology, Corio was able to implement stage 1 (financials and order management) for 15 users within 10 weeks. Virender Ahluwalia, head of finance for Vertical, says this was "only a fraction of the time an internal build would have taken us. "What's more," he adds, "my staff and I would probably have to spend all our time working on the transition." This situation doesn't change once implementation is complete. Corio's staff now serves as Vertical's IT department for the hosted solution, which frees Vertical's IT people to focus on furthering the company's core business.

However, Vertical not only avoided the headaches of a protracted on-site installation and conserved its internal staff and other resources, it made a manageable up-front payment, pays affordable monthly leasing fees, and got a state-of-the-art hosted solution for approximately 40% of the price of an installed one. Vertical estimates that the total cost of ownership for an installed solution over five years would have been near $5.6 million. The Corio solution, including hosting, upgrades, implementation, network connectivity, and support personnel, should come in around $2.4 million over the same period, for an ROI of 169%.

Permission courtesy of Corio, Inc.

Infrastructure Service Providers

As mentioned earlier there are four platform components common to all ASPs—hardware, network, software platform, and hosted applications. As the ASP industry rapidly matured and diversified, however, another class of service provider evolved to complement the basic functional services. Generally known as *infrastructure service providers*, these players offer different combinations of overlapping outsourced services (Figure 2–5).

Infrastructure service providers offer services like the following: access to and management of broadband WANs they own or lease, data center space, data backup, servers, and various types of storage.

Instead of building these from scratch, an ASP leases them from infrastructure service providers to get into business fast, to avoid huge up-front infrastructure costs, and to exploit efficiencies and economies of scale possible to

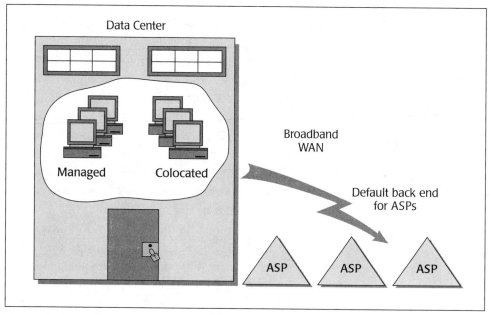

Figure 2–5 The infrastructure service provider functions as the "back end" for multiple ASPs

companies specializing only in infrastructure provision—not also hosted applications or other services. Many players of this type will offer similar services (for instance, a high-end hardware platform and secure data center) for multiple ASPs, becoming in essence the default back end for those ASPs' hosted applications.

Infrastructure service providers can also negotiate different types of deals for their outsourced resources with ASPs. They can lease only network connections and secure data center space, while the ASP furnishes the space with its own servers and manages the applications running on them. Or they can manage servers they own and lease to the ASP. To leverage their legacy competencies and to differentiate themselves from other infrastructure providers, many will also specialize in one or two value-added services like outsourced enterprise storage or e-commerce software for processing ASP/customer transactions.

SUCCESS STORY

Infrastructure service provider: Digex, Inc.
Customer: Continuity, Inc.
**Key elements of the solution: Turnkey deployment, advanced hardware/
software platform, world-class data centers and network, proactive
customer service, impressive capitalization**

Today's customers take good customer service for granted. After all, with
so many companies migrating their sales services to the Internet, customers expect prompt support anywhere and anytime. Indeed, customer
service has become a major competitive differentiator for BAMs and dotcoms alike. Continuity, Inc., a CRM software vendor, saw this pressure to
perform as an opportunity, not an obstacle. If it could offer CRM applications as an ASP, it stood to reason corporations that needed to offer virtual customer service fast would flock to their new venture.

Although Continuity had the dotcom mentality to conceive of such a
venture, and the required customer service technology and methodologies, it was out of its depth when it came to high-end infrastructure back
ends required to support dependable ASP operations. By partnering with
Digex, a well-known ISP that now features infrastructure service provision for ASPs, Continuity could launch Continuity Solutions, a pure play
ASP offering hosted e-CRM. Its hosted PinPoint application now delivers
a full array of CRM services like real-time chat and screen sharing that
promote better company-to-customer interaction.

"In our market, 'first-mover' advantage is absolutely critical," says
Douglas Brockett, Continuity Solution's vice president of sales and business development. Leveraging Digex's value-added hosting components,
Continuity ramped up its hosted solution with preemptive rapidity. "Because Digex was there for us," Brockett says, "we were able to be the first
to deliver e-CRM as an ASP."

Digex is a premier provider of ASP managed services and physical and IT resources. With hosted e-business customers like Nike and
integration partners like Andersen Consulting, it maintains a high profile as an infrastructure service provider. But also contributing to this

continued

notoriety are its world-class hardware platform and guaranteed provisioning services. Digex is the largest Windows NT-based hosting company in the world, and last year received $50 million each from Microsoft and Compaq to develop and manage a suite of high-performance application hosting services. With that depth of resources, Digex can afford to offer some very aggressive service levels. Indeed, Digex guarantees deployment of servers within 10 days for any new ASP it supports, and rapid—and nonintrusive—rollout for ASP server upgrades.

It was just such efficient execution that so impressed Continuity. In its data centers, Digex promptly configured the appropriate backup and recovery resources to ensure that Continuity's client data would always be available. Then it took the needed precautions to harden and secure the ASP's servers. Indeed, with redundant power generators, and air-cooling and fire suppression systems, Digex's "SmartCenters" are constructed to withstand virtually any disaster. They also feature keycard and biometric palm reader security technology as well as security guards for optimal physical security.

The rock-solid reliability that ASPs require extends to Digex's world-class network. Digex has partnered with WorldCom for its broadband network that spans more 2,500 points of presence (POPs) throughout North America, Europe, and the Pacific Rim. It's also established peering agreements with most major providers and ISPs. So, in emergencies, ASP customers are guaranteed instant failover to backup networks.

Digex is also fanatic about customer service—diagnosing and resolving unanticipated technology problems quickly. For instance, by monitoring its network for anticipated congestion, Digex can proactively add capacity for an ASP to head off any performance degradation. As a customer service specialist, Continuity was especially impressed with Digex's guaranteed 24/7 support of its continuous customer service operations.

All of these service components come standard with Digex's app-Link Partner Program, which makes it easy for ASPs just to "plug into" its managed hosting infrastructure and value-added services. As an app-Link member, Continuity qualified for services like dedicated support personnel, access to the Digex portal, which lets ASP customers view elements

continued

of the Digex operating environment like trouble ticket status, as well as Digex's testing platform, where ASPs can configure and test new applications. "There are a lot of people out there offering hosting services," says Brocket. "The problem is, they don't always have the capability to provide the application environment and quality of service."

Digex is one infrastructure service provider that does. And it proved this by going live with Continuity's first ASP customer in only seven days.

ASP-Enabling Software Platforms

Although not yet an integral element of many ASP architectures, ASP-enabling software platforms will proliferate because they help the ASP more quickly integrate hosted applications into the ASP network/hardware/software infrastructure. Such platforms offer shared services and a common interface into which ASP application developers can plug hosted applications. Offered by platform vendors or third-party developers, some provide integrated functional services like software for the database, collaboration engine, Web server, and application server. Others offer a set of core business applications like general ledgers, expense tracking, purchase requisitions, and human resources. In any case, like traditional product suites or rapid application environments, they operate as a single application that accelerates the integration of certain types of ASP software platform back-end and middleware environments (like IBM/Lotus databases, operating system, Web and application servers) with hosted applications of a similar flavor (like Lotus collaborative applications such as Notes and Domino). Or they provide commonly needed business functionality like e-commerce ordering and billing that the ASP may use to charge its customers for hosted and other services.

Value-Added Services

ASPs differentiate themselves further with value-added services that help ASP customers with custom tasks that the ASP's 80% hosted applications don't address (Figure 2–6).

Some ASPs further customize their 80% applications to map more accurately to your existing business processes. Although this slows down deployment,

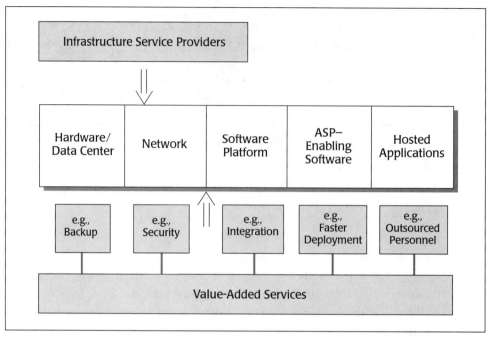

Figure 2–6 Infrastructure service providers, enabling software and value-added services enhance the ASP IT infrastructure

you save money in the long term because of the better efficiencies that result. Customers also invariably reengineer their processes, merge with other companies, and add staff and new positions as they grow—all of which may require an ASP to refine the hosted application later to address these changes.

Some ASPs partner with software vendors and integrators to offer hosted services and to retain the option of later converting customers to more complex and profitable installed applications. They, of course, charge additionally for subsequently converting the hosted application and integrating it with legacy computing platforms.

Although ASP customers expect basic technical support and customer service, levels of both differ among ASPs. In general, levels of each vary according to criteria like troubleshooting response time, level of data security, extent of data backup, and so on. Whether these services are classified as technical support or customer service varies from ASP to ASP.

Many ASPs offer accelerated deployment schedules for premium fees—for instance, 14, 21, and 60 days for a progressively higher cost. For large, complicated hosted applications with hundreds of seats, the routine "turn-on" procedure may be quite time-consuming. It may involve tasks like creating user IDs, populating hosted applications with legacy data from customer repositories, and ordering leased lines or VPN access for network functionality. So a customer that needs to get to market fast may pay extra for faster deployment. Customers with tighter budgets and less time-sensitive applications, on the other hand, may opt to wait longer and pay less.

Customers like dotcom start-ups short on staff may benefit by outsourcing personnel from an ASP instead of committing salaries and benefits to permanent staff. After all, a start-up's first priority is creating and launching a product with a limited amount of venture funding. So some ASPs outsource highly qualified IT staff like database administrators and others that are now in short supply in the computing industry at large. Some will even outsource executives like chief executive officers and chief information officers with general experience in launching businesses and with special competence in the ASP business and IT models.

ASPs also offer technological functionality like additional enterprise storage, data backup and security as value-added services.

Key Concepts

- ASP—Partnership among players with expertise in hardware, networking, software applications, and vertical markets for the purpose of leasing hosted applications to remote customers over broadband networks
- Hardware platform—Should be robust and massively scalable
- Hardware players—Hardware vendors, IXCs, RBOCs, CLECs, and ISPs
- Networks—Should be reliable, high capacity, and scalable, and may offer quality of service
- Network players—IXCs, RBOCs, CLECs, ISPs, and SIs
- Hosted software applications—Web-enabled, scalable, 80%, sometimes modular
- TBAs—VARs, integrators, and specialists outside the channel that provide, often via their own brand, vertical market expertise to ASPs
- Infrastructure service providers—Lease resources like data centers and servers to ASPs and function as their common back end
- ASP enabling software—Speeds integration and provides common business functionality
- Value-added services—ASP Services that help customers with tasks that 80% of applications don't address

CHAPTER THREE

The ASP Hardware Platform

This chapter discusses

- Dedicated server provisioning
- Shared server provisioning
- Clustered servers
- Load balancing across clustered servers
- Caching Web content on servers
- Why smaller ASP servers are better
- Server "capacity on demand"

An ASP's services to its customers are guaranteed in the SLA. Given this fact—and assuming there is no special hardware stored on the customer premises—you might wonder, "As long as the ASP provides the required service, why should I worry about what hardware it uses in its data center?"

The short answer is this: to make sure it's the best hardware platform for your required solution. Why waste money on a superplatform, if you only have to support 20 users with Lotus Notes? Why save money on a mid-range platform if you risk poor support for 1,000 users with SAP ERP?

Your own IT staff has to address more specific concerns like, depending on the application, whether the hardware should be input/output (I/O) intensive versus transaction intensive. In general, though, ASPs should "overprovision" to ensure their SLA guarantees are bulletproof. That's why, despite how an ASP describes its infrastructure, services, and SLA guarantees, you should always visit the data center and examine the hardware. For instance, confirm the power and model of processors, determine how the servers are configured for maximum power and flexibility, and note the ASP's contingency measures when a server fails. Even if you are providing the hardware and simply housing it in the ASP's data center, confirm that it's properly maintained and managed.

With this in mind, there is no universally "right" ASP hardware platform. The best hardware platform for you depends on numerous variables like customer size, number of customers, growth rate of users, cost of leased data center space, and so on. The discussion of hardware that follows, then, is not prescriptive. These are general recommendations about the kinds of components, characteristics, and capabilities most suitable for hardware in an ASP environment.

Hardware Components

As discussed earlier, most ASPs deploy various types of servers, and each server's function is determined by the type of software loaded on it. Application servers store the hosted application operations, and their software interprets data in the databases; database servers store and process the customer's data; Web servers deliver Web pages and let the hosted software transmit data to standard Web browsers; and thin client servers host thin clients on the customer's site and function, in essence, as remote application servers for the ASP.

Some combination of such servers comprises the middle layer of what's known as a *three-tier computing architecture*. A client tier contains logic related to the presentation of information (in other words, the graphical user interface) and makes requests to applications through a browser using Web-optimized software like Java. Web application servers contain the business logic and processes that control the reading and writing of data. Other servers provide data storage and transactional applications used by the Web application servers. Clients access the servers from the customer premises and initiate application functionality on the servers, which in turn access relevant data in the data repositories.

Hardware Provisioning

ASPs can provision the servers for you in several ways. Whether they house the servers in an infrastructure service provider's data center or in their own, ASPs can offer you "dedicated" or "shared" provisioning. With dedicated provisioning, servers are dedicated to one customer: Only that customer's applications run on those servers. In this model, either the ASP's infrastructure service provider or the ASP itself installs and configures the servers in the respective data center, and then manages the servers and applications running on them. With shared provisioning, you share servers and applications running on them that the ASP owns and manages.

Each model has its advantages. With dedicated provisioning, the ASP procures, installs, deploys, and manages a new server and application "instance" (a copy of the application like a duplicate ERP application) for each new ASP customer. In a dedicated model, the provider's hardware platform grows in large increments of, for example, servers 1 to 10 for customer 1 + servers 11 to 20 for customer 2 + servers 21 to 30 for customer 3 = the sum functionality of the increasing number of servers that the ASP must buy and manage. Obviously, as more servers are added, managing them becomes more costly, complex, and personnel and technology intensive. This could present eventual problems for you as a customer. Obviously, if the ASP's costs are higher, it's likely your leasing rate will be too. Also, with an additive hardware strategy, unless the provider increases its profit margin, the additional equipment, personnel, and time diminish its returns as your application grows in size and complexity. And, of course, size and complexity increase not only the number of IT specialists needed for the application but also the intensity and difficulty of their routine activity. At some point they may even have to redesign the system to suit your server requirements. Shortly you'll see how ASPs can alleviate these problems by "clustering" servers.

With shared provisioning, the ASP manages the applications of multiple customers on the same servers. All customers lease a common set of hosted software applications residing on common operating systems and middleware, and their data is securely, but only "logically" (not actually), set off from other customers' data, although it resides in the same databases on the same servers. Because each new customer requires only space for its data—not new servers and application instances—the hardware platform grows in much smaller increments of, for example, servers 1 to 10 for customer 1 + customer 2 + customer 3, servers 11 to 20 for customer 4 + customer 5 + customer 6, . . . = the shared functionality of fewer servers that the ASP must buy and manage. Shared provisioning lets the ASP reap economies of scale as it hosts more customers. Because its hardware costs are less for each customer, every new customer brings in more profit but incurs less and less additional cost. Eventually, of course, more customers will exhaust each server's capacity, and new servers may need to be added. However, in the overall scheme, the ASP's equipment and management costs are much less than with dedicated provisioning.

Nonetheless, some customers feel less secure sharing their servers with other customers. For others, like very large corporations, the large number of servers needed may prohibit sharing. You really need not worry about *data confidentiality* with shared provisioning though. ASPs encrypt each customer's data differently and use other methods to ensure confidentiality. You're more likely to encounter problems with another customer's application affecting the *availability* of your application—for instance, if some activity of another customer affects the operating system you share with them. This said, if the ASP's infrastructure is sufficiently robust, this should never be a problem. In any case, you the customer must decide whether you can live with the trade-off between lower price and these possible risks.

Server Clustering

ASPs can deploy servers as stand-alone computers with one or more processors, or as clustered computers that back up each other and share applications. In any enterprise environment, but especially in an ASP environment, servers must be able to scale readily as applications and users are added. Clustering enables easier scaling as well as other benefits that are especially useful for ASPs.

Server administrators scale stand-alone servers by adding processors. However, as they add more, the applications on the servers scale with decreasing returns. Stand-alone configurations are adequate for many applications—even for simple applications hosted by ASPs. But installed enterprise applications and multiple enterprise applications hosted by an ASP typically require a more robust, elegant, and reliable configuration like clustering.

In a networked server environment, a cluster interconnects multiple servers so they perform as a highly efficient, single-server system, which is much more affordable, robust, reliable, and scalable than stand-alone servers. Various resources like a Web server, database, and network file server may exploit the combined functionality of the server cluster for more affordable server allocation. As users call on each resource in turn for intensified activity, the active resource can pull from the combined functionality of the server cluster for better performance. If one server in the cluster fails, another takes over for it for improved reliability. Often clusters are designed so at least one server is inactive while the others are engaged. If one of the engaged servers fails, the inactive server engages in its place. And adding servers to the cluster lets it scale to accommodate more users, applications, or intensified activity.

As mentioned earlier, stand-alone and clustered servers scale differently. Stand-alone servers dedicate all of an additional server's functionality to a limited set of resources. In clusters, the additional server's potential functionality gets contributed to the cluster's functionality pool from which multiple sets of resources can draw as needed. With stand-alone servers, the performance of the fixed set of resources is limited to the maximum performance of the single computer. With clusters, the performance of a larger set of resources is limited to the sum of available functionality of the entire cluster. The resources pull from different combinations of servers at different times. Thus, although fewer servers support more sets of resources, each set has more functionality available to it than if it were supported by a stand-alone server (Figure 3–1).

When implemented with SANs—a common strategy for ASPs—clustered servers permit faster data transfer between data repositories and client software, so users experience much less latency (delay in getting information) in system performance. Clustering also helps reduce the number of servers an ASP must support in the limited space of its data center.

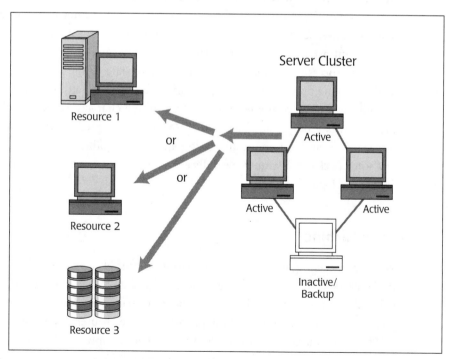

Figure 3–1 A server "cluster" dynamically allocates functionality to multiple resources

Load Balancing

Load-balancing software distributes user request loads for application functionality across servers so individual servers in a cluster never become so overloaded that system performance deteriorates. However, the load-balancing software presents only one virtual host image to the clients making the requests, so the clients behave as if they are accessing one, albeit larger, server.

Basic load-balancing packages distribute requests sequentially across the pool of clustered servers: Request 1 to server 1, request 2 to server 2, and so forth, until, for a six-server cluster, request 7 goes to server 1 and the cycle starts over. These packages are inexpensive and easy to implement but operate blindly—they can't receive feedback about a server's current load or availability. So users whose requests they send to busy or disabled servers experience frustrating delays until the request finds a less busy server or a system administrator intervenes to bring up or replace the failed server.

Basic load balancing also operates democratically. It doesn't discriminate between powerful and less powerful servers. Load-balancing software that sends the same number of requests to a server with slower processing and I/O rates than those in the cluster with faster processing and I/O rates will quickly overload the slower server and undermine overall system performance.

By contrast, intelligent load-balancing software can direct requests to servers with the processing power and I/O rates appropriate to the request. Intelligent load balancing prevents slower servers in a cluster from getting overloaded and lets administrators combine servers with differing characteristics to exploit best their aggregate power and capabilities. What's more, such software can detect server failure and automatically route requests to another server in the cluster, and some packages also automatically engage a backup server to take over for the failed one (Figure 3–2).

Web Server Caching

Web server caching is the practice of storing commonly accessed Web content on ASP servers so customers have faster access to it than if they requested it from the original location on the Web. Caching moves Web content that may be located 20 "hops" (sections of Internet network between the "routers" that direct data to and from destinations) away to ASP servers that are only one or two hops away. Some caching servers can hold a terabyte or more of Web content, easily enough to handle customers' most common Web requests.

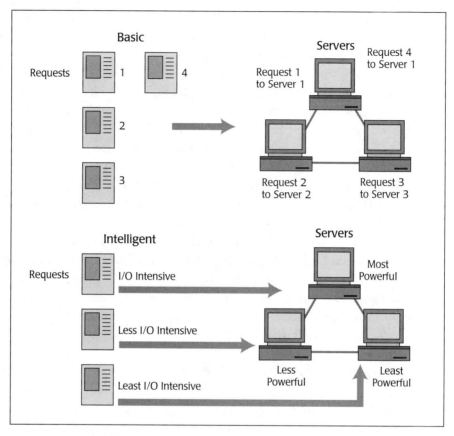

Figure 3–2 Intelligent load balancing allocates requests to the servers best suited to handle them

Characteristics of ASP Servers

Although mainframes, minicomputers, workstations, and PCs can all be used as servers, if an ASP wants to leverage the benefits of clustering and load balancing, it will deploy many smaller servers rather than fewer larger ones. This is not to say mainframes and minis are inefficient servers. They can be deployed as back-end servers in a client/server architecture right alongside PCs. Indeed, if an ASP is leveraging legacy infrastructure to save on server investments, mainframes and minis can be designed as powerful stand-alone servers. But these older, larger computers allow for less flexibility in the way the ASP exploits all of its server resources. Smaller servers, as well as being less expensive, can—with the right strategy—be easier to manage and consume less electric power. When it comes to ASP servers, smaller is usually better.

This is true for another obvious reason: Data centers have limited floor and rack space, so the more servers the ASP can pack into its data center, the more customers it can accommodate and the fewer data centers it needs to lease or build as its customer base grows. This keeps their costs down and they can pass on the savings to you, the customer. Most of the major hardware vendors have launched new server lines that feature smaller, more powerful servers with denser form factors, more powerful processors, and higher I/O rates.

Also, there's a movement among hardware vendors known as *capacity on demand* that accommodates ASPs' needs for scalability. Vendors now enable affordable and fast scalability, for instance, with servers that add power by simply adding processors to individual computers. Some vendors also let ASPs store servers at their data centers to ensure they are on hand and can be promptly deployed. Thus, deployment is quicker than a field upgrade or installing additional servers. But adding servers should not entail expensive and time-consuming system reconfiguration. ASPs benefit when they can scale without significantly redesigning the system or replacing hardware.

Scalability also requires server flexibility—or expandability. It helps if an ASP can upgrade individual servers by expanding I/O and memory after installation. It also helps if this process can be accomplished without interrupting system operations—a technique known as a *rolling upgrade.* And it helps if the hardware vendor designs the servers to be optimized in clustered configurations and by adding software enhancements like load balancing.

If an ASP needs to support customers with different legacy environments, it will need servers that operate well with different clients, operating systems, databases, and storage devices. In addition to standard Web browsers and interactive PCs, state-of-the-art servers should support wireless devices like laptops, PDAs, and even cell phones. This requires compatibility with remote device operating systems like Windows CE and wireless standards like the Wireless Access Protocol (WAP). With the explosive growth of the affordable Linux open source operating system, more customers who may have run an exclusively UNIX- or Windows NT-based software platform in the past are now developing some applications on Linux too (for example, for departments or special projects). And although many customers have standardized their environments on, for example, Oracle databases, this is not to say that they don't also deploy Lotus Notes, Microsoft

Exchange, and other databases for messaging and other uses. Thus, ASP servers must be able to process data in these repository formats too, even if it's just to transfer the data from your legacy systems to their in-house data center repositories. Most ASPs storing vast amounts of customer data do so on their own SANs, so their servers should be optimized to integrate easily and operate well in SAN environments.

As wireless technology improves and more users can access data and applications via wireless devices, ASPs will have to develop anytime/anywhere, device-independent system access. Doing so requires more than one-dimensional system/device wireless compatibility. Users who normally access an application from an in-house interface on their PC will want access via a similar interface when they are on the road using a wireless device. If they're used to subsecond response times in-house, they'll be loathe to wait five seconds or more to access those applications on the road. By the same token, system administrators will be able to tolerate only so much additional management complexity in enabling users access from multiple types of devices. They not only will have to manage more devices, they'll have to troubleshoot more technology- and user-caused problems with the newer devices.

In the face of increasing technological and logistical complexity, ASP data center administrators will need simplified management practices, processes, and tools. For instance, they can streamline troubleshooting by offering both proactive and reactive scalability. Proactive scalability allows them to scale up a system in advance to accommodate additional, anticipated activity. Reactive scalability automatically and dynamically allocates resources to handle unanticipated activity. A server environment designed to share resources on demand dynamically—like a clustered architecture—enables both types of scalability.

More traditional server architectures, in which one application is run on one server, underuse system resources because most applications experience widely varying levels of usage at different times, such as an e-mail system at 9 AM on a Monday versus 2 AM on a Friday. To safeguard against unanticipated overloads, traditional server strategies typically allowed as much as 20% more capacity on each server than its highest previously experienced demand. But overengineering the system was expensive because much of the equipment was never fully exploited. Similarly, as systems got larger and more complex, more personnel were needed to manage them, and management became increasingly decentralized. So, companies were paying more for extra equipment and personnel.

Many server vendors are now designing their servers to be deployed and managed in a more integrated fashion. Whereas the traditional approach deployed each new application on its own unique server that functioned independently of other applications and other servers, the new strategy treats servers, storage, and network interfaces as one integrated system, dynamically supporting many different applications as needed. Such a configuration "logically" represents a set of physical resources for use by the system. Administrators can reconfigure such a system on the fly—without interrupting system operations—by adding and dropping servers and by changing the storage network and computer network routes between servers. Most important, all the applications in the configuration can exploit all of its resources. Applications can share all data in the storage layer, and all elements in the configuration are inherently redundant and automatically back up similar elements in the event of device failures. You might think of this strategy as *value-added clustering.*

However, each configuration also functions independently of other such configurations. Administrators can run mission-critical applications in a configuration isolated from another one supporting less stable applications. Run in the same configuration, the less stable applications may incapacitate the resources needed by the mission-critical applications. In general, then, an integrated server approach centralizes resources that support multiple servers, which simplifies management of the servers and resources, reduces the risk of system failure, and cuts costs by more intelligently leveraging equipment and personnel.

Finally, bear in mind some often-overlooked factors affecting server environment performance. Although it's critical that servers be able to handle a high number of transactions, Web site hits, and Web page and database requests, they must also be able to back up data to SANs at fast rates. After all, data centers typically support many customers and schedule only so much slow time for backup activities. Depending on the legacy infrastructure of an ASP and its customers, servers may also have to interoperate with other servers of different brands. Also, the more applications an ASP runs, the more likely it is one computer will have to support multiple instances of application server software. Doing so should not undermine its performance. And, of course, the more intelligently an ASP manages its server and related resources, the lower its overall cost of operation, which means it can pass on its savings to you in the form of lower leasing and other fees.

Key Concepts

- Dedicated provisioning—ASP dedicates certain servers to one customer; additive server scaling; costly and complex management
- Shared provisioning—ASP manages multiple customers' on the same servers; logarithmic server scaling; less costly management as a result of economies of scale
- Server cluster—Networked multiple servers that perform as a single-server system that's more affordable, robust, reliable, and scalable than stand-alone servers
- Load balancing—Distributing user requests across servers in a cluster so no server gets overloaded and system performance doesn't deteriorate
- Web caching—Storing commonly accessed Web content on ASP servers so customers get faster access than if they requested it from the Web location
- Smaller ASP servers are better—Easier to cluster and manage, less expensive, and use less electricity and data center rack space
- Capacity on demand—Adding processors or storing servers on hand for faster deployment, instead of installing new servers

CHAPTER FOUR

The Data Center

This chapter discusses

- A business impact analysis
- Recovery time objectives (RTOs)
- Backup and recovery
- Real-time backup
- Responsiveness
- Disaster recovery tests
- The ASP's SLAs with its supporting service providers
- Disaster recovery plans of an ASP's supporting service providers

Unlike, say, hardware, data centers must meet some basic criteria independent of the applications hosted from them. Of course, the data center infrastructure has to be disasterproof and physically secure. So you should always verify the measures ASPs have taken to withstand events like thunderstorms and earthquakes, and to secure the center from entry by unauthorized personnel.

However, building and preparing such a center is only the first step in the ASP's ongoing process of protecting your data. The means and processes of data center management are equally important. For instance, many companies don't need "deluxe" ASP data center support. They can prioritize their data availability and security needs by indicating to the ASP which functionality (such as a customer service Web site) must always be available and which data (like e-commerce orders) must be retained nightly instead of weekly. These strategies save you money and simplify an ASP's management chores.

Availability

The data center is the heart of the ASP. The hardware and software platforms, hosted applications, and broadband network, as well as storage devices for all customer data are located here. Data center requirements differ depending on the ASP's customer base, its geographical location, and other factors, but every data center must demonstrate fundamental dependability and security if customers are to trust their data to the ASP (Figure 4–1). Application hosting is a virtual IT model, so many ASPs promote their data centers with virtual site tours via the Internet as well as actual personal tours. Because the data center will function as a second home for your hosted hardware, data, and applications, visit it. Video tours are great marketing vehicles and they help you short-list data centers, but site visits are the only way to verify the nature and the extent of physical security, backup measures for data security, personnel and equipment devoted to server management, and so on. Experiencing the ASP's physical security processes, for instance, is the best way to determine if they are adequate.

As stated earlier, dependability requires availability. "Availability" is the percentage of uptime that a system can be used. Although customers would prefer 100% availability—operating 24 hours a day, 7 days a week, 365 days a year—it's just not feasible for every ASP. In general, uptime for mission-critical applications such as e-commerce financial transactions should be 99.99%. Best practices dictate different standards of availability for ASPs and their customers in different industries, and 99.9% availability may be adequate for manufacturing applications whereas 99.9999% may be required for financial service ones.

Any ASP should be willing to share its availability history detailing its uptime and downtime since its inception. If service has failed, you need to determine the cause and the length of the outage, and decide whether your business could survive such downtime.

Data Backup

ASPs offer different levels of backup and recovery to ensure system availability. It's always critical to determine whether backup and recovery are a standard

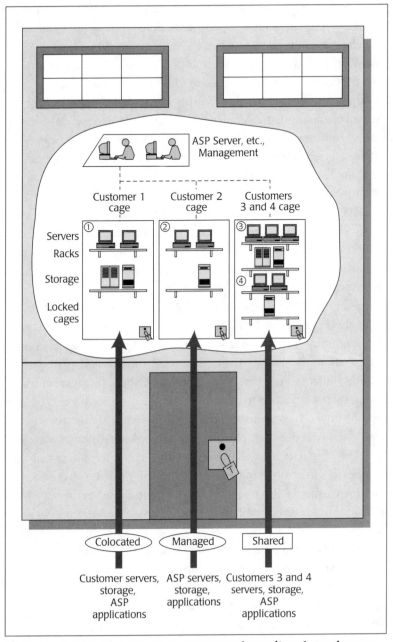

Figure 4–1 The data center manages and monitors leased space and computing resources

component of the SLA, how much is the charge for adding it to the SLA and, if it is not, how your company will perform backup and recovery internally.

Before evaluating ASP facilities, though, you should determine your data security risks by first assessing your internal operations. A business impact analysis estimates the financial damage incurred as a result of the loss of specific functionalities. The larger the loss, the higher the priority assigned to the operation or department. Essential operations like customer support or the IT department are typically high priority. However, you should also prioritize supporting applications, machines, staff, files, or records. In the event of disasters and the like, you should stipulate the ASP should recover the highest priority operations first. You should also establish RTOs for each application and business function to ensure the effectiveness of the plan. RTOs are the windows of time—usually measured in hourly increments—during which you must recover your applications or data. Once you determine your RTOs for each application, find out if ASP prospects can meet them.

Backup and recovery means the ASP copies data to a separate disk drive so it can be recovered if the original storage drive is harmed. Every ASP should have a backup and recovery plan comprised of a list of backup procedures for all data and applications. It should indicate the time intervals for data backup. Mission-critical applications like e-commerce that affect hourly business operations and visitor traffic to your Web site demand real-time backup. This means the ASP instantly "mirrors" new data to another site. Others, like human resource applications, that you use less frequently, the ASP will back up at longer intervals, say every 24 hours. Backup to an independent storage site is usually done at least daily. If the ASP does not perform this type of backup over a network, then it should back up data to tapes and manually send them off-site daily and/or store the tapes in a fireproof vault on-site. If the ASP provides electronic vaulting services, then it should also maintain a log of their backup activity. It's worth noting that you should consider different types of database backups. Do you need cold backups (the database is off-line) or hot backups (the database is on-line)? Consider the costs and benefits of both and specify your preference with the ASP.

The plan should also list management policies and staff dependencies related to backup and recovery that documents standard policies and each employee's specific responsibilities in the backup and recovery procedure. Employees will follow these procedures if automatic backup fails. The plan should further indicate how often the ASP trains its employees in such procedures. With the high staff turnover in many technology companies, the ASP should avail new employees of training opportunities fast. Best practices, such as those of International Standards Organizations (ISOs) 9002-registered companies, assign responsibility for business operations, application support, and the backup and recovery process to at least two employees, and train staff annually at least, and quarterly in some cases. Such measures guarantee continuity of expertise in the event an employee leaves or is incapacitated or unavailable during a service interruption.

Natural Disasters

A data center cannot be too impregnable to severe weather such as blizzards, tornadoes, hurricanes, earthquakes, and flash floods. Thunderstorms, because they are so common, are especially threatening to the ongoing operations of such structures. An ASP should take the precautions necessary to protect its data center from natural disasters common to its location (Figure 4–2). If it's located near fault lines, for instance, it should be specifically reinforced against earthquakes.

Local conditions could call for any of the following measures:

- Below-ground and above-ground power feeds
- Multiple power and driving routes to the building from the power provider
- Multiple power providers, the second possibly in a location not affected by the same forces as the first
- An uninterruptible power supply (UPS) that supports all data center equipment relevant to the customer's business for a period that covers maximum possible downtimes

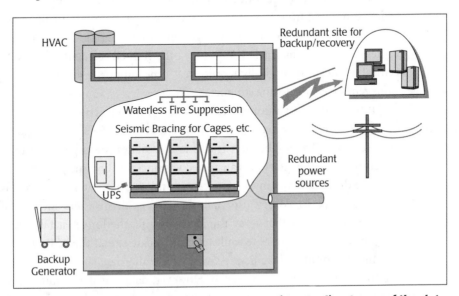

Figure 4–2 ASPs must take numerous precautions to disasterproof the data center

- A backup generator that supports all data center equipment and does not have to be refueled for a period that covers maximum possible downtimes
- Multiple telecommunications paths into the data center
- Multiple telecommunications carriers, the second possibly in a location not affected by the same forces as the first
- Alternate means of communication, such as satellite or wireless
- An emergency action team to support personnel on-site
- Ready supplies and instructions on their use during a disaster
- Alternate processing sites, the second possibly in a location not affected by the same forces as the first
- Equipment at the site secured to withstand relevant natural disasters

Responsiveness

Whereas "availability" refers to hours of live, dedicated staff and customer support (such as a 24-hour technical support help desk), "responsiveness" is the time interval between the initial customer query and the provider response (such as an e-mail response within one hour of the query). The way the ASP staffs customer support and help desk operations determines the level of responsiveness to customer queries.

An ASP will field queries either in real time (dedicated staff will take phone calls) or nonreal time (you'll leave inquiries in staff's voice mailboxes, contact them by e-mail, and so on). Many large companies operate customer support call centers 24/7, whereas smaller ASPs may offer limited call center hours. Mission-critical applications typically require real-time support, whereas other applications require nonreal-time support.

If the ASP has an automated application running its help desk, then after the customer places an initial phone call or e-mail, the ASP's support staff issues a trouble ticket. The application tracks and escalates the urgency of the trouble ticket to ensure the query gets answered within a certain time period.

The distance between the data center and alternate sites can also affect storage, backup, and recovery, especially for large-scale disasters such as failure of power grids. The farther away the alternate site, the longer it takes to transfer tapes from the ASP's on-site vault to the alternate site. If the ASP uses electronic vaulting to an off-site facility, recovery at the alternate site is much more rapid and the process can be automated. However, data transfer requirements across multiple connections to reach the storage destination can be costly.

MANAGEMENT SERVICE PROVIDERS (MSPs)

A subset of infrastructure service providers, MSPs manage hardware, software, and network resources for multiple ASPs and other organizations via a remote connection on a subscription basis. MSPs can deploy and configure an ASP's technology, but they also often define the process by which the technology is used. For instance, they might establish change management procedures by which servers and software are upgraded, or might determine cycles for automated data backup. Typical MSP services include performance monitoring and reporting, performance load testing, desktop management, and service-level tracking.

MSP services provide both end user and the ASP detailed and real-time information on the availability, security, and performance of the IT infrastructure. The ASP can then use that data to assess the end user's experience with its hosted service as well as to monitor and measure the performance of its ASP partners to confirm they are meeting their respective SLAs.

MSPs use advanced tools to collect, summarize, and organize performance data automatically like transaction rates, and then present it to appropriate ASP personnel who can act on it to troubleshoot systems problems or to optimize system performance. Certain tools also autonomously carry out critical management tasks like Web server load balancing. For example, an MSP might place a Java applet on the ASP customer's home page so they can confirm at any time that the ASP is meeting relevant SLA performance levels.

More specifically, much the way network service providers conduct "pinging" and other actions to measure the throughput of a WAN, MSPs run test scenarios comprised of "virtual transactions" that mimic the activities of real transactions so the MSP can measure the ongoing performance of the hosted application. Proactive monitoring like this detects system anomalies before they can hurt performance.

By engaging MSPs, ASPs benefit in numerous ways: They reduce their risks in deploying expensive and complicated technology and in retraining staff on upgrades and new releases, they lower their entry costs and time-to-market by leasing MSP services instead of deploying their own, and they supplement limited internal staff with experts who are less costly to retain than full-time personnel.

SUCCESS STORY

MSP: Lucent Technologies Worldwide Services
Customer: NaviSite
Key elements of the solution: Outsourced staff, VPN performance and security optimization, ongoing performance monitoring, resold MSP services

NaviSite, an infrastructure service provider specializing in hosting e-business Web sites for companies like Restoration Hardware, was adding customers so fast it had to scale up its network to accommodate the increased demand. In working with Lucent Technologies Worldwide Services on reconfiguring its network, NaviSite was so impressed it retained the company for ongoing performance, SLA, and security monitoring.

With the shortage of qualified IT specialists, however, NaviSite did a lot of research before deciding on Lucent. "It's a real challenge for us to find qualified network engineers to support our rapidly growing network needs," said Ted Crawford, director of product architecture at NaviSite. "We chose Lucent . . . because their engineers are skilled in the specific technologies we were interested in, especially Cisco routers, software, and local directory technologies, as well as WAN issues. Our original statement of work was for staff augmentation," he continues, "but it quickly evolved as we saw the depth of their network knowledge. . . . Lucent . . . engineers were soon helping us develop our network architecture and assisting us with strategic planning," he adds.

Network redundancy was an especially critical factor in maintaining NaviSite's quality of service. However, Lucent engineers helped NaviSite design its core infrastructure with no single points of failure, so it could offer customers an end-to-end service guarantee of 99.9% or better for its core database services, Web server services, and facility and network infrastructure. Together, the companies also redesigned the network to be flexible and scalable enough to handle large, unpredictable peaks of bandwidth usage, and worked with various network providers to rebalance the routes across all carriers with which NaviSite had peering arrangements.

continued

> When NaviSite expanded its two major data centers, Lucent engineers helped it develop and deploy a security infrastructure that included firewalls, intrusion detection software, lightweight directory access protocol (LDAP) servers, and token-based authorization. At the same time, they set up NaviSite's VPN which features authentication, login facilities, and a firewall at the main data center in Andover, MA.
>
> Today, the heart of Lucent's ongoing support is its VitalNet network performance monitoring solution that lets NaviSite accurately monitor, analyze, manage, and predict network performance. VitalNet continuously gathers and aggregates performance data from routers, switches, WAN links, and servers so NaviSite can benchmark network behavior, efficiently troubleshoot network problems, and optimize the performance of network devices. It presents all data in standard and custom reports that allow IT staff to identify and resolve bottlenecks, verify carrier compliance with SLAs, and reduce WAN costs.
>
> With Lucent MSP specialists performing its regular network baseline, manageability, and security audits, NaviSite is reselling these services to its customers. Indeed, in addition to offering hosting services, it has now repackaged *itself* as an MSP.
>
> ---
>
> Permission courtesy of Lucent Technologies Worldwide Services

Updating and Testing Disaster Recovery Plans

ASPs should update their disaster recovery plans at least twice a year after each testing phase. They should also update plans when they lose, gain, or change personnel within their operation, when they add new hosted applications or change corporate locations, or when they make a major hardware or software purchase such as a SAN. Monthly or quarterly updates are recommended.

They should also periodically test their disaster recovery procedures. Disaster recovery tests evaluate emergency procedures and provisions for hardware, applications, networks, recovery sites, workspace, and staffing. There are five kinds: tabletops, walkthroughs, simulations, scheduled alternate site tests, and automated tests. At a minimum, the ASP should perform one or more of these tests at least twice a year, and you should participate directly in at least one of these. Best practice dictates ASPs perform three: usually an alternate site, auto-mated, and tabletop or walkthrough.

A tabletop test is conducted as a workshop during which each disaster recov-ery team verbally reviews the processes to recover data and applications. A walk-through test is similar but more in depth. Emergency management personnel as well as relevant staff members in each of your business or information systems units report on their duties and detail how to implement specific tasks and con-tact other staff members involved in the process. Simulation exercises are more complex. Your staff actually play their respective roles in the disaster recovery plan to determine the plan's effectiveness against a fictional set of disasters, and the tests can last from several hours to two days.

Alternate site testing ensures the alternate site operates correctly during the recovery process. You define the company's objectives, prepare a test plan, and write your data validation plan about three months prior to the test. These plans provide guidelines and set expectations for the testing process. The actual alter-nate site test works much like a simulation exercise, with one major difference: the servers, applications, and databases at the test site are brought on-line, and validation procedures are run to verify that the RTO is met. Team members responsible for validation perform the procedures to ensure the alternate site functions properly and the data is accurate.

Automated tests require very little interaction from team and staff members. They involve the ASP's robotic monitoring systems that perform queries on soft-ware and applications on a regular basis to determine their operational status. If the software does not respond to the query, an automated response mechanism sends a message to the team member responsible for the operation or to the soft-ware vendor to initiate recovery activities.

Typical SLAs offer customers two eight-hour days of testing annually per-formed on-site at the ASP, with an option to purchase more time. ASPs with numerous customers may not be able to test all of them at once. Instead, they may establish a revolving test schedule that tests one set of customers, then another, and so on, until it's sufficiently tested the entire customer base.

ASP Partner and Alternate Site Backup

Whether an ASP owns or leases a data center also influences backup operations. If the data center is leased, then the ASP's SLA with the infrastructure service provider determines your SLA with the ASP, so you should review that SLA.

Similarly, disaster recovery also depends on external sources such as the ASP's infrastructure service provider or MSP. It's important to understand how the ASP is affected by its partners' recovery plans. Partners should allocate sufficient employees to the ASP's recovery process so that even if the ASP is on the end of the recovery list, it isn't incapacitated unduly long.

The same applies to the ASP's alternate backup sites. For instance, they should be adequately staffed and have testing programs that ensure backup and recovery procedures remain up-to-date. By the same token, the ASP should dedicate sufficient staff to its own clients' recovery.

Environmental Control

Data centers should meet basic heating, ventilation, and air-conditioning (HVAC) requirements. It's also a good idea to have redundant air-conditioning systems for any physically separated room containing IT equipment, as well as raised floors for ventilation and wiring security.

ASPs should use waterless fire suppression and should construct separated fire zones and special cabinets to contain fires within a single building unit.

To protect against earthquakes, the ASP should harden and stormproof the data center facility, and install special cabinets with internal seismic bracing.

When ASPs share rooms, cabinets, or racks in a data center, unauthorized parties should be denied unsupervised physical access to those areas, and labels identifying ownership of customer equipment should not be visible from outside the cabinet or rack.

Key Concepts

- A business impact analysis—An estimation of the financial damage incurred from the loss of specific functionalities
- RTOs—The windows of time, usually measured in hourly increments, during which you must recover your applications or data
- Backup and recovery—Copying data to a separate disk drive so it can be recovered if the original storage drive is harmed
- Real-time backup—Instantly "mirroring" new data to another site
- Responsiveness—The time interval between the initial customer query and the provider response; queries fielded either by ASP in real time (with dedicated staff) or nonreal time (using voice mailboxes, and so on)
- Disaster recovery test—Evaluating emergency procedures and provisions for hardware, applications, networks, recovery sites, workspace, and staffing

CHAPTER FIVE

The ASP Network

This chapter discusses

- Network reliability
- Network capacity
- Network scalability
- Network players
- Network quality of service
- Network traffic load balancing and distribution
- Frame Relay
- Network overhead
- ATM
- Frame Relay/ATM interworking
- Network traffic management
- Network traffic shaping
- Wave division multiplexing (WDM)/DWDM
- xDSL
- Cable modems
- Wireless networks
- IP

Networking may be the most complex component of computing, but it is the most important element of an ASP solution. Therefore, it's probably a good idea that nontechnical managers understand the networking terms and technologies ASPs may use. With this in mind, the following discussion aims at being inclusive at the risk of repeating information about networking that you may have encountered elsewhere or that may be too technical for you. If you already know information or it's too technical, just skip it. The most important goal of this chapter is to give you an easy-to-understand and comprehensive reference to at least 90% of the information that could impact ASP networking.

The ASP Network—An Overview

In the data center, the ASP's various servers reside on it's own high-speed LAN or storage network. The LAN links to the ASP's network service provider WAN, which in turn may link to other providers' WANs to reach distant customers. Near the customer location, the WAN links to your *local loop* which links to the LAN on your site. Here your workers access the ASP's hosted applications from LAN-linked desktops. Via wireless devices like laptops, PDAs, and cell phones, your mobile employees may also access data and various ranges of application functionality from the same or different ASP equipped with wireless capabilities (Figure 5–1).

Access—ASP to Broadband WAN

An ASP can access its WAN link to you using LAN links of various capacities via different networking protocols. To connect data center servers to the data center's LAN backbone, the ASP will use the following types of connections as it needs more robust throughput: 100Base-X Ethernet, 1000Base-X Ethernet, Token

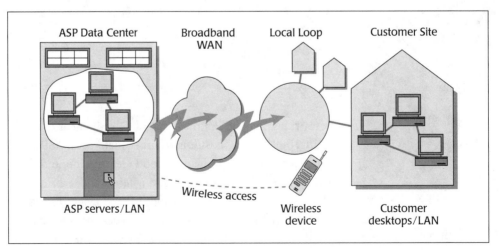

Figure 5–1   The ASP network links the Data Center via a broadband WAN to the customer site

Ring, or ATM. What's more, to ensure reliability, the ASP should create alternate LAN paths to dual network interface cards in each server to provide fault tolerance. Fault tolerance ensures that, if a hardware or network element fails, a duplicate element will back it up.

The LAN backbone linking the data center's server network to the broadband WAN must be more robust still. Because they need increasing capacities here, ASPs can use Switched 100Base-X, Switched 1000Base-X, or ATM. Whatever they choose, they'll also need to create redundant network paths to every server on the LAN, and to implement redundant hot-swapping power supplies in all LAN components to provide fault tolerance.

Obviously, an ASP's customer base determines its bandwidth requirements. Generally, the larger the customer—a G2000 versus an SMB versus a small office or home (SOHO)—the more bandwidth required. However, lots of smaller customers can also drive up an ASP's bandwidth needs.

The ASP's link from the LAN backbone to the broadband WAN can span a range of capacities and protocols as well. As an ASP needs greater capacity, it can use T1, T3, or fiber optics with synchronous optical network/synchronous digital hierarchy (SONET/SDH) links. In any case, the ASP should create alternate network paths to the WAN and provide redundant hot-swapping power supplies to back up routers linking the LAN backbone to the WAN (Figure 5–2).

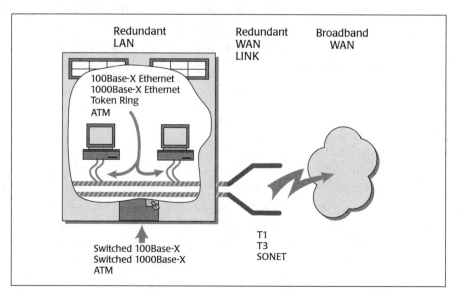

Figure 5–2 The data center LAN-to-WAN network section consists of a robust and redundant LAN and broadband link to the ASP WAN

ASPs with multiple, geographically dispersed data centers must be able to distribute and load balance inbound traffic from the WAN to the most cost-efficient data center. Network load balancing is a way of distributing traffic across a network such that no one section is so overburdened it creates a bottleneck that slows down all traffic having to pass through the section. Based on current load, availability, performance, and other factors, ASPs must also distribute and load balance traffic among the servers within each data center.

THE T CARRIER LEASED LINES

T1 and T3 describe dedicated physical network connections—connections comprised of network devices like wires and repeaters—between provider and customer. The link is a circuit that creates a transmission signal that is "boosted" every 5,000 to 6,000 feet by "repeaters" to maintain its rate of throughput. T carrier lines have specific speeds called their *digital signaling rate,* abbreviated as DS-1 for a T1 with a speed of 1.544 Mbps or DS-3 for a T3 with a speed of 44.736 Mbps. T1 connections are the most popular in the world because they offer good throughput in duplex (both directions) for both voice and data, and they're affordable for most medium and large businesses. T3s are less prevalent because they carry many times the capacity of T1s and are more expensive. In parts of the world other than North America, T1 and T3 are known as E1 and E3, respectively, and offer slightly faster throughput.

The larger and more numerous its customers, the greater must be the capacity of an ASP's link from its data center LAN to the WAN. As an ASP needs greater capacity here, it can deploy T1, T3, or SONET-based fiber optics. A router connects the link to the WAN and can perform load balancing and distribution. Of course, any device that can fail should be backed up by an identical redundant element. This is especially true because, if the ASP leases the WAN from a network service provider, the provider is typically not responsible for problems that occur from the router to the servers, only for problems on the WAN beyond the ASP's router.

SONET

SONET is an American telecommunications standard that lets carriers with optical networks transmit multiple signals from different sources at different speeds through a synchronous, optical hierarchy. With SONET, network providers with legacy networks that do not use optical lines can connect to an optical section of a network and have the varying types of signals transmitted in a standard way. This has great benefits for both the service providers and their users. If a provider could not link its legacy networks to optical infrastructures to achieve faster throughput, it would have to build complex and expensive optical networks to replace its older ones. If users had to commit to one provider's proprietary optical network, providers could lock them into expensive, although less than optimally efficient, contracts. SONET lets providers leverage their legacy networks, build their own optical networks at an affordable pace, and (because they can better manage costs) charge customers reasonable fees. Customers, in turn, can more easily switch providers if cost and service dictate.

The Broadband WAN

There is no definitive ASP broadband WAN, but ASPs deploy broadband connections of three types. They may deploy leased T1 and T3 lines to you and their other customers. If so, they never connect to the overlapping broadband networks of regional, national, and international network service providers. They could also use their own private WAN. In this case, they won't connect to that mediating infrastructure either. (Leased lines and private WANs are inherently secure because each is dedicated to a single customer.) And, of course, they can lease a WAN from a network partner like a long-distance carrier or an infrastructure service provider. Then the WAN will link to that multiprovider "cloud," and all customers will share the infrastructure. Because ASP customers require data security, WANs of this type must be VPNs. VPNs encrypt each customer's proprietary data in broadband tunnels through the Internet so that transmissions are secure. In this way, they leverage the geographical reach of the Internet but deploy security and broadband capacity to service customers better. Dedicated leased lines, privately owned WANs, and shared leased VPNs are the primary WAN infrastructures for ASPs.

Frame Relay

Most WANs used by ASPs are based on Frame Relay, ATM, or a combination of both technologies. Frame Relay and ATM are distinctly different types of networking technologies with unique strengths and drawbacks. Frame Relay is a "packet-switching" technology, which means that transmission data is broken down into uniform packets of content that are packaged with "overhead" information about the packet's destination address, the beginning and end of the packet, and a measure of the packet's quantity of content. The overhead data directs the packet, defines individual packets, and confirms whether a packet has been "corrupted" (content has been altered in some way) during transmission. If the packet has been corrupted, it's automatically discarded and the original content is retransmitted. Each packet contains different content that may be packaged identically or differently, but it is always the same quantity. Packets offer network service providers a standard measurement (that is, per packet) for charging for and performing transmission.

Overhead indicates how much a packet must be handled to reach its destination from its transmission source successfully. The more detailed the overhead data, the more sophisticated the packet handling. But, the more a network must handle a packet, the slower it reaches its destination. Most network technologies strike an acceptable trade-off between sophisticated routing, error detection, and speed of transmission. However, because of limitations in the available routing equipment, earlier network protocols like X.25 had to handle packets excessively to achieve acceptable routing accuracy and error detection, and handling slowed transmission speed. Newer Frame Relay routing equipment is more efficient, so it can handle data less and still deliver it without errors to the correct destination, but at much faster speeds. One reason for this is that Frame Relay error checks the packets at the transmission source and destination only. X.25 error checks packets at every joint linking network sections along the way. ATM, on the other hand, uses vast overhead to handle data in a very sophisticated fashion. This technology is so much faster than earlier network technologies that granular management is still possible without unacceptable degradation of speed.

Frame Relay is, more precisely, a "fast packet-switching" technology that improves speed by reducing the overhead associated with older packet-switched technologies. It also creates permanent virtual circuits (PVCs) to transmit data. A PVC is a network connection between source and destination in which routing decisions are made when the connection is created. With PVCs, greater throughput speed results from less handling, but dynamic routing to avoid congestion isn't possible. On the other hand, a switched virtual circuit (SVC) is a network connection between source and destination in which routing decisions are made in route at linking devices. With SVCs, throughput speed results from dynamic routing to avoid congestion, not from less handling. Frame Relay carries only voice and data, is used exclusively in WAN infrastructures, and transmissions occur at speeds varying from 56 Kbps to 2.048 Mbps.

Because Frame Relay accommodates both voice and data traffic, it must accept converted signals from voice devices as well as from different types of LANs (Ethernet and Token Ring). Once converted at the edge of the WAN, all traffic on the Frame Relay WAN is digital, and can be packaged into packets and transmitted. However, Ethernet and Token Ring packets are different sizes, and voice must be transmitted with no discernable interruption (continuously) to maintain high audible quality. Frame Relay addresses these challenges by offering a large-size packet and "interleaving" voice and data traffic.

Both Ethernet and Token Ring packets easily fit into the larger Frame Relay packets (4,096 bytes). Because voice calls are comprised of pauses as well as talking, there is latent available capacity in any Frame Relay network carrying voice and data. Interleaving lets the network provider intersperse voice data within a data stream and data into the breaks in voice transmission caused by pauses between talking. Interleaving, therefore, permits fast data transfer and continuous voice transmission over the same technology.

With Frame Relay, providers can charge for both voice and data without the expense of building separate networks, and users can get cheaper transmission rates because providers can charge less because they save on infrastructure costs. Because of these benefits, as well as the very high reliability and throughput using one transmission standard, Frame Relay is the world's most widely deployed WAN technology.

ATM

ATM, like Frame Relay, also uses packet switching, but it uses a particular type known as *cell relay* in which a data cell (a fixed-size frame consisting of a five-octet header for routing and other information and a 48-octet payload for the data content is the unit of transmission. Whereas Frame Relay transmits voice and data over WANs, ATM transmits voice, data, video, and multimedia over WANs, LANs, campus area networks (or CANs—linking LANs in close proximity like on a college campus or apartment complex), and metropolitan area networks (or MANs—

linking LANs throughout a metropolitan area (Table 5–1). Prior to ATM, providers had to use separate networks for voice/data and video, and often for voice and data and video.

Deployed over fiber-optic networks that already have unprecedented innate capacity, ATM enables the fastest network speeds available, starting at 1.544 Mbps and ranging to 622 Mbps now, with 2.488 Gbps projected for the relatively near future. In addition, ATM offers what is known as *quality of service*—the inherent ability to define different speeds for different types of data in different transmission modes (known as *categories of service*) for different customers. It also permits very precise traffic management. The provider can proportionately allocate the right amount and kind of bandwidth when certain kinds of transmissions (from mission-critical applications or voice, for instance) require instant or continuous transmission or when certain sections of a network (between manufacturing plants with interdependent activities, for instance) require massive throughput, and other sections (between regional sales offices, for instance) require minimal throughput. Such measures conserve network resources and save money for both provider and customer.

ATM spans heterogeneous networks comprised of different kinds of LANs, CANs, MANs, and legacy WANs by supporting numerous protocol interfaces where different types of networks join the ATM infrastructure. Although it would appear that so many protocol conversions in one interconnected network might cause unacceptable overhead, this isn't the case with ATM. Despite so much handling, ATM transmission speeds are many times faster than Frame Relay. Even if it was slower, because ATM is the only method for spanning such

Table 5–1 ATM Functions on More Types of Network than Any Other Network Protocol

Network	Selected Protocols	Ethernet	Token Ring	Dial-up	X.25	Leased Line	Frame Relay	ATM
LAN		✓	✓					✓
CAN								✓
MAN				✓		✓		✓
WAN				✓	✓	✓	✓	✓

Table 5–2 ATM Has the Fastest Transmission Speed of Any Network Protocol

Selected Protocols	Range of Speed
Ethernet	10–100 Mbps
Token Ring	4–16 Mbps
Dial-up	56 Kbps
X.25	56 Kbps in North America and 64 Kbps elsewhere
Leased Line	T1, 1.544 Mbps; T3, 44.736 Mbps
Frame Relay	5.6 Kbps–50 Mbps
ATM	1.544–622 Mbps

heterogeneous networks, users and providers would embrace it (Table 5–2). It's this aspect of the technology that offers the savings possible with "interworking"—integrating ATM with older networks so providers don't have to build entirely new desktop-to-desktop fiber infrastructures on which to run "pure" ATM. "Pure" ATM networks are rare and expensive, so bear in mind that ATM networks are almost always hybrids, comprised of ATM and some other networking technology. However, the capacity and other capabilities of ATM provide huge benefits even when deployed strategically in sections of a network.

ATM Traffic Management and Shaping

Once you commit to a category of service, the provider must manage the collective traffic of you and all other customers over one network with a fixed amount of bandwidth that far exceeds any one customer's needs but may be strained by particularly intense activity by multiple customers. The provider does this with "traffic management," which attempts to give all users equal access to the network's available bandwidth by using devices to monitor and, when needed, to manipulate the traffic flow. To maintain adequate performance for all users, providers can either change the route of traffic, the amount of traffic, or the amount of time it takes the traffic to reach its destination.

ATM networks manage traffic on an ongoing basis by leveraging and manipulating the intelligence inherent in various network devices. Network administrators, for instance, can reroute traffic from congested areas to uncongested routes to ensure all traffic meets its respective continuity and speed guarantees. They can also discard data at numerous points before or along its route. If the network is too congested when a transmission is sent, some networks discard the data before it enters the network. If congestion develops en route, the network may discard data at the destination so as not to overload the recipient's network resources. In any case, the transmission is resent until it is transmitted according to the parameters of the customer's SLA.

Whereas traffic management ensures that the provider meets the SLAs of all customers, "traffic shaping" ensures that the network also accommodates SLA demands in the most cost-effective way for the provider. Traffic is shaped either "over" or "under" the network's capacity. If data using the network's available bandwidth prevents the provider from meeting all SLAs, then some is discarded and resent repeatedly until congestion dies down and transmissions are successful. If the existing traffic is underusing the available bandwidth, then the dormant bandwidth normally allocated to certain customers is instead reallocated to customers generating more traffic. Traffic shaping dynamically balances traffic levels throughout the network to conserve the provider's network resources optimally, improve your performance, and save you money.

ATM and Frame Relay Interworking

Because ATM is such a powerful and flexible networking technology, it's very expensive. A single ATM switch can cost hundreds of thousands of dollars. Thus, providers and customers typically deploy it in the WAN "core," the highest-capacity sections of the network where traffic from diverse sources is directed and then superefficiently transported to respective destinations. Frame Relay is deployed in the rest of the WAN because it's already so widely installed, cheaper to maintain, and largely paid for. Frame Relay provides broader geographic access to end users over legacy networks operated by corporations, IXCs, CLECs, and ISPs. "Interworking" is the strategy used to get the two different types of networks to operate together so transmissions can span multiple providers' infrastructures to link far-flung users.

Although there are many networks comprised exclusively of Frame Relay and a few comprised only of ATM, large ASPs handling many customers' applications will need the superbandwidth, geographical reach, and precise routing available with interworked ATM and Frame Relay networks. Mid-size ASPs can certainly accommodate a conservative number of customers using Frame Relay-only WANs, but only if the customer does not plan to scale up its user base or cumulative traffic dramatically, or require sophisticated quality of service. Customers who do will need ATM in the network. Also, if they transmit more types of traffic than data and voice (like video and multimedia), and if they must span LANs, CANs, MANs, and WANs, only ATM will do. Only ATM can accommodate the equipment with such capabilities.

ROUTING EQUIPMENT

Any WAN will use various types of bridges, routers, gateways, and switches to direct traffic to its destination more efficiently.

A **bridge** is a device that connects two different types of LAN or WAN networks or partitions a large homogeneous network into more efficient subsections. Bridges can detect users' computer addresses on either side of the partitioned network and allow transmissions originating on one side onto the other side only when the destination address is on the other side. This helps improve performance by managing traffic so it's not routed across unnecessarily circuitous paths.

A **router** is a more sophisticated bridge used only in WANs. A router knows the addresses of all computers at the network's access points, as well as those of all other routers and bridges linking network sections because they are listed in its "routing tables." It can also detect the least congested path among all these devices and route transmissions so they always most expeditiously reach their respective destinations. Whereas a bridge merely stops traffic on one side of a partition or not, routers always pass the traffic through but actually *route* it via the best path.

Gateways are used to link different types of networks and actually to translate the format of one network into the format of the other. In WANs, they are deployed mostly for translating proprietary mainframe or minicomputer network formats into the predominant WAN format.

Switches are more powerful routers that can transport data at much higher speeds, but lack sophisticated routing capabilities. They're essentially a type of router and are often just called *routers.* There are two types of ATM switches: core switches that do not route at all but transport data at extremely high speeds, and edge switches that do all the routing from the core of the ATM network to the end user's computer.

WDM

To this point we've explained how various protocols, equipment, and management techniques affect WAN transmission. However, a huge factor in network dependability and speed is the physical material from which the network is made. The older, much more pervasive, telephone line infrastructure is made of copper. Copper transmission quality was fine for less-dense analog voice transmissions. But then the Internet enabled newer data applications like e-mail and file transfers, and growing traffic loads overwhelmed the available capacity of legacy analog and digital networks. Increasingly, providers replaced or augmented legacy copper with a higher capacity fiber-optic infrastructure because of the volume of people using newer applications, and to accommodate more inherently bandwidth-intensive applications like telephony and multimedia. However, Internet traffic continued to grow until it was taxing the capacity of available fiber. Laying fiber-optic cable in the ground is a time-consuming and expensive process. Network equipment manufacturers knew that, although more fiber must be installed, they also had to find a way to expand the capacity of fiber optics. Otherwise, they'd be in an endless race to deploy fiber to accommodate perpetually increasing capacity demands. Wave division multiplexing (WDM) proved to be the solution.

Fiber-optic lines transmit data using light signals beamed over two standard wavelengths—one from the originating end first, then one from the receiving end in response—to achieve two-way transmission. Using electronic equipment at either end of the fiber-optic line, WDM generates multiple wavelengths over the same cable to carry as much as 30 times more data. The breakthrough created greater bandwidth for users, but at much lower costs and with greater ease of implementation for providers. Now, to augment capacity, providers simply install WDM devices at either end of the fiber link instead of having to lay new fiber in the ground.

WDM was subsequently improved using a method called Dense Wave Division Multiplexing (DWDM). DWDM generates more wavelengths of light over the same fiber cable to create even greater fiber-optic capacity. DWDM can generate 16 different wavelengths on a single fiber, and experts are predicting 128 wavelengths in the near future. DWDM can now carry between 160 to 400 Gbps—128 wavelengths will permit 1.2 Tbps.

Although DWDM over fiber optics is a vast improvement over the capacity of copper, it offers further benefits as well. Fiber optics permit two to three times fewer transmission errors than copper, is cheaper, and, unlike copper, which is vulnerable to interference and carries only analog signals, is not undermined by radio or electromagnetic frequency interference, and can carry both digital and analog signals. So, DWDM offers the digital infrastructure as well as the unprecedented capacity and dependability required by broadband applications like those offered by ASPs today.

Access–Broadband WAN to Customer

Depending on the size of the ASP customer, the connection from the WAN to your LANs might have several configurations. As its bandwidth needs increase, a large enterprise will link its LAN backbone to the WAN using a T1, T3, or SONET fiber-optic connection. Its LAN backbone could scale in parallel from Switched 100Base-X to Switched 1000Base-X to ATM, whereas its LAN workgroup would scale similarly from 16/4 Mbps Token Ring to Shared 10/100 Mbps (to PC desktops) or Shared 100Base-X (to high-end workstations) to Switched 10/100 Mbps (with a 10/100 Mbps port for every ASP desktop).

SMBs will link to the WAN with a T1 and, as bandwidth needs increase, will use one of the following for their LAN workgroup configurations: 16/4 Mbps Token Ring, Shared 10/100 Mbps (with a shared 10/100 Mbps port for PC desktops and Shared 100Base-X segments for high-end workstations), or Switched 10/100 Mbps (with a 10/100 Mbps port for every ASP desktop).

SOHO customers or branch offices of enterprises will use a T1 for the WAN-to-LAN link or, for smaller offices, integrated services digital network (ISDN), xDSL, or cable modem (discussed in the next section). The LAN workgroup configuration will be Shared 10/100 Mbps to the desktop (with a Shared 10/100 Mbps port for every ASP desktop, or Shared 100Base-X segments for high-end workstations).

The customer WAN/LAN infrastructure should support all of your concurrent users without unacceptable performance degradation. Obviously, your network administrator should also configure the LAN to accommodate heavy, moderate, or light users of the hosted applications with more or less robust throughput. And, of course, you are typically responsible for troubleshooting the LAN while the network service provider maintains the WAN-to-LAN link, unless the ASP owns the WAN, in which case it will do that maintenance.

The Local Loop–ISDN, xDSL, and Cable Modems

Today many companies also support remote users called *telecommuters* who access applications from home via wire-line ISDN, xDSL, or cable modem connections. SOHO businesses may use ISDN to link their LAN to the ASP WAN.

ISDN is an established and inexpensive digital technology that carries voice, video, and data over phone lines at either 128 Kbps or 1.544 Mbps, so it's more robust than 56 Kbps dial-up connections but more affordable than leased lines.

xDSL lets customers receive broadband voice, video, and data transmissions over their phone lines via xDSL modems installed at the customer premises. The technology is much cheaper than leased lines because it can convert analog data into digital signals while still using the local loop copper infrastructure. Thus, the provider can deliver broadband service without costly installation of fiber-optic lines or other enhancements.

The most popular flavors of xDSL are asymmetric DSL (ADSL) and ADSL Lite. The first accesses transmissions from the network at relatively high speeds of 1.5 to 8 Mbps, but sends transmissions to the network at relatively low speeds of 16 to 640 Kbps. It offers excellent price and performance for users who access the Internet a lot but send over it a little. It's appropriate for lightweight two-way applications like e-mail or production one-way applications like document imaging. ADSL Lite, known as G.Lite, is a slower, less expensive version of ADSL with access speeds of 1.5 Mbps and send speeds of 500 Kbps, and can handle most residential end user applications like Web surfing. xDSL has one inherent limitation: Because of the transmission capabilities of copper, it can be deployed no farther than about 18,000 feet from the local loop.

Whereas xDSL uses the phone connection to transmit converted analog transmissions, cable modems use the cable link in the small business or home for broadband transmissions to and from the network at speeds of 1 to 36 Mbps via a modem located on the customer premises. xDSL installation and service is generally costlier than that for cable, but ADSL Lite's lower price may soon change that. Moreover, to achieve a two-way cable connection, customers must always pay for a fairly expensive upgrade to their cable link—a cost of doing business for cable companies that will never go away.

In general, xDSL offers better reliability than cable modems, and for this reason will likely be the near-term choice of telecommuters and SOHOs using ASPs. Because users share cable bandwidth, the more users on the local cable trunk, the slower the access speeds. This not only undermines performance, but it also offers an untenable transmission situation for high-bandwidth, continuous-transmission applications like multimedia or voice.

Although residential customers prefer cable modems because of their lower price, ADSL Lite will make xDSL more competitive in that market. Meanwhile, SOHO users prefer xDSL because they need dedicated, constant bandwidth for high-end applications. So, although most SOHOs will leverage xDSL or T1s to access an ASP's WAN, less bandwidth-demanding telecommuters are likely to use ADSL Lite or cable modem connections to keep down costs.

Wireless

Wireless networks use broadcast towers and other technology to transmit voice and data to and from remote users via mobile devices like cell phones and laptops without the use of conventional wire-line connections. For a number of years now, wireless network providers have promised eventual anywhere/anytime/any device voice and data computing for mobile users, but this promise is still unrealized. Although wireless voice is generally acceptable, wireless data transmission has always been hampered by performance problems: Transmissions tend to be slow, the restricted bandwidth cannot accommodate dense data, signals are limited in geographical reach and are susceptible to interference, and other factors that affect quality. Also, although certain vendors like Microsoft have attempted to promote de facto wireless standards like Windows CE, they've had at best only limited success. Lack of a common standardized application platform has slowed wireless data application development and mass user adoption.

However, although these problems have not been satisfactorily resolved, the number of mobile devices like laptops, PDAs, and cell phones continues to grow. At the same time, the explosion of Internet use and applications has whetted the appetites of both knowledge workers and general consumers for wireless Internet access. Although wire-line data services are the dominant growth area in telecommunications, the conjunction of so many technological, competitive, and market demand factors is precipitating a renewed vendor preoccupation with improving wireless services. Whereas high cost and inconsistent performance are the major problems vendors need to address, more subtle issues also affect ASPs that want to offer wireless.

In all networks, but especially in wireless ones, performance is not solely a function of network capacity. It is the result of the interplay of many factors that have to be managed by telecom experts. For instance, because of "latency," users never fully exploit the advertised capacity of a wireless network. Latency is the total delay in transmission caused by all network factors like congestion, overhead, interference, and suboptimal network engineering and management. Although users may pay for a 14.4 Kbps wireless connection, they will never achieve this data bit rate—other users may be using that bandwidth and may be sending messages with attachments that further congest the network, and so on.

Obviously, the absence of a dominant worldwide standard creates interoperability problems between devices using, for instance, different mobile operating systems. However, it also creates policy and management problems for network administrators. If different departments in an enterprise are using different wireless operating systems on different physical devices with different interfaces, then managers have to learn and administer more systems. But if in, say, two years a new standard or device emerges that offers better performance or bang for the buck, users may switch, and the managers' learning process must start over again.

Experts predict that latency caused by technology will diminish dramatically during the next few years. The consensus seems to be that average wireless bandwidth will improve from 8 to 56 Kbps, and more, rather quickly. Similarly, dominant wireless standards like WAP promise better Internet access from wireless devices. However, although these positive developments will drive increased wireless usage, more users and devices may create greater management problems. It's incumbent on wireless device vendors, therefore, to incorporate more functionality for more data types in the same device. Voice/data convergence on cell phones is a good start. Whereas mobile phones are now used primarily for voice, soon approximately 70% will also be able to access Web content and enterprise applications. Of course, it's debatable whether a new device accessing legacy data and applications actually simplifies IT management.

Despite these challenges, during the next decade wireless will be a boom market, and most ASPs will want to support wireless connectivity. Currently, however, most wireless ASPs behave more like integrators and consultants than conventional ASPs. They earn most of their revenues through a variety of professional services like customizing common hosted applications for wireless connectivity and developing their own applications for special markets. Regardless of their eventual business focus and customer base, their market opportunities are legion.

IP

IP is another "packet-based" networking technology. It's the networking protocol of the Internet and, as such, will be deployed vastly more than any other type of network in the coming years. From 1997 to 1999, Internet traffic just about doubled every four to six months. Almost all of that traffic was data. Before long it became apparent that data traffic would eclipse voice traffic sometime around 2003. For network service providers, this was an unprecedented new market opportunity; but, with that opportunity came an unprecedented challenge. The telecom industry would have to invent and build broadband networks in record time to accommodate the new demand for data services.

Although telecom is still in the early phase of IP network development, it appears that within a few years the voice/data traffic balance will have reversed. Most experts predict that data over IP will be the dominant traffic, voice and data providers will spend more trying to add value to data services than preserving margins on traditional voice services, and much long-distance voice service will be transmitted over IP for little or no cost to the customer. To complete this transformation, IP must address some serious existing limitations.

The raw Internet infrastructure does not offer inherent security, mission-critical reliability, or predictable performance. Most of the telecom advances discussed earlier address these issues. VPNs, for example, offer users transmission security over the Internet infrastructure. Optical infrastructures and DWM technologies are creating the kind of unlimited bandwidth needed to accommodate millions of simultaneous users. And ATM, with its quality-of-service capabilities, lets providers guarantee various levels of performance according to what customers can afford. Achieving universal broadband Internet access is only a matter of time.

By 2010 or so, most companies conducting e-business will do so over a hybrid global network, the core of which will be fiber optics enhanced with DWDM, and supporting ATM with its various qualities of service. Meanwhile, the edge of this global infrastructure will be predominantly IP. This means that most users will access a broadband structure within the narrowband Internet via an IP link that may be a 56 Kbps modem, xDSL, cable modem, ISDN, T1, T3, wireless, or whatever other technologies evolve by then. This broadband infrastructure will support an array of advanced applications like voice over IP, IP and multimedia that, at best, are possible in imperfect forms to only the richest corporations now. What's more, bandwidth will be so abundant and cheap that most users will be able to afford most of the advanced applications.

ASPs will profit from this trend. Much the same way they lease enterprise applications to SMBs as affordable services now, ASPs will lease multimedia and other sophisticated and bandwidth-intensive applications as more affordable services to businesses and consumers in the future.

Key Concepts

- Network reliability—No unscheduled downtimes long enough to jeopardize the customer's business
- Network capacity—Should be sufficient to meet the customer's peak bandwidth requirements cost-effectively
- Network scalability—Enough ASP network capacity to accommodate more users and applications in a reasonable time
- Network players—Larger ASPs partnering with larger network service providers (IXCs, RBOCs, major systems integrators); smaller ASPs partnering with smaller providers (CLECs, ISPs, smaller systems integrators)
- Quality of service—The ability of ASPs to charge different customers different fees for different levels of network service
- Traffic load balancing and distribution—Routing inbound traffic from the WAN to the most appropriate data center and server within each data center based on least cost, availability, performance, and so forth
- Frame Relay—"Fast packet-switching" network technology in which transmission data is broken down into uniform packets of content and such "overhead" information as the packet's destination; improves speed by reducing overhead of older packet switched technologies; carries voice and data over the WAN only
- Network overhead—How much a packet must be handled to reach its destination successfully; the more detailed the overhead data, the more sophisticated the packet handling, but the more handling, the slower the transmission speed
- ATM—A type of packet-switched networking technology called *cell relay* that permits the fastest transmission of voice, data, and multimedia across LANs, CANs, MANs, and WANs as well as advanced traffic management and different "quality of service" for different customers
- Interworking—Using protocol translation devices and network engineering to integrate ATM with older networks like Frame Relay so that network service providers don't have to build completely new fiber-optic infrastructures for "pure" ATM
- Traffic management—Practice used by network service providers to maintain adequate performance for all users by changing the route of traffic, or amount of traffic, or the amount of time it takes the traffic to reach its destination
- Traffic shaping—Practice used by network service providers to balance traffic levels dynamically to meet all customer SLAs and to conserve the provider's network resources cost-effectively
- WDM/DWDM—Using electronic equipment at either end of a fiber-optic cable to generate multiple wavelengths over the same fiber to carry more

data, allowing users greater bandwidth and providers lower costs and easier implementation

- xDSL—The delivery of broadband voice, video, and data over customers' phone lines via DSL modems installed at the customer premises; cheaper and slower than leased lines
- Cable modems—The delivery of broadband voice, video, and data over customers' cable links via modems installed at the customer premises; cheaper and slower than leased lines
- Wireless network—A network system using broadcast towers and other technology to transmit voice and data to and from remote users via mobile devices like cell phones and laptops without the use of conventional wireline connections
- IP—The "packet-based" networking protocol of the Internet; used for accessing the Internet, so will be the most widely deployed type of network in the near future; still suffers from security, reliability, and performance problems

CHAPTER SIX

Varieties of ASP

This chapter discusses

- ASPs' pedigrees and partners
- Pure-play ASPs
- Full service providers (FSPs)
- Large VAR ASPs
- Small VAR ASPs
- Large service bureau ASPs
- Small service bureau ASPs
- ASP Application Aggregators (AAAs)
- Large SI ASPs
- Mid-size SI ASPs
- Independent software vendor (ISV) ASPs

Any categorization of ASPs will be somewhat arbitrary for several reasons. To begin with, there are no "pure" categories. Most ASPs (even "pure plays") also offer services that may qualify them as some other type of ASP. For instance, if an ASP offers accelerated deployment schedules, is it strictly an FSP? If it offers virtual storage, is it only what is called a Storage Service provider (SSP)? What if the "SSP" also customizes applications? As we all know, most new companies offer whatever services they think will prove profitable, and ASPs are no different.

Second, all ASPs, with the possible exception of pure-play ASPs, have business pedigrees. A pedigree is like a company's heredity. Its past successes, corporate culture, technology, market focus, and the like, will always influence how it operates in the future. For instance, major ERP vendors always made most of their revenues on integration, not their ERP software. If they offer hosted ERP services, they will tailor them so they don't cannibalize their future high-end installed software and integration business. The surface value proposition for their hosted services may be that they are deployed faster and cost less. But part of their service portfolio will likely be complementary services creating revenues that will make up for the integration revenues on installed ERP systems that the vendor may forfeit by offering hosted ERP services.

Third, all ASPs have partners, and partners' core technology and market competencies, and corporate strategies and culture will always affect how the ASP does business. Even pure-play ASPs typically have equity partnerships with companies like software vendors whose applications they host, and network service providers whose broadband WANs they rely on.

Fourth, just about any ASP with enough financial backing can achieve technological parity with any other ASP. It's just a matter of spending enough money to buy, for instance, a powerful SAN. But just about all technology an ASP may need is also available for leasing. Conceivably, a team of IT experts could rent an office, lease a data center, network, applications, security from a Managed Security Provider (MSecP), SLA monitoring from an MSP, and found their ASP brand on their own market and technology expertise, not the infrastructure they leased. They would differentiate themselves not only by the power and scale of their leased IT platform, but also by how they uniquely combined applications, data center, virtual storage, and other infrastructure components to address their target markets.

Fifth, ASPs are differentiated by all the assorted elements of what is generally defined as customer service: technical support help desks, on-line customer service reps, 800 numbers, different SLAs for different prices, answers to Frequently Asked Questions (FAQs) on a Web site, and so forth. The extent to which an ASP promotes customer-friendly technologies, processes, and practices is a measure of its competitiveness. With the rise of CRM, most businesses know they have to capitalize on every opportunity in the customer interaction cycle to improve customer relations and to reinforce customer loyalty. Although hosted services emphasize simplicity of implementation, administration, and billing, ASPs who ignore customer service shoot themselves in the foot. All else being equal—IT infrastructure, types of hosted applications, security, and so forth—better customer service will be the intangible factor that helps an ASP win and keep customers.

This said, several ASPs in one market may offer multiple services, have similar pedigrees and partners, similarly combine their IT components, and offer comparable customer service programs. Yet one may claim it's a pure-play ASP, another that it's an FSP, and another that it's an SSP. So which providers are actually what they claim and why? The answer is this: They all are what they claim because their label identifies what they *most* are. And, unless they are misleading prospects by marketing themselves wrongly, the label of each should best define their central value proposition.

With this in mind, here are some general guidelines for recognizing different types of ASPs and understanding their strengths and weaknesses.

Pure-Play ASPs

Pure-play ASPs (or *pure plays*) are probably what you think of when you hear the term *ASP*. They typically have some kind of equity partnership with the software vendors whose applications they host. They don't merely license the software at reseller rates. They may also have equity relationships with their infrastructure service provider and/or network service provider, and other partners like hardware and storage providers. Or they may actually own any or all of those components like data centers, network, SAN, optical jukeboxes, and servers.

Whatever the constitution of the owned and/or leased components, pure-play ASP management usually assumes end-to-end accountability for the entire solution because they own or *control* all the components. At the high end, pure-play ASPs tend to offer best-of-breed IT combinations—for instance, a state-of-the-art data center, a global network leased from an international carrier like AT&T with peering arrangements with comparable carriers like MCI, the leading applications in their niche (Siebel CRM, SAP ERP, Lotus Notes groupware, etc.), a SAN from EMC, and so forth. At the mid range, however, pure plays may simply offer *their own* solution—for instance, a proprietary imaging/workflow application hosted from their data center over their own regional network with optical jukebox storage only. Although this may not be best of breed, you should not summarily dismiss the offering. If the pure play has done its homework, this solution will be a good match for its target customers' IT, vertical market, and budget requirements. If the mid-range pure play bids against a high-end one for a regional bank's loan-processing workflow business, it's likely the smaller ASP would win—based on price and knowledge of the customer's business.

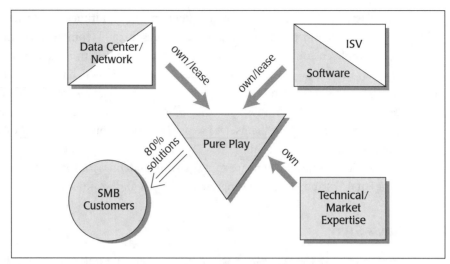

**Figure 6–1   The pure-play ASP leases 80%-hosted applications, but few
value-added services, to SMB customers**

In general, pure-play ASPs don't necessarily put a premium on value-added services like custom integration. They specialize in 80% solutions that customers can deploy more affordably and faster than installed ones because there is minimal customization (Figure 6–1). The upsides of pure-play ASPs tends to be end-to-end accountability and faster and cheaper deployment. The downside for smaller ones may be less than state-of-the-art technology and, for larger ones, lack of value-added services.

FSPs

FSPs are ASPs that differentiate themselves with value-added services (Figure 6–2). They may lease or own any or all of the ASP IT components, and they may or may not have equity relationships with their software and other partners. However, they definitely will offer services like accelerated deployment, advanced integration, outsourced IT staff, application testing in their data centers, consulting, and most other personnel and IT services that companies may need to implement hosted services.

"Full service" does not mean serving all markets with any application from cross-platform IT platforms. Although FSPs could offer multiple applications to multiple markets and offer, say, applications based on both Windows NT and UNIX, so could any ASP.

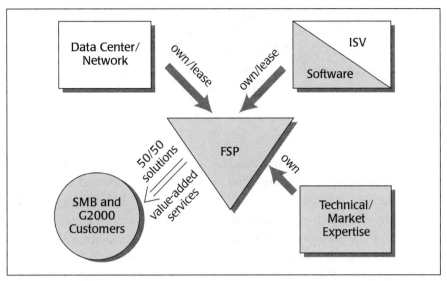

Figure 6–2 The full service provider (FSP) leases 50%-hosted applications and many value-added services to SMB and G2000 customers

FSPs typically focus on certain markets and certain applications, but offer very "deep" solutions in these areas. For instance, an FSP might help a dotcom customer define the scope, budget, and requirements of a CRM solution, customize the generic hosted CRM application right in its data center to conform to the customer's specifications, then implement it on an accelerated schedule. This is hardly representative of the "lease-and-go" computing utility model generally associated with ASPs.

FSPs are essentially one-stop shops for all your hosted services. They may even outsource executive IT and management staff to help launch a dotcom using its hosted e-commerce application or may actually integrate their hosted applications with your legacy ones. Their comprehensiveness and flexibility essentially define their value proposition and allow them to compete better with other providers like traditional integrators and pure-play ASPs. Unlike SIs, FSPs can manage the application after building it and, unlike pure-play ASPs, can troubleshoot the application better because they built it.

FSPs also tend to scale you up through their various offerings over time, which helps retain you in the long term with "after-market" sales opportunities as your business evolves and expands. You also get better accountability because you are always dealing with the same provider for all services.

Generally, FSPs offer more of a 50/50 generic-to-customized hosted solution and can address most problems you may have. Their upside is that they are a flexible, one-stop shop that can adapt to your customization requirements in the short term and fulfill your changing requirements as you grow over the long haul. The downside is that FSPs can get expensive because their solutions are not generic.

VAR ASPs

Pedigree is the dominant defining factor for all the other types of ASPs. It largely determines their partnerships, value-added services, and technology mix. For instance, the ASP strategy of VARs who launch hosted services will largely be influenced by their size and their relationship with their legacy ISV.

One prefatory remark bears stating before discussing VAR ASPs. If channel players initiate hosted services before an ISV has its own ASP model in place, it's likely they think they can license the software under the old installed model but resell it under the new hosted one—in other words, buy one software license from the ISV and resell it many times to their ASP customers. This strategy, of course, shrinks their software costs. The ISV may permit this until it has its own ASP program in place, or until it realizes it's leaving money on the table. In any case, it won't do it for long. Once the ISV develops an ASP licensing model by which it charges VARs for software to its own satisfaction, channel players must figure the new price into their costs.

This said, large VARs with sufficient capital will likely create much of their own ASP infrastructure—data center, servers, storage, and middleware. Unless they have an existing broadband network, they will lease one with sufficient scope and bandwidth because it simply takes too long to build one. Their primary partner in hosted services will be the ISV whose software they resell. But it's probable they will want merely to license the software and then do whatever they can to differentiate their hosted service from typical installed solutions. Large VARs will also pursue hosted services as a way of winning new business in the mid-range market.

If the VAR's ISV hosts its own software, then of course the VAR must decide whether it can compete with that offering in its geographical, vertical market or technology niche. Often the VAR's specialized expertise is enough to differentiate it from the more horizontal ISV-hosted service. However, if the ISV chooses to compete aggressively on price with VARs in their own specialty areas, large VAR ASPs must make some tough decisions. Do they compete with the ISV on hosted services and cooperate on installed solutions? Do they partner with a different but comparable ISV that does not compete with them in their specialty area? Do they give up their own infrastructure and simply resell the ISV's hosted services for a standard markup fee?

Large VARs with sufficient differentiation and a solid track record in their specialty areas can usually make a go of hosted services. The ISV would be stupid to try to compete with a VAR that's earning it big revenues. Even if it could out-compete the VAR in its specialty area, it would likely take a serious hit in cash flow for several years to win that market from its reseller. Most ISVs won't risk guaranteed profits now for potentially greater profits later.

However, the ISV can raise its software licensing fees for VARs that want to implement hosted services, and can beat them on price by leveraging their greater economies of scale. The ISV typically has more customers than any one of its VARs, and it can offer its ASP customers incentives like free services to win customers from a VAR. ISVs may feel justified in using such a competitive strategy on VARs with poor performance in their niche or who merely resell software without adding value like vertical market expertise. The ISV saves on channel expenses, wins customers, and only risks losing easily replaced VARs or low performers.

However, irreconcilable differences may also affect the ISV/large VAR relationship. For instance, the ISV may have a long history of selling direct in the VAR's territory without informing the VAR. In this case, a large VAR may decide high licensing fees for hosted services is too much to tolerate and may partner with another ISV.

Small VARs are more dependent on the ISV for infrastructure, financing, marketing, and their own education about the ASP model. With less disposable capital, small VARs usually can't build their own ASP infrastructure. To break into hosted services, they must lease or rely on the ISV or some other partner to provide it.

Of course, the ISV may choose to raise licensing fees on hosting licenses and force the small VAR's hand. In such a situation, the most viable solution would be for the small VAR to lease the ISV's infrastructure and resell the hosted software for a standard markup. In this way, the small VAR justifies its presence in the ISV's channel by bringing in additional revenues through hosted services, and the ISV won't be inclined to compete with the VAR on hosted services. What's more, the small VAR does not have to jeopardize its cash flow, so it's profitable from the start. But just as important, offering affordable hosted services is a safe defensive strategy. It thwarts other VARs from stealing the VAR's customers for installed solutions by offering their own cheaper hosted service.

Mid-size VARs may adopt either an aggressive or defensive posture on hosted services, depending on factors like cash flow, legacy relationships with the ISV, emerging hosted competition, and the like.

VAR ASPs excel in the same areas as traditional VARs. They understand their vertical market and technology specialty, and their more intimate relationship with customers means they understand each customer's unique requirements better than, say, an ISV trying to offer hosted services to those customers. But, depending on their ISV relationship, both large and small VARs may offer a less-than-optimal hosted service. If a large VAR must pay inflated licensing fees to the ISV, the customer will pay more for the VAR's hosted service. If the small VAR is merely reselling the ISV's hosted services, there may be little incentive for them to perform the softer services like customer support, unless they are getting paid well for it. Indeed, customers may lease through the VAR but get support from the ISV and have to deal with two providers. To a certain extent also, small VARs tend to miss the big picture because they are so focused on their chosen niche. So they can get wed to technology solutions that may be a bit behind the curve. They also may not be able to offer the economies of scale of an ISV and large VARs, so they may not be able to compete with them on price—all the more reason for small VARs to resell an ISV's hosted services, not launch their own.

But the biggest downside with VAR ASPs may be this: They are loathe to cannibalize their installed system revenues with hosted services. Installed solutions are VARs' bread and butter. Even if they offer hosted services, the services may be used to induce you to buy other professional services like consulting, integration, and other value-added services like document conversion and virtual storage. So you must decide whether the total cost of the package has, in the end, better value than another ASP's offer. If this is the VAR's strategy, then it may not be fully committed to the *best* hosted services, only to hosted services that best bring in professional service revenues.

Service Bureau ASPs

The service bureau ASP and VAR ASP categories overlap. Both service bureaus and VARs resell software and do on-site customization. However, service bureaus tend to build their core business around tasks like performing document conversion at the service bureau's own location. By contrast, VARs tend simply to resell software for a standard markup and/or perform system integration at your site. Factors similar to those affecting VARs will determine if and how service bureaus adopt the ASP model—namely, the size of the service bureau and the legacy relationship with the ISV.

Large service bureaus will tend to tip the balance of power with an ISV in their favor by leasing their infrastructure from a third party or building their own. Their overhead is already high, and if they are successful they have compensated for those facility, equipment, software, and personnel costs by retaining large customers at healthy margins. Their key dilemma is understanding how to offer hosted services to customers that are large enough to justify the bureau's time and investment, but that likely also want to retain control over their own IT infrastructure. A large service bureau making 35 to 40% margins on installed services will be hesitant to cannibalize that revenue down the road with lower-margin hosted services. Their challenge is this: Knowing when the time is right either to adopt hosted services defensively to ward off competition or to migrate from high-margin installed services to lower-margin but higher-volume hosted services.

Large service bureaus can build an ASP business without endangering its high-end outsourcing business by selling hosted services downmarket. Large service bureaus will likely find SMBs are quite happy to leverage the bureau's high-end facilities for lower periodic leasing fees. The bureaus themselves can refine their processes so that when they do offer hosted services to high-end customers, they're more cost-efficient, can extract greater margins, and are still competitive. The SMB experience will likely show them which value-added services customers actually need, and offering these services will help offset the lost revenues of slimmer margins both in the short term with SMBs, and later with larger customers. This argument is moot, however, in the face of serious competition from other service bureaus offering hosted services.

Of course, the large service bureau must ask itself some tough questions about its ISV relationship. Is the bureau bringing the ISV enough business that the ISV will continue cooperating, and not start competing, with the service bureau? For instance, if the ISV offers hosted services to high-end customers, will that threaten the service bureau's high-end installed business? One way to counteract this kind of move by an ISV is to partner with them. If the large service bureau can put together a hosting infrastructure before the ISV does, then it may behoove the ISV to use the bureau as its infrastructure service provider—or as one of them, say, for a geographical region or vertical market. In this way, both parties benefit. The ISV doesn't alienate the service bureau, which is usually one of its big software customers, but it can still aggressively pursue hosted services because it is growing the service bureau's overall business.

SUCCESS STORY

Service bureau ASP: Critical Technologies/FilesOnTheNet.com
Customer: Loyola University
Key elements of the solution: Accelerated deployment, reduced processing costs, central storage, and simultaneous remote access of documents

Applications, transcripts, and letters of recommendation are only the start of a record flow when a high school student applies for admission to Loyola University. When a prospect becomes interested in attending, he first applies for financial aid and initiates a chain of documentation that includes financial applications, tax returns, school records, and appeal letters. Then, when the candidate is accepted, enrollment generates class registrations, schedule records, class changes, and grade transcripts. As a result, the record and document management demands faced by Loyola University are a relentless year-round challenge. Traditionally, these important documents have been retained in paper files and handled by a variety of staff, administrators, and counselors involved in the various admission decision-making processes. Often these demands are compounded by staff being located at multiple campus locations.

Universities are like any other business. They want to meet the functional needs of their various departments, and they want a cost-effective application process. To achieve those goals, Loyola demanded certain capabilities from any hosted document management system it leased from an ASP:

- Personnel had to share records and data at various campuses.
- Files had to be centrally stored.
- All data had to be secure.
- The system had to be easy to use.
- And it had to be cost-effective.

continued

Loyola's Old Document Management System

Loyola University has traditionally stored their paper documents in manila folders spread over various departments on separate campuses. In the old system, staff circulated these folders for review, processing, and consideration. Some records, after they were no longer active, were permanently archived on microfilm. Others were warehoused in boxes or, after a set retention period, destroyed. In the past, these were reasonable enough solutions, though admittedly the process of retrieving and processing records requests was slow, and occasionally documents and folders were misfiled or lost.

The Benefit of FilesOnTheNet.com

FilesOnTheNet.com presented a time-saving and cost-effective solution for Loyola. Now users simply log on to the FilesOnTheNet.com system from any Internet browser to access and share electronically stored documents and records from any department at any campus. As new documents arrive at the various locations, system users scan and index them so they are readily available for viewing. Documents are indexed, and can be cross-referenced, by student ID number, name, and social security number with just a mouse click.

As well as ease of use and quick retrieval, every department has also experienced several bonus benefits:

- Admissions counselors are often working on the road, and FilesOnTheNet.com allows them to access working documents using a browser, so an applicant's request or query gets a quick response.
- Financial Aid Counselors are required to meet strict federal compliance guidelines, and FilesOnTheNet.com is a quick and efficient way to track documentation to verify compliance.
- Many documents are original copies of important student records, so a complete backup is written to tape daily, and tapes are stored offsite in a data vault where disaster recovery procedures are already in place.
- Loyola saves money because, in using an Internet-based service, they avoid expensive equipment or maintenance costs.

continued

- Finally, there are no startup costs. FilesOnTheNet.com's affordable monthly pricing is based simply on the number of concurrent system users.

Loyola has always prided itself on high academic standards and an excellent scholastic reputation. However, as at so many cash-strapped colleges, funding to improve administrative efficiency sometimes merited lower priority than money spent on academic programs. FilesOnTheNet .com changed that. Now document management in admissions is a virtual process that lets staff evaluate and admit new students in record time.

Permission courtesy of Critical Technologies/FilesOnTheNet.com

Small service bureaus are in a different situation. Like small VARs, they may feel compelled to offer hosted solutions defensively to ward off competition for their installed business from other service bureaus offering hosted services. However, building an ASP infrastructure is hardly a foregone conclusion for them. They probably don't have the cash flow to do so. They may not even have the downtime to learn the ASP model, and to research infrastructure and other service providers. Their best option, in this case, is just to resell hosted services from the ISV to customers in their region. In this way they need make no investment but still win incremental revenues and ward off competition from other providers' hosted services.

On the other hand, some smaller service bureaus will embrace hosted services—although they will still not build their own infrastructure—because they allow them to go after bigger fish with a small rod. Because they can leverage an infrastructure service provider's state-of-the-art data center and network, they can sell their services upmarket to larger customers. If they partner with an ISV offering an ASP infrastructure, the ISV may also be able to offer value-added hosted services like a portal through which all hosting customers access applications, upgrades, and data about special discounts and the like. Because of economies of scale, the ISV can spread the cost of an expensive portal infrastructure over all its ASP partners, whereas a small service bureau would be hard pressed indeed to fund and build one.

Regardless of whether they adopt an aggressive or defensive ASP strategy, smaller service bureaus will appreciate the recurring revenue streams of hosted services. Indeed, this factor may outweigh all others. Cash flow is the biggest problem most small businesses face. Most will sacrifice big potential margins for steady, guaranteed revenue to meet operating expenses every month.

In using large and small service bureaus you can reap savings and convenience by migrating from, say, traditional outsourced services like document conversion (where the service bureau converts and delivers documents on CD each month) to hosted services where all documents are stored in the data center and accessed by you over the ASP network. SMBs can also leverage the high-end technology of large service bureaus while paying affordable leasing fees. However, if a large service bureau is competing with its ISV for hosting customers, you risk having the service bureau abandon the ISV relationship down the road and leaving you stranded. If small service bureaus launch hosted services not provided by the ISV, their financial risk is greater than if they simply resold the ISV's hosted services, which may affect customer service if cash flow dries up.

ASP APPLICATION AGGREGATORS

While the ASP market has differentiated into ASP-like service firms like SSPs for virtual storage, MSPs for virtual performance monitoring, and MSecPs for virtual security services, it's become evident to some entrepreneurs that customers would benefit immensely from a solution that consolidates many of the hosted services offered by different providers. AAAs bundle diverse applications from multiple ASPs, software vendors, and related providers behind a common interface through which you can access the applications (Figure 6–3). The AAA partners with relevant providers and resells their hosted services to you, and you get one bill for all services.

Such an approach simplifies management for you, but it also promotes best-of-breed hosted solutions. Typically the AAA integrates each customer's unique set of hosted applications into an XML-based platform and guarantees that they will interoperate. The AAA hosts the applications from its data centers or those of an infrastructure service provider that is a business partner in the AAA operation. The AAA also takes responsibility for maintaining,

continued

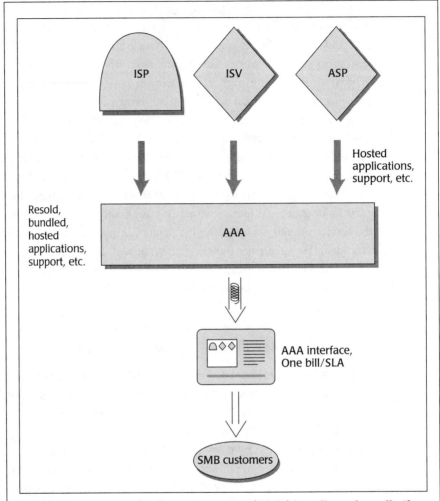

Figure 6–3 ASP application aggregators (AAAs) bundle and resell other ASPs' applications behind a common interface

troubleshooting, and upgrading each application set, and supports each customer's SLA. As internal IT staff need to interact with the applications, they can do so via the AAA's common interface, not the disparate interfaces of the individual hosted applications in their set.

A representative AAA solution may offer customers a Web-based portal through which you and other customers interact with their sets of applications.

continued

To create a generic e-collaboration platform, for instance, it may integrate horizontal applications like e-mail, conferencing, Internet access, and data backup and storage. Some AAAs are specializing in horizontal applications for, say, sales, and are offering customers a large set of applications from which they can select a few for a bundled fee. For instance, of these available services—sales force automation, e-mail, around-the-clock technical support, wireless connectivity, document management, and workflow—an SMB might lease the first three from an AAA for a bundled fee of $500/month per salesperson using them.

In any case, the AAA becomes a VAR for hosted applications, but you no longer must put up with a VAR's extended on-site integration and the attendant customization fees or steep margins on resold equipment. Instead, you pick and choose the applications you need from a Web menu and virtually access them in fairly short order.

Over time, as AAAs refine their business models, they may bundle multiple complex applications and charge a steeper per-application fee plus the monthly aggregation fee. Now, most AAAs charge a one-time setup fee in addition to the monthly leasing fee for aggregation.

Obviously, to be profitable, AAAs must choose application partners who offer their applications at a channel discount and whose software they can easily integrate. AAAs then make accelerated integration their core competence, and leverage the economies of scale possible by reselling popular application sets to multiple customers.

There are also an increasing number of AAA-like operations such as ASP enablers that, as well as hosting multiple applications, do things for customers like ASP-enabling software packages, integrating hosted applications with legacy ones, and performing general IT consulting services. As aggregators diversify, it's likely AAA-like operations will outnumber pure AAAs.

SUCCESS STORY

ASP Enabler: Agiliti
Customer: Achieve Online Services
Key elements of the solution: multiple hosted applications accessed with one login, extensive technical consulting and service, virtual platform and performance monitoring

Achieve Online Services (AOS) is a major provider of IS services to the long-term care industry. Achieve's PathLinks software serves this growing market with an integrated suite of financial and clinical applications. When it decided to offer PathLinks through the software-as-a-service model—a proven route to revenue and market expansion—AOS outsourced its hosting needs. AOS sought a cost-efficient solution offering high reliability and support as well as value-added services in order to be more attractive to its customers. After looking at the competition, AOS turned to Agiliti.

Superior Reliability and Performance

Agiliti calls itself an ASP Enabler that specializes in solutions for ISVs. For example, Agiliti's Tier One data center gave AOS access to a secure hosting environment built on world-class technologies and staffed 24/7 by Agiliti's certified technicians. With guaranteed high service levels, Agiliti ensured the continuous reliability of AOS's IT operations, supported by Web-based monitoring tools enabling the company to instantly check its system performance. According to Bob Harris, general manager, Achieve Online Services, "Our selection of Agiliti provides our clients with improved system reliability and availability due to the sophisticated level of system monitoring and control procedures they have in place."

Working with Achieve's IT staff, Agiliti designed a solution reconfiguring AOS's storage area network (SAN) for greater server reliability. During this process Agiliti was there every step of the way, providing responsive professional services to help AOS handle the migration to its new environment smoothly. Reengineering paid off, enabling AOS to reduce its hardware requirements and put more servers into production.

continued

> **Adding Value for Customers**
>
> The Agiliti solution also offered additional services AOS could include with its offerings to extend value to its customers, including hosted versions of Great Plains and Microsoft Exchange 2000. Agiliti also provided extensive solution support including sales force training, online access to marketing collateral, and co-marketing services to help AOS reach its customers better.
>
> In all, Agiliti's solution enabled Achieve to capture broader market share through a superior mix of world-class hosted applications and aggregation and other services to help this leading company serve its clients better and compete even more effectively in its market.
>
> ――――――――――――――
> Permission courtesy of Agiliti

SI ASPs

Of course, SIs operate on similar business models as VARs and service bureaus. However, large SIs are more likely to have the rudiments of an ASP infrastructure already in place. After all, they have the most experience performing outsourced services like managing a government agency's back office records stored on servers in the SI's data center or at the customer site. Many global SIs like the Big Five also have legacy broadband networks linking their own or customers' regional offices, so it's a small step to launch hosted services over their own infrastructure or to team with an infrastructure service provider to do so.

Large SIs have also traditionally partnered with enterprise software vendors to customize complicated applications like ERP and CRM, and, like those vendors, realize that they have almost exhausted the high-end market for installed enterprise applications. Hosted services offer them a way of aggressively going down-market and winning new customers in volume. What remains to be seen, however, is whether global integrators with massive overhead can profitably provide hosted services to SMBs. Their challenge is perfecting their processes and implementing them quickly for a more "mass" market. They will meet with serious competition from mid-size integrators that already have refined, accelerated deployment methods for installed solutions at fixed prices and guaranteed deadlines.

In some areas, however, large SIs have an advantage—for instance, where they have extensive experience in customizing solutions in one vertical market like banking. In many instances, SIs have worked so closely with their customers that they end up "productizing" custom solutions refined during one long engagement. This relationship ties them inextricably to certain customers. In some instances, they know the customized code and the customer's work processes as well as the customer. It would be very expensive and time-consuming for such customers to switch to another provider. Their best bet is to work with the SI to evolve hosted solutions based on current code.

All in all, though, large SIs are probably the best equipped of any service provider to migrate to a hosted model. They have great integration and outsourcing experience, and they are, unlike, say, hardware and software vendors, service oriented. Their major challenge is moving from a time-and-materials integration model to a commodity service model. Given their heritage, most large SIs will also emphasize value-added services as a way to cover themselves if they are slow to master 80% hosted services (Figure 6–4).

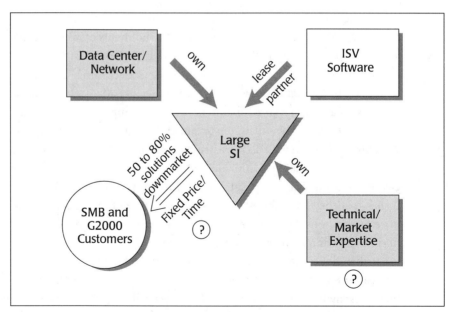

Figure 6–4 Large SI ASPs own the ASP infrastructure and technical/market expertise, and lease hosted applications downmarket

And, of course, all SIs have to deal with long sales cycles for installed enterprise solutions while maintaining a new sales run rate that ensures cash flow. Hosted services that bring in recurring revenue provide a nice hedge against such contingencies.

Smaller SIs are in the same boat as small VARs. Limited time and cash flow may dictate that they simply resell an ISV's hosted services, although some will find a new niche doing accelerated deployment and other services for their larger ASP partners.

So, although large SIs have the outsourcing experience and legacy infrastructure, they lack experience in the mid market and in commodity services. And although mid-size SIs can deploy solutions by fixed deadlines and for fixed prices (Figure 6–5), they may lack the financial depth and technological scale of the larger, more established SIs. The safest strategy for small integrators is probably reselling an ISV's hosted services.

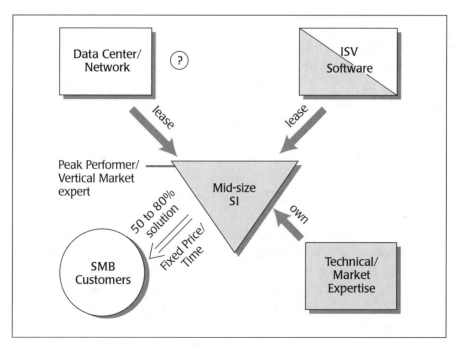

Figure 6–5 Mid-size SI ASPs lease the ASP infrastructure and excel at fixed-price/time-hosted applications leased upmarket

---

THE HARDWARE VENDOR'S ASP PLAY

Hardware vendors' main ASP play will be to enter an equity relationship with an infrastructure service provider to provide massive server farms for ASPs. Some, like Hewlett-Packard, see partnerships like this as a way to gain minority stakes in new ASPs and related companies with great growth potential. Hewlett-Packard, in fact, has gone so far as to front hardware to and help finance start-ups. Others, like Sun Microsystems, remain more hands off but are making a concerted effort to change certain hardware lines to be more modular and powerful to meet ASPs' needs for small footprint, dependability, and scalability. They can then play the role of "arms provider" to ASPs and others in their hosted services programs.

ISV ASPs

Large ISVs of enterprise applications have a number of ASP options open to them. If, like IBM, they also sell hardware and offer global IT services, they can launch their own ASP program to the high end and go downmarket with regional data centers featuring their own servers and storage, linked by their own (or a business partner's) network. If, like Oracle, they have complicated but modular enterprise software, they can initiate an equity partnership with an infrastructure provider like Qwest and essentially launch a new division that hosts, say, select ERP modules to SMBs. If, like SAP, they have a stable of SI and other types of large business partners with some of the ASP infrastructure already in-house, they can leverage them and team with an infrastructure provider for elements like performance monitoring, and can lease service downmarket to SMBs. They won't cannibalize their high-end installed system sales and they'll gain incremental revenues. If, like Documentum, they establish an ASP channel comprised of peak performing or specialist Documentum VARs, they can team with VARs to evolve hosted solutions for certain vertical markets like engineering. The ISV can help with development and marketing costs and take a percentage of each leasing contract in perpetuity. This gives the ISV both a new, recurring revenue stream and new SMB customers. If, like Lotus with its Lotus Notes Partners, they have a massive channel to SMBs already in place, they can evolve ASP-enabling software platforms and software suites that help their partners deploy hosted services faster to end customers.

In each situation, however, the ISV will probably choose a strategy that does not cannibalize its installed system sales or alienate its channel. Generally, ISVs can prosper by teaming with their VARs or business partners and leasing hosted services downmarket (Figure 6–6). If they launch their own ASP program, they can encourage their best VARs to join it, and can grow everyone's customer base.

The upside of ISVs taking the "middle way" is that the customer gets more affordable hosted solutions that are still supported by VARs who know their business processes and requirements. Essentially, the ISV capitalizes on all the strengths of the old model to better ensure the success of the new model. ISVs take a riskier course trying to win margins from their productive VARs by offering hosted services directly. Unproductive VARs that get eliminated from that ISV's channel will have to hustle to win a place in another channel. Customers getting hosted services direct from the ISV will have to wonder about their deployment expertise. Those getting hosted services from successful VARs must realize the ISV can always increase licensing fees. Those looking for a deal with a

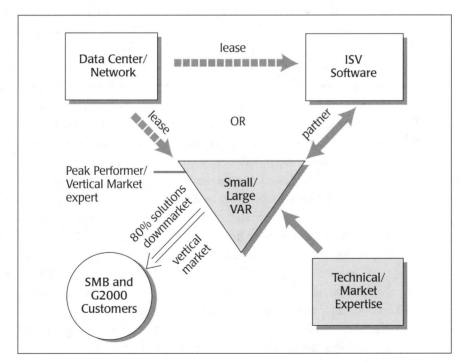

Figure 6–6 ISV ASPs are partnerships between ISVs and peak-performing or vertical market VARs

VAR in transition should realize the VAR may not have mastered the new software yet and is scrambling to maintain cash flow.

ASP ECOSYSTEMS

Often, global corporations provide software vendors with such great revenues that the vendor, in concert with an SI, will essentially tailor custom software for the company. Later the vendor can productize, although not completely duplicate, that experimental iteration and resell it to companies with similar business processes and requirements. Some ISVs feel their biggest customers will want to exert the same control over hosted solutions. To address this need, the ISV can overengineer a general modular solution that can be readily tailored to such a company as well as its business partners and suppliers. Indeed, the largest corporations not only dictate to ISVs, but they also have such leverage that they can dictate to their supply chain on which type of technology platform to standardize. ISVs like Open Text and SAP have adopted strategies to accommodate these supercorporations.

Open Text, for instance, has partnered with high-end SIs and infrastructure service providers, and has struck strategic relationships with vendors that provide software components like middleware, enterprise portals, and Web tools. Its "e-Community Platform for e-Business Innovation" consists of a portal interface, business content (like that in an industry trade association) relevant to the corporation's industry, integration of legacy structured data with hosted applications, e-commerce integrated with electronic data interchange (EDI) for transactions, and knowledge management for doing collaborative tasks like managing processes, teams, and unstructured data. Partners like KPMG use those components to build a platform on which the corporation and its partners can deploy applications like CRM, ERP, and e-commerce. To do business with the supercorporation, members of its supply chain simply plug into the platform instead of building their own. Such a strategy quickly and affordably lays a virtual technology foundation for an existing trading community. Depending on the extent of control the supercorporation requires, it can even host the platform with its own, not the ISV's, ASP.

continued

SAP is pursuing a similar strategy. It has teamed with infrastructure service providers and its legacy customers to create a flexible infrastructure that supply chain members and other SAP customers can plug into to launch e-commerce activities and perform virtual work. Customers simply lease certain SAP ERP modules, the mySAP portal, and a virtual workspace to plug into the existing SAP virtual business ecosystem and to trade with the supply chain's anchor corporation. The ERP modules comprise the supply chain infrastructure; the portal provides an interface to all data, applications, and people involved in it; and the virtual workspace offers the common word processing, e-mail, and other office productivity tools needed for employees of different corporations to virtually interact as members of the common supply chain.

This is a promising strategy for supercorporations that need powerful but flexible, interoperable, and affordable interenterprise IT platforms for all their extranet participants. The model could also be applied to virtual trade exchanges where a company needs to assemble a supply chain quickly using partners that respond to its bids for goods and services in a virtual auction environment. These environments may falter, however, if the ASP cannot exploit secondary revenue sources like advertising to the community at large. Long-term success presupposes a critical mass of demographically appropriate participants willing to buy goods and services from vendors virtually advertising them to the community.

Related Service Providers

Any ASP that offers hosted applications that enable financial transactions can support customer e-commerce initiatives. Often the terms *commerce service provider* (CSP) or *business service provider* (BSP) are applied to such operations. Most ASPs will also use some form of electronic billing system for their own customers. Although e-commerce is probably the most pervasive hosted application, this fact argues against separate categories for ASPs offering e-commerce. Most ASPs will be more accurately defined by the categories outlined previously even if they offer e-commerce applications.

Similarly, ASPs specializing in certain vertical markets are often categorized as *Vertical ASPs* (VSPs) and are lumped together according to the market they serve.

Companies seeking vertical hosted solutions will certainly use market focus as one criteria to select prospective ASPs, but they will also consider factors outlined in this chapter as well as differentiating factors like technology platform, customer service programs, and value-added services discussed in the rest of the book. See Appendix C, Selected ASPs in Major Vertical Markets, for examples.

As for related service providers like SSPs, you should refer to explanations of different ones, and the reasons for using each, elsewhere in the book.

Key Concepts

- No "pure" ASPs—Labels tell what an ASP *most* is and explain its central value proposition
- ASPs differentiated by—Mostly pedigree and partners, but also by technology mix and customer service
- Pure-play ASPs—Equity partnerships, end-to-end accountability, 80% solutions, few value-added services, affordable but inflexible
- FSPs—Some equity partnerships, deep solutions in markets/applications, one-stop shops, 50/50 solutions, many value-added services, expensive but flexible
- Large VAR ASPs—Lease/buy infrastructure, independent, earn big revenues so ISV won't compete with them
- Small VAR ASPs—Need ISV for infrastructure, financing, marketing; best to resell ISV's hosted services
- Large service bureau ASPs—Lease/own infrastructure, partner with ISV as infrastructure service provider for region or market, sell hosted services downmarket, protect high-margin outsourcing business
- Small service bureau ASPs—Need ISV infrastructure, resell ISV's hosted services in region or market, sell some hosted services upmarket, swap some high-margin integration for recurring revenue
- AAA—Bundle hosted applications from multiple ASPs and related providers behind one interface and resell them to end customers who get one bill and SLA
- Large SI ASPs—Own legacy infrastructure and do integration/outsourcing, sell hosted services downmarket in volume, and must profitably move from a time-and-materials, high-overhead installed model to a low-margin hosted one
- Mid-size SI ASPs—Lease ASP infrastructure, mastered fixed-time deployment at fixed prices, better at "e-sourcing" than large SI ASPs
- ISV ASPs—Don't cannibalize installed sales or alienate channel, team with VARs to lease hosted services downmarket

CHAPTER SEVEN

Security Issues for ASPs

This chapter discusses

- Authentication
- Encryption
- Access control
- Integrity
- Confidentiality
- Auditing and accounting
- Firewalls
- Proxy servers
- Security policy
- Security audits
- Background checks
- Physical security
- Managed Security Providers (MSecPs)

With the rise of e-commerce and the extended enterprise, corporations have become obsessed with securing their systems from unauthorized outside access. Although proprietary broadband EDI networks extended enterprises in the past, security risks increased proportionately as the corporate IT real estate sprawled over intranets and extranets, and transmissions came to include financial transactions and other data with mission-critical and competitive value. When a company contracts with an ASP, it essentially adds a new infrastructure to its already complex existing one. New hardware, applications, networks, storage devices, and physical facilities like data centers all present potential security vulnerabilities that customers must rely on the ASP to address. Whether their fears are justified, most customers rate security, along with performance and reliability, as one of their three most important concerns when leasing hosted services.

However, there is no such thing as perfect security. Security is always a function of how much time and money organizations devote to it. Enterprises with limited personnel, IT, and financial resources may have to prioritize their security risks and address only the most threatening ones with airtight solutions. Even organizations with vast resources must exert continual vigilance against unanticipated threats like new viruses, denial-of-service attacks, and malicious activities by disgruntled former and current personnel. Security, therefore, is an ongoing process—not a goal that's achieved and forgotten.

ASPs and their customers must define and implement security policies and services at data centers as well as background service provider and customer sites. This is merely the first step. All involved parties must then manage security during the course of business as new personnel are hired, old ones leave, access and responsibilities change, and the customer leases or installs new equipment and services. What's more, periodically everyone must update their security measures as the state-of-the-art changes, mergers and acquisitions occur, and as diligent hackers persevere in trying to violate safeguards like encryption algorithms that over time can be compromised.

This said, then, although ASPs should be the experts in securing their own services and their customers' exposures, ultimately the customer must perform due diligence on the ASP to guarantee the safety of its own resources. To do so, potential ASP customers first need a base knowledge of security issues, strategies, techniques, equipment, and policies to ensure the ASPs they hire are giving them at least viable deterrence to hackers, and at most the best security they can afford.

Determining Your Security Risks

Your first step in defining a security program with an ASP is to determine your security liabilities once you lease the hosted application. To do so, you might use the following method to determine the seriousness of a liability incurred by the new application. As in Figure 7–1, first plot an x- and a y-axis for a graph. The x-axis should represent the increasing likelihood of a security attack or breach, and the y-axis should represent its increasingly negative consequences. The more likely a breach, the farther out on that axis you should plot it; the more damaging

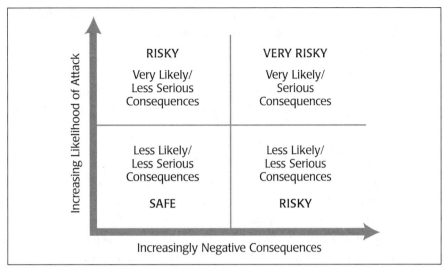

Figure 7–1 Plot your security risks to determine which merit the highest priority and funding

its consequences, the farther out on that other axis you should plot it. After reading this chapter you can assess which security areas like "access control" and "integrity" are most relevant to your organization. Having identified your issues, you should then divide the graph into four quadrants and plot the issues on the graph.

Issues that fall in the upper right-hand quadrant of your graph are likely to happen and to have serious consequences. These issues *must* be addressed. Issues in the upper left-hand and lower right-hand quadrants *may* present security risks, but you'll have to decide whether they are worth the time and money to fix. The object of this exercise is to get you to make the security improvements sufficient to move the relevant issues for the new hosted application from the three "risky" quadrants into the "safe" lower left-hand quadrant.

Types of Security Risk

Most security risks involve theft of data; compromises of confidentiality, integrity, or availability of data; or interruption of service.

Hackers can steal data by breaking into the applications and storage repositories in the ASP's data center or when data is in transit over the ASP's network.

ASPs guard against theft by taking precautions like deploying firewalls between outside networks and their internal applications, and by encrypting transmissions over the network.

Confidentiality ensures that data is disclosed only to parties authorized to see it. Access control typically defines a set of access rights and privileges for people authorized to access certain data and applications. Encrypting network transmissions typically guarantees that only recipients with access to the decrypting key can decode the sender's data.

Integrity, of course, ensures that data gets from the sender to the recipient without undetected alteration. Obviously, there could be serious consequences if sensitive data like bank records were changed in transit. Techniques like "checksums" in transmitted packets confirm that the exact amount of data that was transmitted in the packet is the amount received. If such techniques indicate data has been tampered with, the network discards it. These techniques don't necessarily prevent data from being corrupted, but they do ensure that the corrupted data is discarded.

Techniques ensuring availability of data prevent applications or network components from being sabotaged and disabled so users can't access data. Computer viruses are a common method of crashing applications, and techniques like antivirus software programs guard against these threats.

Interruption of service—also called *denial of service*—occurs when hackers flood a network or application like a Web site with so much artificially generated traffic that legitimate traffic flow is seriously hampered. Legitimate users trying to access the flooded resource, in effect, are denied service because of this data "busy signal."

Security Techniques

ASPs can use the following techniques to secure their networks and applications.

Authentication

Authentication verifies that ASP system users are who they claim to be and permit them access to certain applications and network devices. As in conventional computing models, all users must authenticate themselves to use the ASP system. ASPs assign a unique identifier to each user, typically a user ID along with a password that is unique to the user or the resources (applications, storage devices, and so on) the user is accessing. User IDs let users perform certain activities when using certain resources. For instance, a user's ID may let him view records in a certain storage repository but not modify them.

Authentication procedures typically allow users limited logon attempts so that hackers can't discover a valid user ID by simply trying to log on indefinitely with different IDs. Administrators should disable the IDs of former users so unauthorized parties can't use them to break into resources linked to the IDs. Of course, all authentication data like user ID tables should be securely stored, and only administrators should be permitted to create or change them.

Some situations may merit the use of one-way encrypted passwords, which can only be reset, never viewed. This strategy prevents administrators in one venue from viewing a user's password and potentially compromising the user's security at other sites where he may use the same password.

Applications that interact with each other (like the different modules in an ERP system) may be required to authenticate their peer. For instance, if accounting system users must access a human resource system to assign employees' social security numbers to paychecks, only the authorized personnel in accounting should have the authentication information to access human resource databases. Human resources, on the other hand, may have no reason to access accounting records, so human resource personnel should not have authentication information to access accounting databases. Obviously, rogue users in either department with unauthorized access to authentication information could violate the integrity of corporate data by, say, changing pay records in accounting to embezzle funds, or by compromising confidentiality by revealing sensitive health records of employees.

ASPs should also consider timing out computing sessions on customers' clients after a certain period of inactivity. This is especially important if your employees access hosted applications via laptops or other remote devices that can be used outside the secure corporate perimeter. For instance, a salesperson visiting a prospect may leave his laptop running and unattended. Anyone wandering by could access his corporate data stored at the ASP. Even within a customer's corporate confines, unauthorized users routinely pass by open offices where unattended PCs offer similar opportunities.

Encryption

Encryption is a technique that scrambles a sender's transmission according to an algorithm (key) that the recipient then uses to unscramble and decipher the transmission. Public key security techniques provide both a public key to many users of a network as well as a private key to certain users. Anyone decrypting transmissions must know and use both keys to be successful. Secret key techniques, on the other hand, use only one key for encrypting and decrypting. It must be kept secret by the users sharing it. Because it's less complex, secret key encryption can be thousands of times faster than public key encryption, and should be used when speed is important.

Generally, encryption implemented in hardware is better than that implemented in software. However, although traditionally experts agreed that proprietary encryption was superior to nonproprietary types, this is no longer the consensus. Because only customers of an encryption vendor interacted with proprietary encryption products, experts used to think the vendor's scrambling tricks were less well known. Today, many experts feel nonproprietary encryption like Data Encryption Standard (DES), TripleDES, and others are more secure precisely because they've been used by the IT community at large and, therefore, scrutinized more exhaustively. In their opinion, any flaws in these techniques would have been discovered by now, whereas proprietary techniques may still harbor vulnerabilities that aren't generally known.

DES is a 56-bit nonproprietary encryption technique that is adequate for securing data that is not highly sensitive. Tests have shown that, within 20 to 30 hours, dedicated, powerful computers can unscramble DES. It's unlikely that amateur hackers would have these resources at their disposal. Anyone who did would likely be a competitor and would go after a company's most valuable information.

TripleDES is a 168-bit nonproprietary encryption technique that should be used to protect just such information—data like unique product formulas and pending marketing campaigns that, if exposed, would give the competition a distinct advantage. Even the most powerful decrypting tools need years to unscramble TripleDES.

Both nonproprietary techniques are quite secure in any case because companies using them can routinely change encryption keys so hackers have to keep decrypting new keys to break into the system.

It's probably worth noting that the federal government is adopting a new standard, the Advanced Encryption Standard (AES), to replace DES some time in the future.

Access Control

Access control is the practice of authorizing access to certain resources to certain users based on their company responsibilities and the security classification of the resources. Administrators can grant users individual access to resources based on their user ID. For example, an IT engineer may be given temporary access to his employer's financial records to solve a calculation bug in that department's software, but when his work is finished, his ID is disabled. Administrators can also classify data with different levels of security like "Secret" or "Top Secret," and allow only users with clearance to that security level access to those resources. For example, only executives making strategic marketing decisions for a car manufacturer may be permitted to access data warehouse statistics on the buying patterns of customers.

Of course, only authorized personnel may be allowed into certain physical locations—like the IT facility housing computer equipment—within the corporate perimeter. Access may be determined by the resource's logical location too. For instance, data on a virtual drive in a mainframe may be accessed by only personnel in the finance department.

Integrity

Applications and data have integrity when they are secure from unauthorized modification.

An ASP's files, operating systems, and hosted software can be compromised by computer virus programs. Generally an ASP can prevent this by installing appropriate scanning software at its firewall between the data center LAN and the broadband WAN. Because viruses are typically transmitted in e-mail attachments, if certain applications handle a lot of e-mail, the ASP can also install scanning software in a server located between the ASP firewall and the application. Messaging applications, for instance, may require such double-layer protection.

Hypertext Markup Language (HTML) and other data like Microsoft Word files can also contain macro or script programs that outside parties can alter. These "Trojan horse" programs can do damage to an ASP's applications when introduced undetected from the Internet into the ASP's secure environment. The same techniques for combating viruses are effective for Trojan horses.

"Man-in-the-middle" security breaches occur when data transmitted by a network or other mechanism is intercepted, altered, and passed on as valid information by an unauthorized party. Public key encryption systems are most vulnerable to this strategy because many users know the public key and can intercept and change it, and experiment with ways of discovering the private key. Authenticating the sender and receiver of such transmissions is usually sufficient to prevent this, but using secure network protocols can also help.

Confidentiality

Applications and data have confidentiality when they are secure from disclosure to unauthorized persons or programs.

ASPs should run intrusion detection software to see if anyone is trying to gain unauthorized access to the secure environment. Intrusion detection programs look for patterns in the data packet flow (like an unusually large number of packets from the same IP address) that could indicate denial-of-service attacks or probes of vulnerable ports. However, the software is only as good as the policies governing its use. It's imperative that the ASP regularly review the logs of system activity generated by the intrusion detection software to spot patterns of sniffing.

ASPs should also routinely eradicate all old data from disk space, memory, and other temporary storage before new data is stored on it so that the previous contents cannot be recovered by unauthorized parties.

Nonrepudiation provides confidentiality and authentication because it proves to a third party that a sender actually sent a message. With hosted services, especially those for which the ASP charges on a usage basis, ASPs must be able to prove that a user actually used a service. Similarly, if an impersonator uses services for which you, the customer, will be charged, you need non-repudiation to substantiate the impersonation.

ASPs can also use public key encryption to create "digital signatures" as well as encrypt message contents. Public key systems both authenticate users (because only authorized users with the key can send a transmission) and check integrity of data (because the digital signature or checksum guarantees that the same amount of data sent is received).

Audit and Accounting

Audit and accounting systems monitor the ASP system and maintain records of system and user activity.

ASPs use monitoring and management systems to detect unusual or unauthorized use of system resources. They then use the audit trail to determine how and when someone initiated an event like an unauthorized intrusion as well as the identity of the perpetrator.

Security Equipment

The following sections present standard devices an ASP can deploy to improve network and application security.

Routers

Routers connect network segments and determine which data packets will be forwarded from one network segment to another. They were originally designed to transmit data fast, so for a long time they did not analyze the data type transmitted. Once deployed on the nonsecure public Internet, however, most routers evolved packet filtering to determine which types of packets were permitted across the sections it connected. For example, a router connecting a corporate network to the Internet might only allow packets containing Hypertext Transfer Protocol information to pass between networks.

As easy-to-configure, high-speed network gateways, routers offer basic security against casual, external attempts to access a network. However, tools and techniques for compromising them are also readily available.

Firewalls

A security firewall is typically located between an organization's LAN and the Internet. It's used to keep unauthorized outside parties from infiltrating an enterprise's resources via the Internet, and parties inside the enterprise from accessing resources on the Internet that administrators would rather they not. Firewalls inspect each packet in a transmission and apply predetermined rules to decide whether a packet should be forwarded. These rules may determine types of packets being sent, the source of the packets, and the destination of the packets.

Firewalls are hardware or software based. Hardware-based ones are usually routers with enhanced management and screening capabilities that route data packets to their destinations and filter them for unauthorized activities. Software-based firewalls are installed on PCs and run on top of the operating system software like other applications. Some operating systems also come with firewall software that, when activated, screens all data trying to access them.

When the firewall is in the router, the router becomes the screen between the Internet and the enterprise LAN. When it's on a PC, the PC can be located between the LAN and router or between the router and Internet, depending on its security purpose. Hardware-based firewalls process transmissions faster than software-based ones and tend to be more secure, but software-based ones generally allow more flexible deployment and are less expensive (Figure 7–2).

Firewalls are also categorized according to the way they control traffic access. Network-level firewalls control traffic based on its source and destination addresses and Transmission Control Protocol/Internet Protocol (TCP/IP) port

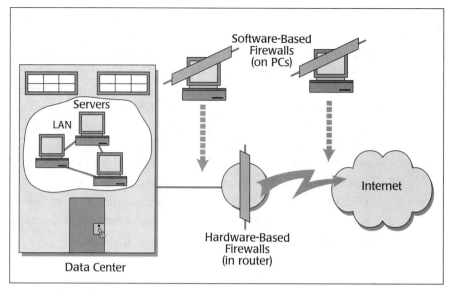

Figure 7–2 Hardware-based firewalls reside on routers and software-based firewalls reside on PCs

information. Because network-level firewalls primarily just filter addresses, traffic can flow directly through the firewall. Thus, network-level firewalls are usually much faster than application-level firewalls. Traffic doesn't actually flow through an application-level firewall. The server on which the firewall exists processes destination and other requests internally and "translates" that data from one network to another. Resources on either side of the firewall never actually make contact. Because application-level firewalls must translate the traffic data, they tend to be slower than network-level ones. However, because an application-level firewall checks more information, it's easier to track and control the transmissions going across them.

Firewalls providing network-level security generally just read traffic coming across the network and accept or reject it. Firewalls providing application-level security may also give users the ability to modify data and code in the application.

More advanced firewalls also analyze the context of the data in transmissions. Many hackers will "mask" unauthorized activity by trying to make it look like normal traffic. Some firewalls look for these contextual inconsistencies, log the action, and don't transmit suspicious packets. However, firewalls can only screen out inconsistencies they've been programmed to recognize.

Firewalls protect enterprises only from unauthorized data that they process. So they are not a deterrent to infiltration that occurs in places other than the networks the firewall screens—for instance, via a dial-up connection. Network-based firewalls also don't protect against viruses, because viruses come embedded inside files, and these firewalls examine only data like the transmission's origin and destination, not the actual contents of the packets. In most cases, examining all packet content would make the network run so slowly it would be useless. No firewall is 100% secure because it performs security based on certain rules. If hackers can decipher the rules, they can usually exploit some vulnerability in them.

Proxy Servers

Unlike routers and firewalls, proxy servers do not process transmission data to detect unauthorized activity. On a PC functioning as a firewall, or positioned inside an actual firewall, they serve as a substitute address for resources inside the enterprise. When outside parties try to transmit to those resources, they reach addresses on the proxy server, not the real addresses of the resources themselves. The proxy server then forwards the transmissions to the correct addresses according to rules linking the proxy addresses and the real addresses. Hackers can never know the real addresses of resources they want to break into, and the enterprise's internal network is never exposed to outside parties.

Some experts explain proxy servers by using an analogy to a US postal service foreign post office box. Letters addressed to the leaser of a foreign post office box are sent to a post office box in the United States, and are then forwarded automatically to the recipient's real address outside the United States. This protects the recipient's privacy because senders never find out their actual location. Proxy servers function similarly. Because outsiders can never discover the real address of the enterprise resources they may wish to compromise, they can't attack those sources directly.

Proxy servers are also increasingly used to cache data that's frequently accessed by users inside or outside the enterprise. Employees inside the enterprise who commonly access certain Internet sites can do so faster if their administrator stores the relevant pages on a proxy server that they access instead. Likewise, customers requesting data like answers to FAQs on the customer service page of an enterprise's Web site may access them faster from a proxy server with a cache dedicated to just that data. In either case, less traffic passes through the enterprise's firewall, which improves the firewall's overall transmission performance.

Customer Requirements and ASP Strategy

It should be obvious that the security equipment and strategies that ASPs deploy depend ultimately on your requirements. It should also be obvious that all of these tools and strategies can be deployed differently by different ASPs. For instance, one ASP may use a proxy server for cache primarily, whereas another relies on it for securing addresses from outsiders. Whatever the tools and strategy, it's always a good idea for ASPs to supplement them with human monitoring to detect unauthorized activities that automated security systems might miss.

Appropriate Security

Prioritizing Security Threats

Security risks are more or less critical depending on the extent of their threat to your business. If a competitor was able to steal the Coca-Cola soft drink formula, Coke's core business would be ruined overnight. If they altered the formula undetected, the change could erode Coke's market share over time. If they launched a successful denial-of-service attack on Coke's supply chain extranet, it could hurt earnings in the short term. Any of these threats could also do intangible damage to Coke's reputation.

Generally, the most serious threats arise from violation of data integrity. In the long term, wrong data usually does more harm than stolen or denied data because it can go undetected indefinitely, and its negative effects ramify the more extensively it's disseminated. Obviously, misinformation can also be the basis for costly lawsuits. The next most serious threat is unavailability of data or applications. During a system failure or denial-of-service attack, a business is dead in the water. Not only can it not make money, but having to cancel orders and the like causes actual lost business in the present, and potential lost business in the future, because of a damaged reputation.

Most laypersons think of data confidentiality as synonymous with data security. In fact, confidentiality may be less of a threat than compromised integrity or availability because breaches of it are easily detected by intrusion detection devices and other tools. Once the breach is detected, its consequences can be controlled.

Similarly, data theft, although immediately damaging, can also be somewhat neutralized after the fact. Once the business knows what data is stolen, it can take steps to limit the consequences of the loss. Of course, this rule does not apply to loss of the family jewels—a unique differentiating asset like the Coke formula, which is the basis of an entire business.

Access control may be the least threatening of the security risks because basic authentication and consistent security policy so effectively combat it. On the other hand, an unauthorized party with malicious intent and access to the system can probably also compromise at least integrity, confidentiality, and exclusive ownership, which are serious threats. Also, access control is notoriously poor inside many companies' hardened perimeters. If hackers can get beyond the corporate firewall, they often can wander at will between actual departments and logical and actual data and application resources. For this reason, many studies indicate that near 70% of security breaches originate from inside the company, not outside from the Internet.

This said, every business is unique, so you may prioritize these threats in a different order. Whatever priority you assign them, doing so helps you best allocate the funds to deal with them because you can address the highest priority threats with the most resources.

Security Tiers

Here are three security benchmarks to help you gauge the degree of security your company merits:

1. Financial organizations with sensitive financial figures and government agencies with secret information usually implement the most secure computing environments. For instance, a brokerage house calculating earnings on stocks can't risk a customer hacking his account and increasing his valid earnings. Similarly, the CIA does not want its list of agents in the Middle East falling into the hands of Islamic terrorists. Organizations of this type, requiring hermetic security, typically encrypt all data, use tokens for authentication, implement firewalls, use VPNs to connect to different clients, and routinely run intrusion detection software to assess user and system resource activity and vulnerability. If you fit this profile, you need an ASP that can provide this degree of security—if you can afford it, of course.
2. SMBs with mission-critical data typically encrypt data, perform authentication, and implement firewalls. However, to save money, they may deploy encryption in software on individual clients instead of building or leasing a VPN.

3. Organizations that require minimal security to prevent accidental security breaches or deter low-level hacking can get by with public key data authentication and integrity checking. Encryption and/or a VPN is not necessary because authentication and data integrity checks ensure that the users are who they claim to be and that no corrupted data is transmitted.

Security Policies

Different Rules for Different Users

ASPs need to create and enforce different security policies for different customers, and for various sets of users within each customer company. Security policies direct how companies secure their systems. Depending on a user's job responsibilities, each will require different levels of access to different system resources. For instance, application developers in a customer's IT department will need access to application development environments to build or modify applications. They will usually be allowed access to these resources, as well as to tools like e-mail and groupware, which are available to general users. General users, however, might be limited to e-mail, groupware, and the core application that they need to perform the primary duties of their job (for instance, a workflow application that claims processors use to process health insurance claims).

Types of Confidentiality

Because multiple clients leverage the same centralized servers and software, an ASP must take special precautions to ensure that your proprietary data is not accidentally revealed to other ASP customers and, possibly, sensitive data in one of your departments is not revealed to other departments.

Many ASPs use virtual vaults to segment customer data; others create separate virtual drives for different customers. In lieu of these confidentiality measures, ASPs may encrypt the data of different customers with different encryption keys to achieve the same goal. Of course, with encryption, the ASP must establish access control over which users have access to the encryption/ decryption keys as well as which ones have access to which applications. If an ASP does not use virtual vaults or drives, then it should use such a combination of encryption, authentication, and access control. Also, security policies should be documented and include procedures that cover all aspects of the ASP's security like strategy, tools, and staff. Without documented procedures, even the best security technology falls short when, for example, staff turnover leaves the ASP without crucial expertise that existed only in a former administrator's head.

Security Audits

Of course, the best way to confirm the ASP can provide the security protection it claims is by getting an independent security specialist to audit the security measures. You can request an audit, security report, or Statement on Auditing Standards (SAS) 70-style report from an accounting firm. The report should capture both the ASP's documented security measures and policy as well as tacit knowledge about security procedures in the heads of the key ASP staff responsible for security. You should be able to use the report to run independent tests of the ASP's security without notifying the ASP.

What's more, ASPs should maintain detailed security logs. In the event of a security breach, you should be able to access log data to investigate possible perpetrators and to repair any security weaknesses. Logs also provide proof if the ASP is to blame in the event there is a data security problem at your site. They also constitute legal evidence if you sue an ASP for, say, proprietary data being stolen. Generally, logs improve an ASP's credibility. Lack of them suggests negligence (even if you never refer to them). Auditing, like security in general, is an ongoing process. You should audit your ASP periodically for your own protection.

PERSONNEL BACKGROUND CHECKS

Suffice it to say, an ASP should perform background checks on all personnel with access to its infrastructure and your data. You may also want to verify data about the ASP staff like employment history, security clearances and certifications, and criminal offenses. In servicing very high-security customers, ASPs that hire personnel with Top Secret clearance in the military or comparable institutions may have a competitive edge over those who don't.

Physical Security

Earlier in the book we discussed some aspects of physical security like disaster planning. Although a data center should be reinforced to withstand unpredictable acts of God like earthquakes, there are also some proven procedures and strategies that ASPs should use to minimize exposing your equipment and its own facilities to unauthorized parties.

An ASP should always control access to facilities like data centers. At the minimum, it should man facility entrances and require that anyone entering sign in. Often, however, ASPs also will use some form of biometric recognition system that recognizes unique human characteristics like fingerprints, for example, or other systems that scan, say, card keys to identify authorized parties. Most ASPs also either prevent access to or provide escorts through data center areas housing customer servers and other equipment.

These areas should be separate from lobbies and offices, and if a general area houses more than one customer's equipment, each customer's equipment should be locked in its own cage or other space that's accessible only to designated ASP and customer employees.

Many ASPs deploy security personnel on the facility grounds as well. Often, they back up that human line of defense with automated security devices like motion detectors and video monitors that detect intruders both in the data center and on the surrounding perimeter, where they keep critical contingency equipment like backup generators.

As a final precaution, the ASP would be wise to store all backup copies of customer data at least on tape and house it at an off-site location secure from unauthorized personnel. Some ASPs even choose a location geographically far enough away that it won't be affected by a local disaster.

In general, the more secure a facility *looks,* the more likely it will deter unauthorized intruders. So the more walls, doors, guards, signs, and security technology an ASP keeps between unauthorized outside parties and internal data, media, and equipment, the better.

MANAGED SECURITY PROVIDERS

For a number of reasons, SMBs are outsourcing security to specialists called *managed security providers (MSecP)*. Today, IT systems and WANs are increasingly complex and decentralized, and the vast majority reside in SMBs. More SMBs are dotcom companies that have neither the time nor the money to invest in security technologies, strategies, and personnel. Moreover, with the e-business boom, security threats from the Internet are growing for all types of organizations. What with new viruses, changing technology, and hacker ingenuity and perseverance, the types of threats are constantly changing.

It should come as no surprise, then, that ASPs are also teaming with MSecPs to gain better credibility with ASP customers. MSecPs provide a full array of security services. They:

- Perform vulnerability assessments to alert ASPs to possible security weaknesses in their infrastructure, personnel, and policies.
- Conduct audits to ensure ASP customers that the ASP has taken sufficient steps to correct any vulnerabilities. They also perform specialized audits like the "Information Security Exam for Financial Institutions" and "HIPAA" audits for health care to confirm the ASP meets the regulations for data handling in certain industries.
- Install security technology where necessary at the ASP site and then remotely monitor all ASP facilities like data centers and security equipment like firewalls. This, of course, entails dedicating MSecP specialists to administer and upgrade equipment as needed.
- Perform intrusion detection to alert the ASP if unauthorized parties are attempting to access ASP systems.
- Perform incident response to a security breach, define the breach, and then recommend and implement corrective measures. They also gather and archive all evidence associated with the incident so it can be presented in court as needed for suits, criminal proceedings, and other matters.
- Help formulate an ASP's security policies and guard the actual policy copies from unauthorized personnel.
- Perform background checks on all ASP personnel.
- Offer ongoing routine security education to all relevant staff.

continued

MSecPs' services vary. Some offer only certain services like security monitoring or periodic audits, whereas others provide a full complement of services including education, policy creation, and background checks. The more security services an ASP needs, the more scrutiny the MSecP will apply to mapping the ASP's IT infrastructure and documenting its, and its customers', unique business processes and practices. Whereas outsourced security was once the exclusive province of the Big Five and comparable consulting companies, these newer, smaller, and more specialized MSecPs now offer a viable security outsourcing alternative for ASPs and other businesses (Figure 7–3). Whether an ASP employs an MSecP will probably depend on the SLA conditions you stipulate and on how dramatically the ASP wants to differentiate itself with value-added security from competing ASPs.

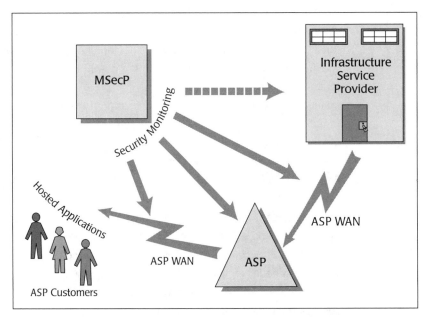

Figure 7–3 Managed security providers (MSecPs) are xSPs that manage the security of multiple ASPs' IT infrastructure

SUCCESS STORY

MSecP: Netegrity, Inc.
Customer: Corio, Inc., an ASP
Key elements of the solution: Simplified, one-point access across multiple hosted applications, extensive customization of security software, scalability

Corio, a marquee pure-play ASP, leases integrated hosted applications to help companies more quickly and cost-effectively manage rapid growth and business processes across the enterprise. All applications are turnkey and preintegrated on Orion, Corio's ASP hardware/software platform. Hosted offerings include software modules like Peoplesoft's finance and manufacturing, Siebel's sales force automation and CRM, and Broadvision's e-commerce.

In addition to providing powerful, affordable, focused functionality, customers expect that ASPs will secure proprietary data from unauthorized access and render it impervious to external denial of service and other attacks. Corio certainly wanted to allay these fundamental customer fears by accurately managing each user profile and authorizing all users' access to the appropriate applications. But it also needed a comprehensive security solution that could scale to accommodate its fast-growing customer base. And, beyond that, it was seeking a method of tracking customers across all of its hosted applications. In keeping with the one-bill/one-provider ASP model, Corio also desired simplified user access to applications through single sign-on technology that let users log on at a central location and, without reentering passwords for separate applications, access personalized information across all their hosted applications.

As a pure-play ASP, Corio keeps its focus on leasing and serving its turnkey hosted applications—not on the arcania of securing them. So it opted to engage the MSecP, Netegrity, Inc., particularly because its SiteMinder user management and security software promised enhanced security, single sign-on, and user authentication via predefined privileges. In concert with Netegrity, Corio engineers also developed and

continued

added an entitlement management system (EMS) to SiteMinder. EMS essentially secures and simplifies customer access to Corio's hosted applications, and manages users across all of the applications from one central console. Through independent lab testing, Netegrity further proved that SiteMinder was capable of the superior scalability and performance needed to support Corio's future growth.

With SiteMinder as an integrated component of its Orion platform, Corio can now guarantee customers secure business transactions, centralized user and access management, single sign-on, secure and personalized content for large numbers of users, as well as unparalleled scalability and performance. What's more, SiteMinder is reducing Corio's overall operating costs by eliminating the need for administrative personnel to support its security efforts.

Netegrity is more than a point service provider for Corio. In addition to establishing user policies, installing the appropriate security technology, and monitoring the SiteMinder solution, it also worked hand-in-hand with Corio to understand the ASP's user requirements and to customize SiteMinder suitably to address them. In doing so, Netegrity helped Corio create the kind of unique security program that will help this pure-play ASP differentiate itself from other providers offering hosted turnkey applications.

Permission courtesy of Corio, Inc.

Key Concepts

- Authentication—Verifying that ASP system users are who they claim to be so they can access certain applications and network devices
- Encryption—Scrambling a sender's transmission according to an algorithm that the recipient then uses to unscramble and decipher the transmission
- Access control—Authorizing access to certain resources to certain users based on their company responsibilities and the security classification of the resources
- Integrity—When applications and data are secure from unauthorized modification

- Confidentiality—When applications and data are secure from disclosure to unauthorized persons or programs
- Auditing and accounting systems—Monitor the ASP system and maintain records of system and user activity
- Firewall—A transmission filtering device typically located between an organization's LAN and the Internet that keeps unauthorized Internet parties from infiltrating an enterprise's resources and enterprise parties from accessing certain Internet resources.
- Hardware-based firewalls (in routers)—Process transmissions the fastest and most securely of any type of firewall
- Software-based firewalls (on PCs)—More flexibly deployed and less expensive than hardware-based firewalls
- Network-level firewalls—Filter traffic as it passes through by checking its address to see if sending and receiving addresses are authorized
- Application-level firewalls—Filter traffic by "translating" address and other information from one network to another so, although the transmission gets checked, resources on either side of the firewall never make contact
- Proxy servers—Located on or inside firewalls and house substitute addresses for enterprise resources, so when outside parties transmit to them, they reach proxy addresses that forward the transmissions to the real addresses, thus protecting the internal network from outside parties
- Security policy—Security rules for users within each ASP customer department and for different customer companies that, depending on a user's job responsibilities, require different levels of access to different system resources
- Security audit—Identification and documention of an ASP's security measures by independent security specialists
- Background checks—Verifying data about ASP staff, such as employment history, security clearances, and criminal offenses.
- Physical security—Measures and policies like guards, video monitors, and sign-in logs (not IT infrastructure measures like encryption) to protect internal data, media, and equipment from unauthorized parties
- MSecP—Service provider to whom ASPs outsource any or all of their customer security responsibilities

CHAPTER EIGHT

ASP Service-Level Agreements

This chapter discusses

- Network SLAs
- Hosting SLAs
- Application SLAs
- End-to-end SLAs

An SLA is a contract that specifies the deliverables, terms, and conditions between service providers and consumers. For instance, most SLAs state terms like the length of the contract, the start date of the service, and the terms of payment. Most SLAs also define the following deliverables and conditions:

- Services supplied by the provider
- Standards the provider must meet in providing the services
- The provider's reporting requirements (real time or historical) to the end customer
- The nonperformance penalties (to the provider) and remedies (to the customer) if the provider fails to deliver services at specified standards

ASP SLAs typically address three component services—network, application and hosting—that the ASP or its partners may provide. Each of these services may justify its own SLA.

A network SLA typically covers the network connection between you and the ASP. A network SLA is the network service level promised by a network service provider or infrastructure service provider to the ASP.

An application SLA covers the hosted application's functionality and may be guaranteed by the software vendor partnering with the ASP. Of course, this functionality can be affected by the performance of the hardware, software, and network platforms.

A hosting SLA covers the support services like leased servers, leased storage, data center infrastructure, or performance monitoring that an ASP might acquire from a company like an infrastructure service provider or an MSP.

These are typically "background" SLAs that the ASP creates with its partners. They define an acceptable range of performance, like throughput for system components like broadband networks supplied by partners like infrastructure service providers. An ASP may have multiple background SLAs with multiple partners like an infrastructure service provider and an MSP.

The ASP must take these into consideration when defining the "end-to-end" SLA that it offers you. The end-to-end SLA is the binding contract between the ASP and you for all service components offered, regardless of whether they are provided by the ASP or its partners. If any partner fails to meet its SLA with the ASP, the resulting performance degradation may affect the ASP's service to you, and you will hold the ASP responsible according to the end-to-end SLA. The ASP, therefore, must establish realistic SLAs with its partners to guarantee you only the levels of performance in the end-to-end SLA that its partners' SLAs can support.

SLAs can get confusing if you, not the ASP, engage both the ASP and your own other service providers like MSPs. However, engaging MSPs and MSecPs to monitor ASPs' performance and security is probably going to be routine for the foreseeable future. So, to simplify your interaction with the ASP and any supporting providers, it's probably best to establish flexible and cooperative relationships among all parties. If, for instance, your MSP alerted the ASP that it fell short on a network metric like throughput, the sensible thing to do is for the MSP and the ASP to cooperate on improving the performance for the next billing cycle, and for the ASP to offer a service rebate. Unless there are repeated discrepancies between what the providers claim, niggling finger-pointing only hurts you by alienating the provider. If there are repeated discrepancies, you probably should replace one or all providers.

Network and application SLAs address similar conditions that are defined slightly differently in a network or application context. The conditions covered in

Table 8–1 Network, Application, and Hosting SLAs Make Up the End-to-End SLA

SLA	Service Covered	Service Provider
Network	ASP to customer network	Infrastructure service provider, network service provider (for the ASP)
Application	Functionality of hosted applications	ISV (for the ASP)
Hosting	Special support services the ASP leases from the MSP, MSecP, SSP, etc.	Infrastructure service provider, MSP, MSecP, and SSP (for the ASP)
End-to-end	All services the ASP provides the customer	ASP (for the customer)

hosted SLAs are not nearly as predictable because the services offered by the hosting providers are so various. For this reason, they won't be discussed here. However, in negotiating a hosting SLA, you'd be well advised to use the network and application checklists (Tables 8–2 and 8–3) as guides to the major categories of service on which to focus.

The Network SLA

You should confirm with the ASP its unique requirements for these conditions affecting performance of telecommunications networks.

Network Availability

Availability specifies the percentage of network uptime the ASP is guaranteeing you (typically as a 99.x percentage). Obviously, the measurement required will depend on a number of factors, but mostly on the mission criticality of the hosted applications being leased. The more mission critical the application, the closer to 100% uptime you'll require. The provider may also need to specify different uptime percentages for different parts of the network—for example, for different Web sites.

Table 8-2 Define your network SLA by filling in the third column of this network SLA checklist

Condition	Key Metric	Required Performance Range
Availability	Uptime	
Throughput	Speed	
Redundancy	Duplicate components/functionality	
Equipment	Vendor/model	
Scalability	Reach/power	
Peering	Backup/supplemental networks	
Delay	Response time	
Corroboration	Service monitoring/testing	
Reporting	Parameters monitored/reported	
Provisioning	Installation/turn-on time	
Support	Type/availability of technical support	
Planned outages	Scheduled downtime	
Unplanned outages	Maximum downtime for unforseen repairs	

Network Throughput

Throughput specifies the range of the network's throughput speed and takes into consideration possible burst speeds needed to accommodate sudden increases in traffic.

Network Redundancy

Redundancy specifies the duplicate network elements deployed as backup for the primary elements like routers and ATM switches, as well as "failover," or the speed with which they take over operation.

Network Equipment

Equipment specifies the particular equipment such as models of and vendors for routers and ATM switches being used in the network. This condition should specify version numbers and satisfactorily address compatibility issues as well.

Table 8–3 Define your application SLA by filling in the third column of this application SLA checklist

Condition	Key Metric	Required Performance Range
Availability	Uptime	
Performance	Transactions/second, keyboard response time, database response time, etc.	
Redundancy	Duplicate components/data	
Platform	Vendor/model	
Scalability	Server capacity	
Security	Encryption, authentication, nonrepudiation, etc.	
Administration	Percent of customer-controlled management/customization	
Monitoring	Who monitors which performance metrics?	
Corroboration	Service monitoring/testing	
Reporting	Parameters monitored/reported	
Provisioning	Installation/turn-on time	
Support	Type/availability of technical support	
Planned outages	Scheduled downtime	
Unplanned outages	Maximum downtime for unforeseen repairs	

If an ASP is promising particularly fast throughput, it should be willing to indicate to you if and how it is deploying equipment like fiber-optic trunks and DWDM. You may also want to specify when certain equipment must be upgraded or replaced to guarantee competitive performance. For instance, if you sign with an ASP that offers Frame Relay but need certain quality of service 16 months after you sign, you should specify in the SLA that the ASP should have an ATM network functional by then.

Network Scalability

Scalability specifies the ASP network's existing and potential reach and power. You should be able to determine whether the network will adequately service all your existing offices as well as new offices, customers, and remote workers as they need to be provisioned over the life of the contract. Also, if certain power users will make greater demands on their LAN link to the ASP network, you should be assured that router and trunk capacity at that link can accommodate peak demands at the service levels of the contract.

Network Peering Arrangements

Peering arrangements specify the other networks to which the ASP's primary network connects to accommodate greater geographical reach or alternate failover transmission routes. For example, an ASP may own a national VPN but have peering arrangements with AT&T and Sprint for international service and failover.

Network Delay

Delay specifies the network's response times needed to accommodate your applications. Real-time, interactive applications like voice require very fast response times. Nonreal-time applications like e-mail can tolerate slower response times.

Network Service-Level Corroboration

Corroboration specifies the means by which the ASP proves that your service-level guarantees have been met. This indicates how the ASP monitors the network service it provides. For instance, the ASP might retain an MSP to monitor its network platform and to perform proactive testing to guarantee the ASP's service levels.

Network Reporting

Reporting specifies the network performance parameters like average throughput and unscheduled downtime that the ASP routinely monitors and reports to you, and how promptly and often the ASP provides these reports.

Network Provisioning

Provisioning specifies the length of both the installation period for initial service and the provisioning period for new users. For instance, an ASP might guarantee it will install a new T1 leased line to your premises within three weeks, but that it will replace defective existing routers within three days.

Network Support

Support specifies the extent of the ASP's network technical support and the periods during which it's available. This indicates the number of agents on duty at a given time, the response times for problem resolution, periods when the help desk and account management staff are available, and so forth. For instance, to save the ASP resources and you money, the ASP and you might agree that ten help desk staff will be on duty from 8 AM to 6 PM and only two from 6 PM to 8 AM. As part of network support, the ASP should also clearly identify your troubleshooting escalation procedure.

Planned Network Outages

Planned outages specify the periods when network service will be down for routine maintenance and periodic upgrades. They also specify what network capabilities will still be offered during the downtime so you can maintain minimum operations like e-commerce Web site functionality.

Unplanned Network Outages

Unplanned outages specify the ASP's response time to resolve unforeseen network problems.

SUCCESS STORY

ISV ASP: DataCert.com, Inc. and Interliant, Inc.
Customers: Law firms and Fortune 100 corporate legal departments
Key elements of the solution: Proven ASP infrastructure to win credibility with Fortune 100 customers, bulletproof 24/7 support, cost-effective data security

DataCert.com, Inc., headquartered in Houston, TX, provides e-business services for the secure exchange of information between trading part-

continued

ners and applications to help companies eliminate redundant processes and reduce costs. DataCert.com also allows enterprises to create more effective business webs by extending business processes beyond traditional barriers directly to trading partners.

Recently, DataCert.com applied its innovative technology and partnered with Interliant to solve a long-standing challenge in the legal profession. Law firms thrive on billings, yet billing for legal services has long been a cumbersome process. Historically, the lack of a common electronic billing language has made electronic invoicing impossible. Large law firms might use an Electronic Data Interchange (EDI) network. However, EDI is expensive to lease or build and maintain. So most firms have prepared bills in house and mailed them to clients, who in turn have scanned or keyed the billing details into their accounting systems. But if an invoice gets lost or keyed incorrectly, the entire process breaks down.

DataCert.com developed ShareDoc/LEGAL, a Web-based secure document distribution solution, to address the billing challenge. The solution is hosted by established ASP, Interliant, Inc., within a Microsoft Windows Distributed interNet Applications Architecture (Windows DNA)-based application hosting environment. The platform is built on the Microsoft Windows NT Server network operating system and Microsoft SQL Server.

Legal billing personnel use a browser and the Internet to access a Web server that links them to DataCert.com's ShareDoc/LEGAL application. ShareDoc/LEGAL translates the invoices into any accounting or finance system file format that the clients specify and electronically delivers them—quickly, securely, and cost-effectively.

A Foundation of Trust

To move sensitive information between law firms and their clients with complete integrity, ShareDoc/LEGAL relies on digital signatures and secure transfer protocols. It also provides a detailed audit path, which chronicles when the invoice was sent and who received it.

While these benefits are compelling, DataCert.com knew the solution would be difficult to sell unless it could guarantee the reliability, availability, and security of the servers running ShareDoc/LEGAL.

continued

"It's a tremendous benefit to have Interliant host our application," said Eric Elfman, DataCert.com president and chief executive officer. "As a startup company, I don't think that we could have convinced some of our Fortune 100 clients to trust us to keep the servers up and running. We, alone, could not deliver the data center support structure or security level that our clients require. [But] Interliant's ASP Host solution delivers all that and more, and its established reputation helped us win our clients' trust," he concludes.

Interliant, which hosts mission-critical applications for more than 1,300 enterprises, provides the data center infrastructure, system administration and management expertise, along with 24/7 support. DataCert.com handles marketing, help desk services, and billing for the ShareDoc/LEGAL service.

The ASP Advantage

"Both DataCert.com and its customers gain from Interliant's hosting of the ShareDoc Network," said Jim Battenberg, Interliant's vice president of product marketing. "Our application hosting experience enables quicker time-to-market for a company such as DataCert.com," he adds. "And customers don't incur the expense of running and supporting the application themselves. Interliant's staff includes experts certified to work on Windows NT, Internet Information Server, SQL Server, Compaq ProLiant systems, and more. We [also] offer 24/7 support, a level of service that clients might not have in their own IT departments," he says. "Plus, clients don't have to worry about keeping up-to-date with new releases and patches. All they have to do is manage the browsers on their desktops—we take care of everything else."

A Secure Environment

For DataCert.com, the choice of Interliant made sense for two reasons: the ASP's time-tested data center infrastructure, and its expertise in supporting Windows NT-based hosted applications.

"We selected the Windows NT platform because of its depth and breadth," said Eric Smith, DataCert.com vice president of software development. "Our application is built around a secure platform, and Microsoft tools allow access to many layers of that platform," he adds. "We're using the Microsoft Certificate Server and the Crypto32 library. As we expand the

continued

application in the future, the encryption is built into Windows NT for streamlined implementation."

Microsoft development products enabled DataCert.com to bring this hosted application to market quickly, according to Smith. "Since the application's components are all from Microsoft, we have fewer interoperability problems than we would have had if we'd used UNIX and Netscape, for instance," he said.

Big Benefits

Since transitioning its business model from Independent Software Vendor (ISV) to Application Service Provider (ASP), DataCert.com has used the INIT ASP Host solution to win marketplace confidence, reduce time to market, and lower costs. Today, some 1,000 law firms and Fortune 100 corporate legal departments depend on DataCert.com's secure billing solution.

Ultimately, everyone benefits from this new model of document distribution. Law firms gain an efficient and secure billing system, DataCert.com can capitalize on the services and proven strength of Interliant, and Interliant can expand its portfolio of application services.

Permission courtesy of Interliant, Inc.

The Application SLA

You should confirm with the ASP its unique requirements for these conditions affecting performance of hosted applications.

Application Availability

Availability specifies the percentage of application uptime (typically expressed as a 99.x percentage) the ASP is guaranteeing you. This typically covers all application components like databases and directories, and may be different for different components. Obviously, this measurement will depend on a number of factors, but mostly on the mission criticality of the hosted application. The more mission critical the application, the better uptime you'll need.

Application Performance

Performance specifies the capacity of the application, in terms of its transactions per second, keyboard-to-screen response time, database response time, and so forth. It should indicate the performance level at which the application routinely operates, such as an average keyboard-to-screen response time of one second. This measurement will be affected by the number of other ASP customers using the same application servers or database servers. However, although you may want to know how many customers share these resources, this number should not matter as long as you have a guarantee of performance.

Application Redundancy

Redundancy specifies the measures taken by the ASP to ensure all application elements are failover protected. For instance, the ASP may replicate databases on servers at different data centers on different geographical power grids. This condition guarantees that there are no single points of failure in the application architecture.

Application Platform

Platform specifies the components of the ASP hardware/software platform and their capabilities. This condition covers models and vendors of operating systems, middleware, servers, storage devices, and any value-added components like CD creation utilities for generation of reports on CD. This condition should specify version numbers and satisfactorily address compatibility issues as well.

Application Scalability

Scalability specifies the existing and potential capacity of the ASP's servers. You should be satisfied that, as it adds users, the ASP's servers can accommodate them without performance degradation or that the ASP will upgrade or add servers to maintain the service levels of the contract.

Application Security

Security specifies backup and restore schedules and capabilities, unique backup resources—like a duplicate data center where data is stored in the event of a catastrophic failure, location of duplicate user, configuration, and security information, and so forth. It also specifies the ASP's data security measures for you, such as encryption and authentication, as well as number, capabilities, and locations of firewalls, and so forth.

Customer Application Administration

Customer administration specifies if and to what extent your administrators and users can manage and customize application elements. For example, can your administrators add new users to hosted applications? Can they modify the interface of a hosted application to better suit one department's requirements?

Application Monitoring

Monitoring specifies who monitors application performance, which metrics are monitored, and which performance measurements you can view and when. For instance, an MSP might monitor an ASP's infrastructure performance and provide all the ASP's customers with average keyboard-to-screen response times and average database transactions per second in real time.

Application Service-Level Corroboration

Service-level corroboration specifies the means by which the ASP proves the customer's application service-level guarantees have been met. This indicates how the ASP monitors the hosted application and platform components affecting it. For instance, it might retain an MSP to monitor its hardware/software platform, network throughput, and average transactions per second, and to perform proactive testing to guarantee service levels.

Application Reporting

Reporting specifies the application performance parameters that the ASP routinely monitors and reports to you, and how promptly and often the ASP provides those reports.

Application Provisioning

Provisioning specifies the length of both the initial installation period for the hosted application and the provisioning period for new users. For instance, an ASP might guarantee it will install a 1,000-user hosted application in six weeks, and it will subsequently activate new users on the application in one day.

Application Support

Support specifies the extent of technical support and the periods during which it's available. As part of application support, the ASP should also clearly identify your troubleshooting escalation procedure.

Planned Application Outages

Planned outages specify the periods when an application will be down for routine maintenance and periodic upgrades. They also specify which application capabilities will still be offered during the downtime.

Unplanned Application Outages

Unplanned outages specify the ASP's response time to resolve unforeseen application problems.

General Practices

When an ASP fails to meet an SLA, it customarily reimburses you in the form of a rebate of free service for a period of time, not with a financial payment. If you require other penalties for SLA failures, you should state them in the SLA. Rebates can also be relative, based on the scale of a system or network. ASPs may adjust their rebates to account for the number of users affected by interrupted network and/or application service.

Most SLAs range in length from one to three years. If you are very wary of committing to the ASP model, an ASP might offer you a temporary SLA for a trial period of, say, six months.

And, instead of customizing an SLA for every customer, many service providers offer tiered levels of service at different prices to accommodate the various performance and support requirements of different customers while also conserving their own administrative resources.

Lastly, although SLAs can be painstakingly granular in their conditions, you should not lose sight of the big picture in trying to cover all your possible performance liabilities. ASP SLAs guarantee you the ability to do business more affordably and dependably with less management overhead. You should always negotiate SLA details with these ends in mind.

Key Concepts

- SLA—A contract that specifies the deliverables, terms, and conditions between a service provider and its customers
- SLA goals—To define services supplied, standards and reporting requirements for them, and penalties and remedies for nonperformance of them
- Network SLA—Background SLA that covers the functionality of the network connection between the customer and the ASP
- Application SLA—Background SLA that covers the functionality of the hosted application
- Hosting SLA—Background SLA that covers services like data center infrastructure or performance monitoring that an ASP may acquire from a supporting provider like an infrastructure service provider or an MSP
- End-to-end SLA—Comprehensive SLA between the ASP and the customer comprised of all background SLAs and any additional stipulations unique to any customer

CHAPTER NINE

ASP Pricing Models

This chapter discusses

- Flat/flat leasing rates
- Flat/tiered leasing rates
- Variable/tiered leasing rates
- Per-click leasing rates

As stated earlier, several factors eroded software margins in recent years. As more enterprise applications became Web enabled, most client functionality migrated to the server. Vendors couldn't justify expensive client license charges because an increasing percentage were inexpensive "thin" Web browsers, not traditional "thick" interactive ones. Sales of high-end enterprise systems to G2000s were also slowing. Although big vendors had always made more money on services than enterprise software, the lack of *new* installs further pinched that installed software revenue stream. Also, new mid-range system integrators were refining the repeatable solution business model so that they could undercut big vendor/SI bids on high-end enterprise application projects. Because they offered fixed prices and deployment periods, customers began to understand that there was now a viable alternative to traditional time-and-materials pricing for many enterprise application installs.

These and other factors suggested to vendors that they needed to evolve a new way of charging for services that made them more accountable to the prices quoted in bids, gave customers more control over price up front, and was more usage based, so customers paid for focused functionality they actually needed, not "bloatware" packages with gratuitous features and functions designed to address broader and more "mass" markets. In short, the trend in IT overall was combining mass availability and pricing with greater customizability and flexibility of pricing models. Both tendencies dovetailed in hosted services.

The ASP business model also addressed other issues: for example, the pricing complexity and unpredictability that resulted from different service providers using different pricing and billing models. Managers bought hardware per box, software per seat license, network services per SLA, and integration per man-hour. To calculate costs, managers had to use four different models. However, network SLAs and time-and-material integration fees weren't necessarily predictable. Implementation delays and varying usage patterns could drive up costs. Most customers preferred stable up-front fees they could control and on which they could base annual budgets and cash flow. All of these issues were especially troublesome for SMBs because of their personnel, financial, and IT limitations.

ASP pricing models address most of these issues. First, because monthly, quarterly, or yearly leasing models tend to be fixed (as one flat rate or tiered flat rates) or usage based, you either know the price for the service right up front and can budget for it, or you pay only for those services you actually use. Thus the unpredictability of SLA and time-and-material pricing has less influence on final price. Second, deployment time and price are often guaranteed, so extended hours of customization don't change price. Third, you pay a more "mass" leasing rate for a "mass customized" solution instead of purchasing an expensive custom solution, although many ASPs will also further customize a hosted solution for a fee. Fourth, provider and billing management is much less complex. You get one bill each month for your unified hosted services, which includes hardware, software, network, storage, and oftentimes security and performance monitoring too. In any case, services from one ASP don't overlap. You are always dealing with one provider and one bill, and this simplifies administration and improves accountability.

Finally, with the old time-and-materials model, nothing was free. You paid for everything: servers, application licenses, leased lines, integration man-hours, and so forth. With the ASP model, the infrastructure and integration are much less expensive. Data center, servers, storage, applications, and VPNs are built once and resold many times, so the ASP spreads its infrastructure costs over many customers. Integration may even be fixed price or included in the leasing fee.

However, although ASP pricing models tend to be simpler than traditional ones, they are hardly one-dimensional or inflexible.

The Major Types of Pricing Models

ASPs tend to use three parameters—flat leasing rates, tiered leasing rates, and per-click charges—to define their pricing models. In general you reap the economies of affordable fixed flat or tiered rates, or incur charges only for your exact usage (Table 9–1).

Flat leasing rates are fixed prices for certain periods of time, like monthly or annually, often regardless of usage. Often they are based on the number of user licenses the ASP must purchase to service your user base. Tiered rates are prices charged per tier of usage (casual, moderate, heavy), number of users ($X per 1 to 100 users, $Y per 101 to 500 users, $Z per 501+ users), or number or amount of documents, images, and data manipulated (first 50,000 images scanned = $175/month, next 175,000 images scanned = $300/month, next 200,000 images scanned = $450/month, and so on). Per-click rates are charges per instance of activity, such as an e-commerce transaction that's completed or a document or image that's converted, imported, stored, or retrieved.

ASPs adapt their cost models to their target customers' usage patterns—or they should. In general, large customers with lots of activity like document retrieval prefer a flat rate. For instance, a flat fee like $5,000/month for a hosted workflow service might allow your users unlimited document retrievals. If you were charged per click, retrieval and routing costs could get exorbitant. Because there's only one flat rate that can never change without your approval, ASPs call it a "flat/flat" rate.

Table 9–1 Various ASP Pricing Models Yield Different Customer Benefits

Pricing Model	Customer Benefits
Flat/flat	High activity for fixed fee
Flat/tiered	Accommodates variations in use
Variable/tiered	Lower price with increased use
Per click	Pay only for exact usage

ASPs can also charge "flat/tiered" rates. These are tiered rates fixed in advance that you select based on your estimated usage. The ASP may use various criteria to do the estimate: number of users, quantity of documents stored and likely to be retrieved, size of files to be retrieved, and so forth. For instance, an ASP offering hosted CRM might charge $1,000/month for as many as 100 users, $2,500/month for 101 to 500 users, and $3,500/month for 501 or more users. The flat/tiered rate is often used by ASPs with high-volume users whose activity varies or number of users tends to grow, as well as by ASPs servicing customers of all sizes and usage patterns to accommodate customers with different user/usage requirements.

If, for instance, an ASP wants to provide an incentive for you to do more business with it, it might charge variable/tiered rates. So it would charge a tiered rate for documents processed per month, but that rate might fall in each tier the more documents that you process.

ASPs can also charge on a "per-click" basis (Table 9–2). This is strictly a usage-based model in which the ASP charges customers a set fee for each instance of activity. Smaller customers with moderate usage tend to like per-click charges

Table 9–2 Examples Help Clarify the Basic ASP Pricing Models

Model Type	Price	Frequency	Description
Flat/flat	$1,000	Per month	For unlimited use
Flat/tiered			
Tier 1	$1,000	Per month	For up to 100 users
Tier 2	$2,500	Per month	For 101 to 500 users
Tier 3	$3,500	Per month	For 501 or more users
Variable/tiered			
Tier 1	0.05/ document	–	For up to 100,000 documents scanned
Tier 2	0.04/ document	–	For 100,001 to 200,000 documents scanned
Tier 3	0.03/ document	–	For 200,001 to 300,000 documents scanned
Per click	0.05	–	Per document retrieved

because they're more economical. For instance, a small service bureau ASP converting less than 1,000 land records for a state agency each month might charge 0.03 per page scanned and stored, and 0.10 per retrieval after conversion. Instead of paying a flat monthly fee for estimated usage it may never equal, the agency pays only for its actual system activity. Customers whose activity fluctuates wildly may also prefer per-click charges because it's so difficult to estimate their actual usage. For instance, consider a mid-size brokerage house the leases an on-line trading application its customers use to buy and sell stocks. The vagaries of the stock market will determine the number of transactions that occur each month (Table 9–1).

Flat, tiered, and per-click models can be combined in limitless ways. For example, a service bureau ASP might charge three flat/tiered rates of $1,000, $2,000, and $3,000 a month based on the approximate number of paper documents a customer will have scanned and stored. But it might also charge a 0.05 per-click fee for each document scanned in excess of a certain number at each tier—say, 10,000 at the $1,000 tier. A VAR ASP with an ERP software vendor partner may charge a fixed fee per ERP module that a customer leases, but also charge a per-click transaction charge for each transaction in excess of 2,500 a month. An ASP hosting a knowledge management application for a construction company may charge per server and gigabyte of storage needed to support a varying number of building projects that need to collaborate.

This said, probably because of its familiarity and simplicity, "flat/flat" based on the number of users is the most popular cost model—probably because it's the most similar to the old software licensing model (so it doesn't confuse customers) and because it offers the simplicity of a flat, periodic rate that lets customers accurately estimate annual budgets.

Other Fees

Many ASPs also charge you for storage in addition to the base fees. Larger customers typically pay per gigabyte, whereas smaller customers may prefer per-megabyte charges. The rate may also fall the longer the data is stored and migrated to less expensive media—say, from a redundant array of inexpensive disks (RAID) to optical to tape. Sometimes the ASP charges a storage setup fee for preparing its optical disk jukeboxes and SAN.

ASPs may also charge a one-time "setup fee" for preparing their general ASP infrastructure to accommodate your requirements—for instance, to cover costs like adding servers in the data center and provisioning necessary leased lines.

Depending on the value-added services they offer, ASPs may also charge tiered fees for different levels of security, different guaranteed network through-put, and so on.

Real-World Examples of ASP Pricing Models

ASPs must balance several factors when defining their pricing models. They must protect themselves by creating a model that permits them to make their desired profit margin, cover their anticipated costs, undercut their own and their competition's installed system prices, and is appropriate to the usage patterns of the ASP's target market. If the model is too different from past IT pricing models, it may take customers out of their comfort zones. If it's too complex, the customer may suspect the ASP is hiding fees or trying to make it impossible for customers to comparison shop. Also, a complex model essentially undermines the simplicity of billing the ASP model promises. Most customers want a bill that's easy to understand. Also, if the pricing model is too variable, customers will find it hard to adjust their annual budgets accurately. Of all these factors, the two most important are how the model permits the ASP to make a profit and how well it maps to the usage patterns of the ASP's customers.

As stated earlier, the most common ASP pricing model is a flat, monthly, per-user leasing fee accompanied by a one-time setup fee. However, this flat monthly fee doesn't cover the same service and infrastructure components for different ASPs. One ASP may offer storage and security, for instance, as part of the fee, and another may charge you for them. This inconsistency across pricing models for seemingly comparable hosted solutions can make it difficult for you to compare—item by item—the price of services. Thus, total cost may be a better way for you to estimate the value you're getting from different ASPs. This, of course, is the sum of fees paid for all the services you will use—monthly lease, one-time setup, network provisioning, storage, customization, training, technical support, customer service, security, performance monitoring, application aggregation, and so forth. You will probably choose one ASP from several of comparable value on the basis of intangible factors like the ASP's approach to customer service.

However, although one model predominates, there is still great variety in models for different types of customers, applications, and vertical industries. So much so, that identifying a standard model based on market or other criteria is quite difficult and probably misleading. In lieu of standard models, then, the following are a number of real pricing models and the strengths of each. Whether based on usage, flat fees, software modules, support staff required, or other factors, they indicate how uniquely the ASPs have fashioned their pricing models to cover their own costs and keep fees affordable and easy to understand for customers.

Model A

Service: An FSP hosts an ERP application for manufacturing, distribution, and e-commerce.

Pricing: Per-click transaction fee or flat fee per month.

Rationale: If customer usage is hard to estimate, fairly light, or the customers are smaller in size, per-transaction fees let them pay only for the service they use. If usage is easier to estimate, heavy, or the customer is larger in size, a flat fee per month may be more economical and easier to budget.

Model B

Service: A service bureau ASP hosts a scanning, capture, and imaging application for document conversion, storage, and retrieval.

Pricing: Flat/tiered fees based on the number of images converted per month; unlimited access by unlimited users. The cost per tier drops as volume increases. The first 50,000 images are $X/month; 50,001 to 200,000 is slightly cheaper; 200,001 to 350,000 is slightly cheaper, and so forth.

Rationale: Sliding fees encourage more customer activity, and the pricing tiers accommodate the budgets of both smaller and larger companies. Unlimited access is a nice bonus for the customer but doesn't cost the ASP much because most documents are accessed infrequently after 90 days.

Model C

Service: A mid-size SI ASP hosts its own proprietary AS/400-based document conversion, imaging, workflow application.

Pricing: Flat/tiered pricing with light, moderate, and heavy tiers based on the number of documents scanned or electronically imported, but with unlimited retrievals.

Rationale: With workflow customers perform much more document routing and manipulation, but the ASP opted for flat/tiered fee simplicity based on documents converted rather than complicating the model with another usage-based variable for workflow activity. This is a nice bonus for the customer, and it's likely the ASP can give away this aspect of service because it's not paying software licensing fees to an ISV.

Model D

Service: A VAR ASP for a content management ISV hosts content management software for the engineering market.

Pricing: Customers are charged tiered and per click for each document accessed—that is, for annotating or viewing (but not importing) documents. For documents smaller than 100KB (in the first pricing tier), the per-click fee is X cents per document retrieved; for documents larger than 100KB (in the second pricing tier), the per-click fee is Y cents per document retrieved. The ASP also charges a basic storage fee.

Rationale: The usage-based pricing is consistent with the behavior of engineering document users. Many users typically access a few very large documents and make many revisions to them over extended periods. The tiered fees per size of document accessed compensate the ASP for additional network bandwidth and storage needed to accommodate especially large computer-automated design (CAD) documents, and for their many iterations.

Model E

Service: An FSP hosts its own proprietary reporting and analytical applications for CRM, including customer profiling, market segmentation, and customer loyalty analyses.

Pricing: Custom pricing based on the amount of data stored and consulting time spent on the account.

Rationale: These tend to be ad hoc applications that produce business intelligence, not production applications that generate a predictable number of documents per month. So measuring price according to output isn't viable. The model is not strictly usage based either. Data stored is not the same as data processed. Nonetheless, the customer pays only for the services provided, and the ASP always covers its costs.

Model F

Service: An ASP hosts interactive voice and Web collaboration software for e-commerce, on-line customer service, and technical support.

Pricing: Custom pricing based on number of concurrent sessions required.

Rationale: The model is analogous to per-seat licensing, but because it's impossible to predict the number of customers requiring support at a given time, the ASP uses the number of concurrent sessions.

Model G

Service: An ASP hosts a suite of claims processing and other applications for health plan providers.

Pricing: Custom pricing per health plan member per month.

Rationale: Price rises or falls depending on the number of plan members, so customers have a flexible monthly cost that is always proportionate to their revenue stream. Also, it lets small customers start hosted services affordably and scale up as their business grows.

Model H

Service: An FSP hosts a CAD management application that enables engineers to create and route engineering drawings electronically throughout a manufacturing supply chain.

Pricing: Custom pricing—the ASP takes 3% of the customer's contract fee for the design project and charges $X for the first 2MB of storage and $Y per additional megabyte.

Rationale: Engineering drawings are large files, and engineers may revise them numerous times. Thus, storage and network bandwidth are variable cost factors. However, estimating revision and routing activity is difficult. Three percent of the customer's contract simplifies costs, but it can also be spread over the members of the supply chain so no one member bears the financial burden of the system.

Model I

Service: An ASP hosts a remote help application that lets customers deliver help desk support to their customers or employees.

Pricing: Licensed monthly per seat and per support agent.

Rationale: Software licensing plus support agent pricing is flexible enough that customers can scale to more or fewer seats and agents depending on the support SLAs they've negotiated with their customers.

Model J

Service: An ASP hosts a suite of modular transportation management tools that lets shippers, carriers, and B2B marketplaces collaborate on-line to simplify purchasing and transportation for all trading partners.

Pricing: Custom pricing per software module and volume of transactions.

Rationale: It's difficult to estimate the amount of transportation activity companies of different types and sizes will generate. Pricing per module (like scheduling, invoicing, and reporting) lets the customer lease only the functionality it needs and pay for only the activity it generates.

Key Concepts

- Flat/flat leasing rates—Fixed prices for hosted services for fixed billing cycles (like monthly or annually), regardless of usage
- Flat/tiered leasing rates—Fixed prices for hosted services for fixed billing cycles, but they are tiered so customers can select the appropriate price tier based on criteria like number of users, estimated usage, or total documents stored
- Variable/tiered leasing rates—Variable prices for hosted services for fixed billing cycles, and the prices typically decrease with greater volume or number
- Per-click leasing rates—Variable prices for hosted services for fixed billing cycles, and prices are based on a charge per instance of activity such as an e-commerce transaction completed or document retrieved

CHAPTER TEN

ASP Customer Service and Technical Support

This chapter discusses

- Service provision
- Implementation estimates
- System sizing
- Platform preparation
- Client preparation
- Customization
- User policies
- Data conversion
- Testing and quality assurance (QA)
- Training
- Going live
- Maintenance and upgrades
- Monitoring and reporting
- Call centers
- Billing and mediation
- ASP CRM

Several factors contribute to the unique nature of ASP customer support. To begin with, in the ASP business model, the ASP guarantees near-bulletproof operation of the hosted application. So you expect that very little will go wrong and, if it does, that it will be fixed without untenable interruption of your core business. Obviously an ASP must support more than an application. It's also responsible for servers, the enabling software platform, storage, network, and physical infrastructure such as the data center.

The scope of support is much greater than for a conventional IT company like a software vendor, whose help desk personnel need address only a fairly predictable set of problems—things like software patches, hardware compatibility, upgrades, and so forth. With installed applications, especially mission-critical ones, the customer usually keeps support staff on-site or on-call around-the-clock to enable prompt troubleshooting. For the most part, ASP support personnel are not located on-site at the customer premises. In an ASP virtual support environment, staff are much more dependent on monitoring and remote support equipment to solve problems quickly. Obviously, *that* equipment, as well as the hosted application and other components of the total ASP solution, must also be absolutely dependable. Of course, because an ASP is the sum operation of multiple software, network, and other players, the partners are dependent on each other for reliability. And although partners typically have equity relationships or SLAs that provide them incentive to promote top performance, nevertheless, one broken link in the ASP chain can undermine all others. Players like telcos partnering with software vendors, for instance, might not be expert at supporting complex software, even though they are extremely qualified at troubleshooting problems with voice networks.

To complicate matters, the nature of IT support in general has become multidimensional. Call centers, for instance, increasingly handle queries by phone, e-mail, fax, and whatever other medium the customer prefers. They prioritize problems and address them accordingly. They use workflow and other systems to route specialized queries from the customer service representative (CSR) to, say, a database expert. They are increasingly aggressive in marketing their products and services to customers at every opportunity. For instance, if a CSR knows a new software release is ready, he may refer a customer to the sales department to buy an upgrade for $50 instead of to a database administrator for temporary troubleshooting. Yet customers expect all queries to be handled promptly and efficiently. And, with comparable IT functionality becoming more generally available from multiple vendors, vendors now realize that customer service is a key competitive differentiator.

Compared with traditional customer service and technical support, ASP customer support is *complex*. But to you, the customer, it should *never* seem so. Most of you want to call one number and have problems fixed quickly. When you call, you should be able to explain the problem very easily and have the support person understand and deal with it. For instance, you don't want to be on the phone for 30 minutes trying to explain a database problem to a network specialist because the CSR misdiagnosed the problem and transferred you to the wrong expert.

However, with more than 1,500 ASPs operating worldwide, not all of them understand or offer full-featured virtual customer service and technical support. This is especially true of small ASPs specializing in one or two very focused applications. Often these companies were service bureaus or VARs with modest sales and support programs, and they may tend to trivialize this aspect of an IT operation. This is not to say these smaller ASPs are necessarily slipshod when it comes to support. Indeed, their narrow focus may require fewer value-added services like complex support.

On the other hand, customer service—like security, storage, and infrastructure back ends—will likely become more outsourced and specialized as the industry matures. One call center may support six different ASPs by using the ASP's staff or by training their own. Such personnel could easily handle these low-level problems and pass on more difficult ones to an in-house support department at each ASP. Infrastructure service providers and MSPs will also absorb many platform monitoring and maintenance tasks from ASPs. It's not unlikely that they will specialize in supporting certain ASP operating systems, hardware platforms, networks, applications, and, possibly, vertical markets. However, although diversification and specialization are inevitable in any industry, the ASP industry will have to counterbalance that tendency with its marketing promise of providing a simple, all-in-one solution on a single bill.

Up-front Customer Service

ASP customer service starts as soon as you log on to the ASP's Web page or call its sales department to inquire about leasing an application. If you are inquiring about pricing and deployment time and it's not clearly conveyed by the Web site or by the sales rep, then that shortcoming may be indicative of the service your hosted application will receive later.

If you decide to lease, you can subscribe to out-of-the-box applications, like hosted e-mail, usually right on the Web site by virtually signing up and choosing your price/service level like Silver, Gold, or Platinum. Service can be up the same day. More complicated enterprise applications that require integration may take months. Many turnkey enterprise applications, though, require much less preparation, and subscribing is relatively quick and painless. Part of the subscription process also involves defining the terms of the SLA. Many ASPs offer standard SLAs that you can't amend, whereas others will negotiate special terms.

Then the ASP must provision the service by setting up, turning on, or ordering the following components before deploying the application:

- Network—Capacity, quality of service, connection to customer via local provider, and so on
- System platform—Extra storage devices, client installation/upgrade, middleware, and so on
- Application—User names, and so on
- Servers—Shared or dedicated, disk capacity, chip power, and so on
- Billing—Customer billing data, and so on
- Reporting/monitoring—Real-time or historical, the metrics to be monitored, and so on
- Security—User profiles and policies, and so on

This activity, however, is still preliminary to the service relationship between you and the ASP throughout implementation.

Hosted Application Implementation

The ASP implements the hosted application in roughly chronological phases. First, the ASP has to decide the functionality that is needed to meet your business requirements. If you lease a turnkey, generic hosted application, the ASP can commit to a predetermined schedule. After all, little customization between legacy and hosted applications is needed. However, if customization is required, the ASP must estimate the extent of it and work out the fee it will charge you. For example, the fee might be based on time and materials for the whole project or be a flat fee for specific work.

Next, the ASP must size your solution. This phase, too, can be less or more complicated according to different factors. If the ASP makes you conform to its own system platform, sizing is easy. You have already decided to forego customization and will adapt your work processes to the hosted package. If you require that the generic application be customized, then the ASP must tailor the software to your unique specifications.

To size hardware, the ASP must decide the number, type, and use of computers to be deployed, and the system architecture of the solution. For instance, will different types of servers be used as firewalls, database, and Web servers? At this phase, the ASP also will typically decide on disk space for each computer and storage capacity for storage devices. This estimate should take into account user data accrued over the period of the contract. The same goes for servers. The ASP must estimate "headroom"—how many additional servers and how much rack space you'll require—as well as whether the servers will be dedicated to you or shared by you and other customers. Any hardware architecture decisions like whether to cluster servers should be made at this point. And, of course, the ASP must choose processors powerful enough to drive those servers.

Actual platform preparation usually involves loading the operating systems, partitioning drives (logically dedicating drive capacity in the same server to different users, departments, and so on), loading the servers and storage devices into the racks, and deploying network firewalls at your customer premises and the data centers.

Client Preparation

If the leased application uses a client/server architecture, then the ASP must load the client software on your on-site desktops. If it uses thin clients, then the ASP must load the appropriate communication protocol on them.

If you've contracted for VPN services and are deploying encryption software on your own users' PCs (not in a router or other device), the ASP loads the appropriate security software on the clients now.

Finally, if you've elected to have the ASP remotely manage the application so it can do things like virtually add, delete, and change users, the ASP must now load that software on the clients.

Customization

Although ASPs roughly configure the application to your requirements when they install it in the data center, if you require customization, the ASP makes the actual code changes at this stage.

As mentioned earlier, customization ranges widely in the extent of its complexity. For instance, you might want your legacy applications integrated with the hosted application. Obviously, this cannot be done from the data center, and it requires expertise in additional applications. Also, you might not want your mission-critical applications inextricably tied to a hosted application that you may discontinue using in the future. It's up to the ASP to gauge the type of APIs and tightness of integration to your level of commitment to the solution. Depending on whether the ASP offers integration as a value-added service, and often even if it does, these charges are additional to the leasing fee. Some ASPs will bundle integration into the fee, but this is likely only if the required time and materials are easy to determine.

Typically during this phase, you experience for the first time the ASP's value-added services like outsourced IT personnel and accelerated application deployment. So customization is a key indicator of the quality of the ASP's future customer service.

SUCCESS STORY

IBM Global Services
Customer: CareTouch, Inc.
Key elements of the solution: Accelerated deployment, extensive application development and integration, one-stop shopping for the complete solution

An estimated 52 million people in the United States today have taken on the responsibilities of life care: that is, caring for sick loved ones with a continuing health condition who cannot live fully independent lives. Often these caregivers have no prior experience. Yet, the current healthcare system, its resources strained to the limit, provides little support in this vital area. This leaves an even bigger burden directly on individuals and families and indirectly on their employers. For example, lost productivity from employees caring for elderly relatives and friends cost American business between $11 and $29 billion yearly.

CareTouch, Inc. offers a powerful remedy to reach and support this often-isolated group of caregivers. The company was conceived in January 2000 by the world's largest not-for-profit healthcare delivery organization, Kaiser Permanente. Moving at Internet speed, CareTouch launched its call centers and the most robust, comprehensive e-commerce site of its kind www.carepanion.com six months later. In fact, it built its Web

continued

e-commerce solution in just 85 days with the help of IBM and the use of leading IBM WebSphere platform technologies such as WebSphere Application Server, WebSphere Commerce Suite, and VisualAge for Java.

"We saw a huge, unmet need in the healthcare marketplace and we're using the Internet and IBM e-business technologies to meet this need—there are a number of Web companies out there trying to do a part of what we're doing, but not with the same speed or scale," explains Dr. Peter Juhn, MD, president and chief executive officer. Prior to founding CareTouch, Dr. Juhn was the founding executive director of the Care Management Institute, Kaiser Permanente's national disease management, outcomes measurement, and clinical policy entity.

A Robust, Scalable e-Business Solution

Speed-to-market is essential for any new company. Still, CareTouch had to make sure it built a robust e-commerce foundation that could handle future growth. Through its parent company, Kaiser Permanente, it would have instant access to more than 8.5 million potential customers. Down the road, it could potentially reach a worldwide audience on the Net.

To get it right, the CareTouch executive team decided to work with a technology partner to launch the Carepanion e-Commerce System. After a spirited competition among several leading firms, it chose IBM and its WebSphere platform solution. Scalability and robustness were the decisive factors. As Juhn says, "We are planning for success—we fully anticipate we'll have millions of customers using our site on a daily basis."

In fact, IBM Rochester benchmarked the system prior to its launch, showing it could readily support up to 2,500 concurrent users with its current architecture. And, it can scale up easily to support double that number.

"With the architecture IBM developed, we simply add more servers to support more users," adds Dr. Prasuna Dornadula, vice president, Web development, and acting chief technology officer. "With WebSphere Application Server and Commerce Suite," he continues, "we have a proven solution that has been used to build a number of major e-commerce

continued

sites—we consider it to be more robust and easily scalable than any other alternative we considered."

A Proven Technology Partner

Beyond the technology, CareTouch also had high confidence in IBM as a partner. IBM had already proven its mettle in helping Kaiser Permanente implement a Clinical Information System. According to Dr. Eric Aguiar, MD, executive vice president and chief business officer, "It was an 'A' team and that's what we needed to jump start our project—time is serious money in the dot-com world."

Not only that—the Kaiser brand name has been carefully protected over the years and represents a huge corporate asset. The company wanted to ensure that its e-commerce solution would continue to maintain the value of that brand. CareTouch was counting on IBM's expertise to ensure they got it right from the word *go*.

"IBM has repeatedly demonstrated it has the ability to ramp up not just the development effort, but to scale a solution to support hundreds of thousands and potentially millions of users," says Aguiar.

A Comprehensive, End-to-End Solution

The time was early May 2000. The target launch date was late September. After six weeks of intense design meetings, the joint CareTouch and IBM Global Services team went to work. CareTouch developers worked with Jasper Design of New York to create the look and feel of the Web site. IBM, meanwhile, focused on building the e-commerce engine and doing back-end database integration.

CareTouch briefly considered an Oracle database as part of the end-to-end solution, but, says Juhn, "We concluded that for overall robustness and compatibility with other applications, DB2 was our best choice—we couldn't afford to get hung up down the road trying to work out an integration problem."

"Time-to-market was key," reiterates Jeff Lucas, vice president, sales and market development. "One of the reasons we chose IBM was that it gave us one-stop shopping with access to today's leading IBM Web technologies. We could use a DB2 database and the WebSphere platform

continued

environment, including VisualAge for Java, and it's all designed and pretested to work together smoothly," he adds. "In addition, IBM could provide the hardware, Web hosting services, and the integration services needed to pull it all together. Frankly, without the IBM total solution, we wouldn't have been able to hit our September 30 launch date."

A Highly Productive Development Environment

The Carepanion e-Commerce System runs on heavy-duty IBM RS/6000 servers located at IBM's server farm in Rochester, New York. Approximately 75% of the application code was based on WebSphere Commerce Suite. IBM Global Services developed the remaining code using VisualAge for Java Enterprise Edition, deployed on WebSphere Application Server.

"WebSphere Commerce Suite gave us the built-in functionality we needed to drive credit card transactions through our e-commerce engine," says Dornadula. "We estimate it saved us anywhere from two to four weeks' worth of development time and reduced the cost of building the solution by approximately $1.4 million," he continues. "All we needed to do was tweak the interface to link it up with the CyberCash system, a leading payment solution," he adds. And, he concludes, "We got additional support for this work from the IBM Toronto Lab team which helped us move forward quickly."

CareTouch used IBM's formal project implementation approach to manage the project. It's an iterative approach with overlapping phases that gives developers the opportunity to respond to changing conditions and scenarios. The phases include:

1. Requirements definition/macro design
2. Micro design
3. Build and test
4. Production readiness and deployment.

A team of four IBM and four CareTouch developers used VisualAge for Java to develop additional functionality, including a Java-based calendar function, care registry, and address book. Caregivers can use these resources to schedule home care services for their loved ones, share

continued

information with family and friends, and also reach out to a wider community of people facing similar challenges.

"We looked at alternative Java developer toolkits," says Dornadula, "but we found VisualAge for Java offered superior debugging capabilities. Sometimes building interfaces can be a challenge," he adds, "but with the integration of VisualAge for Java with WebSphere, it was very easy—we estimate it reduced our development effort by an additional 10%."

In building future applications, Dornadula anticipates his team will be able to reuse at least 50% of the code developed for the Carepanion e-Commerce System. In addition, they are planning to use Enterprise Java Beans to further improve reuse and achieve significant cost savings. For their next project, the CareTouch team is evaluating the feasibility of developing a wireless capability, which will allow caregivers to access Carepanion via palmtops and other portable computing devices.

A High-Revenue e-Business

In its first year of operation, CareTouch anticipates it will generate millions of dollars of revenue through targeting three distinct areas of need. Juhn calls these "our corporate ABCs" and they include:

1. Advocacy support, giving patients and caregivers a forum to get the advice and assistance they need to make important healthcare decisions—for example, the site provides tools members can use to build a CareCommunity that brings together patients with similar problems.
2. A brokerage function, which leverages the buying power of large numbers of consumers to help people get healthcare products at special discount prices in a business-to-business environment.
3. Concierge services, which help caregivers put together all the essential support services they need, including grocery shopping, home cleaning, in-home nursing, and more.

"Caregivers are often thrust into the role without prior experience or an instruction manual," says Juhn. "They must provide care services, seek

continued

information, investigate, and shop for and buy medical and health products that are available to solve the needs of the patient," he continues. "The Carepanion e-Commerce System is especially designed to put them in touch with all the resources they need to navigate through what can be a fragmented, confusing world of options and find the most effective, economical answers available to them today," he adds. So, he concludes, "The fact that we have partnered with IBM to build this solution will help us deliver the highest level of service to these people as they face the enormous challenges of caregiving."

Permission courtesy of IBM

User Policies

Policies determine who can use what functionality and when. There is some leeway in which administrators—the ASP's and/or yours—will create and/or enforce them.

Policies affect both networks and applications. Network policies are an integral part of traffic management. Via network policies, network administrators grant different types of traffic like data, voice, and video from different companies or departments greater or lesser availability and bandwidth as their users require. Although you have input into the network SLA, once it's determined, the ASP or its network supplier enforces network policies.

For instance, the network section linking a company's inventory warehouse with its sales force might need 24-hour availability and T3 bandwidth, so orders placed by salespeople are filled in time by the warehouse, whereas a customer service engineer troubleshooting on-site equipment problems might need only a wireless link from 8 AM to 7 PM on weekdays.

Administrators can also create policies so specific that only certain users are allowed to access certain application features over the network, and only at certain times of the day. If a large bank processes all the preceding day's checks from midnight to 4 AM the following morning, then the administrator can prioritize appropriate network sections for that purpose during that period.

Policies affecting applications authorize certain users access to certain applications or application resources like databases or screen fields. A sales rep, for example, might be able to enter an order on a screen but not have access to the *Approved* field. Only his manager does because she has to approve all orders. Conversely, the manager may not have access to the *Credit Limit* field on the same screen because, when the sales rep enters the order, the order entry system automatically fills that field with the amount by which the customer has exceeded his credit limit.

As with network policies, you have input into application policies to determine the SLA, but afterward the ASP enforces those policies. However, if you specify, some ASPs will permit your IT staff some administration authority like adding new users. Obviously, however, the ASP must be promptly alerted when such changes are made.

Data Conversion

SMBs without in-house IT departments may fail to take into consideration the often necessary step of data conversion. Larger companies are probably experienced in the process because they've run different applications in different departments and had to load data between applications and reformat it during the process. In the ASP model, data must be loaded from your legacy-installed applications to the ASP's hosted applications.

If it's transferred between similar systems from the same vendor—say, from an installed SAP ERP system to a hosted SAP ERP application containing identical modules—then conversion isn't needed. The data is typically copied to some storage medium at your premises according to the ASP's specifications, and loaded onto the hosted application in the data center. If it must be converted from one or several formats into a format usable by the hosted application, then actual data conversion—rather than data transfer—takes place.

ASPs either outsource conversion or do it themselves. If they outsource, then they hire consultants, service bureaus, integrators, or other service providers to handle the process, and then the ASP loads the converted data into the hosted application. The ASP might pass on the fee for the service to you as a charge independent of the leasing fee. For instance, a pure-play ASP that offers no value-added services would likely outsource conversion. If the ASP does the conversion, it assigns its own staff to go on-site and either actually do the conversion or oversee it to make sure you convert the data according to the ASP's specifications. An FSP offering integration as a value-added service would likely be efficient at conversion, do it profitably, and be able to bundle the cost into the overall leasing fee to your satisfaction.

Testing and Quality Assurance

ASPs must maintain a separate testing environment to "test drive" hosted applications loaded with your data on a computing platform like the one it has sized and configured for you. The test environment is like a Y2K platform where, after an upgrade, applications are test run to see if they are Y2K compliant. Most test environments are fairly standardized, not customized literally to replicate the hardware and other equipment of each new customer. For instance, if you lease an application for 200 users, the ASP can create a simulation environment with 200 "logical" seats, not actual PCs.

However, the ASP does use the testing platform to configure and customize the actual hosted application, as explained earlier, and then to run it through various user scenarios to see if it can hold up to the performance guarantees of each customer's SLA. The test driving is generally what's considered "testing."

Training

Training your users is an ongoing process, but initial training should take place before the hosted application is used for actual business. To get good training, you may stipulate that course materials and presentations cover any functionality, tasks, and policies uniquely created by the customized hosted application. This means that standard materials from the software vendor of the application should be revised accordingly.

Generally, too, the best training offers content in several modes—written, presented, and in interactive workshops—so that users who learn better in certain modes are exposed to the content in their preferred mode. Interactive workshops also expose users to actual common screen sequences that occur during routine work scenarios. For instance, sales reps who will have to create orders using a sales automation package usually benefit by doing so in a demonstration rather than having to transfer knowledge they learned from screen shots in a workbook. This said, multimode training is nice to have; not a "must have."

Train-the-trainer strategies are also a cost-effective way of shortening the ASP's period of involvement with your users and ensuring that ongoing training occurs after the initial sessions. Using this approach, ASP personnel train one or two users who then train the rest of your users. It's a good idea to choose initial trainee/trainers who are proven managers or who excel in the area of expertise that the hosted application addresses. Often their feedback helps the ASP make the application more user friendly and to more accurately handle the company's work processes. Also, their proven competence makes them the best candidates for reinforcing "the right way" of using the application to your other users in the future.

Often, to expedite an installed application's launch, training occurs while the application is still being tweaked during the final stages of customization. This may be necessary to cut costs and stay on schedule, but it can be very frustrating for users who may encounter different functionality in the finished application than in the version on which they were trained. With hosted applications—especially in the case of accelerated deployment—this may be necessary. But the consequences for your users will probably also be more harmful. A bulletproof application is the best training ground, and ASPs should always strive to approach that ideal.

Although during customization your "techies" develop a relationship with the ASP (this is where an ASP first proves its "tech" competence), during training your users develop a similar relationship (this is where the ASP proves it has a nice personal "touch"). Although the ASP model stresses a high-tech/low-touch approach, if an ASP takes a "no-touch" approach, it can backfire. For instance, the ASP might ignore your users' input during training, so even if the live hosted application works fine later, the users' resentment from training may undermine their acceptance of the application. This hurts their productivity and your bottom line. The importance of this cultural factor to the long-term success of your relationship with the ASP cannot be overstated.

Going Live

Going live is a matter of the ASP replicating the customized application from the testing environment to the production environment in the data center and, if needed, at your site. Once the hosted application is live, you should be able to use it to conduct legitimate business.

Routine Maintenance and Upgrades

As a fundamental tenet of the ASP business proposition, most maintenance and upgrades are included with the leased application. How much of the cost for these activities is included in the leasing fee and how much is a billable service depends on the ASP. Some ASPs may charge a premium for especially redundant backup or for extra storage, for example. As a rule of thumb, though, these activities come part-and-parcel with the hosted service.

You should also expect certain key upgrade activities to be covered by the maintenance/upgrade agreement, have input on the date of upgrades, and expect the ASP to take sufficient change management measures to ensure the upgrades do not unsatisfactorily interrupt work. The ASP should routinely upgrade, either remotely or on-site, needed client software as well as the operating systems on the servers in the data center. It should also locate and install or develop patches for all software bugs in its vendor's software. (If the ASP has an equity relationship with the vendor, the vendor is likely to be more responsive in creating patches.) The ASP should also keep at your reasonable disposal a database administrator certified on the databases used by the hosted application.

Of course, the ASP should also routinely backup, restore, and archive data. The media on which data is stored is determined in the SLA, but most ASPs will back up data each night and store an extra copy on tape off-site. Some may offer less frequent backup intervals for lower fees.

Technical Support

Users take it for granted when an application runs smoothly, but it's usually the harried activities of the IT department that ensure bulletproof performance. By hiring an ASP, an IT department is often seeking a way of relieving the pressure on its own personnel to support users. In many cases, unlike users who might gripe incessantly about poor technical support (but have little power in improving the situation), IT managers might scream once or twice and then just pull the plug on the hosted application. If your ASP fails to address technical support, it's a serious problem.

Most of the major areas of technical support like upgrades, backup schedules, and SLA monitoring have been discussed to some extent in other chapters, but certain procedures deserve elaboration here.

Monitoring and Reporting

Monitoring and reporting, whether done by the ASP itself or outsourced to an MSP, is, ideally, proactive. The ASP should be so adept at scrutinizing the performance metrics that it can predict, say, network congestion, warn you, and fix it before service is affected. Such foresight comes with increasing experience with each customer, but the ASP should also have developed a "feel" for the application during the earlier "testing" phase. Similarly, the ASP should be able to run test scenarios (say, in off hours or on the testing platform) to determine whether system performance will degrade in the event you need to upgrade the application, for example, to accommodate additional users.

Any ASP should monitor most key components of its infrastructure like network, servers, databases, and applications. However, the ASP should also never overlook any equipment integral to the application's performance—like a SAN in the data center. Routine maintenance will usually also entail activities like managing storage and other assets, as well as administering user access.

Reports submitted to you corroborating SLA performance guarantees must also contain data that's *relevant to your typical production work periods.* For instance, an ASP submitting a measurement of transactions per minute taken at midnight when four users were on the application is of no use to a company performing production work from 9 AM to 5 PM, when the system has to accommodate 500 users without performance degradation. Test results from artificially generated data scenarios are also not accurate enough to be relevant.

Of course, monitoring should also not interrupt the users' work or the application's performance.

The ASP should generate reports analyzing *all* relevant performance trends. These may vary from customer to customer. An FSP may have to monitor transactions per second for a customer leasing an e-commerce application but may not have to for a customer leasing a messaging application. Monitoring and reporting systems should scale as the application scales and be readily integrated with the appropriate help desk or other departments whose staff will troubleshoot problems.

Call Centers

As mentioned earlier, you should be able to contact the ASP support call center in multiple ways like phone, fax, and e-mail. Most ASPs will offer 24/7 support, sometimes for a premium fee. This said, though, the predominant mode of contact is phone calls to live agents.

Ideally, an ASP call center should enable the agent to access your service history, including all services you are leasing, all bills and payments you've made since services were turned on, and all previous support interactions (from users' questions about billing to actual troubleshooting). Some ASPs provide agents copies of questions that customers commonly ask, and suitable answers and actions for solving common problems. Some call centers also keep logs of how problems were escalated from agents to experts and record the actions taken at each stage of escalation. Such preparations expedite near-term service and refine call center business processes over time.

If the ASP uses multiple call centers or subcontracts some of its support to an outside company, you should be able to call one toll-free number and quickly reach the appropriate personnel at all centers.

Some ASPs will also place FAQs and responses and other information on their Web sites so your users can conduct their own self-service for low-level inquiries. This frees call center agents to deal with more substantive customer support issues. If the ASP lets you add, delete, and change users and otherwise mutually administer the application, then it should also offer some method by which you can do so remotely from your premises.

Billing and Mediation

Two aspects of billing are unique to the ASP model—consolidated, itemized services from multiple providers on one bill and tracking application activity to calculate usage-based fees. Contact center agents with access to your billing/payment history can probably handle general billing inquiries, but for rebates and other areas of negotiation, your ASP should probably assign a representative—either an agent or some other form of account manager—who acts as the primary liaison between you and the ASP. Most customers appreciate it when an ASP "puts a human face" on their virtual relationship. You will probably find that a single rep reinforces the sense of accountability and single-source service that define the ASP model.

Because the model is virtual, you may expect to be billed in the same mode that you lease services—over the network—although all ASPs may not offer this option. If they do, they may institute common e-business billing practices like electronic bill presentment and payment, and electronic funds transfer. If the ASP outsources bill presentment, the final bill should only represent the ASP, not the subcontractor. If the ASP is leasing different applications to different departments and you prefer that each department pay for service out of its own budget, then the ASP should be prepared to bill each department accordingly with separate statements. Of course, these practices hold true for ASPs offering traditional billing methods as well.

Usage-based pricing models require that the ASP track your activity for the relevant equipment such as database, storage, and scanners used to deliver all services. This pertains not only to per-click pricing, but it is necessary also for pricing models like "variable/tiered" ones where you're allowed a certain amount of usage within the price tier and pay a premium if you exceed it. Key service components like average network bandwidth, transactions per second, and response times are captured as a matter of course in the application monitoring process. However, particular usage metrics for billing purposes require actual, not average, data records and monitoring equipment tied to specific pieces of equipment like, for instance, scanners (for recording number of documents scanned), databases (for number of transactions), clients and servers (for number and initiator of retrievals), and so on.

Tracking usage is complicated. The ASP may have to track multiple metrics for multiple pieces of equipment like network, clients, different types of servers, storage devices, and so on. It may also have to identify the user or department that initiated an activity like a document retrieval. When the hosted application is bundled with other hosted applications or integrated with your legacy applications, the ASP may track the interrelated activities of multiple applications where certain actions initiate other actions for which you're billed—for instance, a business transaction in an e-business application might involve a document retrieval in a workflow application.

General Expectations

Although certain ASP players like software or hardware vendors may not traditionally excel at service, if they are involved in an ASP coalition, their partners should. Inasmuch as ASPs offer services virtually, and CRM has become a common practice, you may differentiate ASPs according to how well they carry out major CRM practices. Although not mandatory, ASPs may aspire to achieve CRM benchmarks to be more competitive.

CRM is the process of combining an ASP's best business practices, optimized work processes, apt technology, and relevant knowledge to service customers better and retain their business. However, CRM is not merely a means of guarding the customer assets that an ASP already has. The business intelligence and opportunities for customer interaction that it engenders also help the ASP more effectively market to customers and grow the services they use. This attitude transforms customer service from a reactive chore into proactive prospecting for increased business. Although this is good for the ASP (it transforms customer service from being a cost drain into being a profit engine), it is good for you too (it uses the ASP's basic business motive, profit, to promote superior customer service). Accordingly, although an ASP may win more of your business, your value for your dollar usually increases dramatically via bundling discounts and other bonuses.

To begin with, ASPs should minimize confusion by designating which of their employees may have contact with you. If certain IT personnel worked for months with your IT staff to customize the application, the ASP might capitalize on that personal relationship by also having one or more of that group do ongoing troubleshooting for you. Similarly, specific call center agents, customer account managers, and other liaisons often deal consistently with the same customers. These more consistent and intimate human encounters, whether it's an account manager solving a problem or a sales rep making a new service suggestion, are known as "moments of truth" in the customer interaction cycle. By exploiting them, ASPs keep you happy in the short term and keep your business in the long run.

By managing the customer interaction cycle from end to end with appropriate technology, the ASP can humanly "touch" you more often and more efficiently *and* boost its bottom line. For instance, an ASP might use integrated telephony tools to enable customer service personnel not only to communicate with you but also to access your service and billing history and to compare notes to satisfy you better.

Minimizing wasted time is also key to superior customer relations. Studies have shown, for instance, that the average user can tolerate about a two-second response time in applications they use regularly. Greater delay usually upsets their work rhythms so that, for instance, a manager approving loans forwarded to her in a workflow system might forget why she accessed a document, especially if phone calls interrupt, by the time it appears on the screen. The cumulative affect of such delays undermines service personnel efficiency.

Likewise, studies indicate that customers contacting a call center can tolerate about a four-second wait to speak to a representative. Most professional call centers make it mandatory that agents pick up before the third ring, for example. However, if they then put you on hold for 10 minutes, they've ruined a good first impression. Instead of putting you on hold, agents should always direct you to an expert who can resolve your issue. Prompt communication is especially important in an ASP setting because your user cannot physically contact the ASP. With installed applications, IT personnel and users tend to get to know one another and users will, if needed, walk down to the IT department and get someone to fix a time-sensitive problem. Users of hosted applications have no such outlet for their frustration.

The more methods an ASP uses to *quantify* its staff's customer service activities, the better. The ASP can offer bonuses to individuals who excel in this area, assign them to the busiest shifts in the call center, use them to train less adept agents, and so on. For instance, if—to resolve issues—an agent averages three minutes per customer call and rarely hands off to other experts or rarely makes multiple callbacks to customers, you have no grounds for complaint. However, if another agent averages 15 minutes per call and makes excessive handoffs and callbacks, then they are wasting your time.

Although putting the best agents on the busiest shifts is generally a good call center policy, putting more of them on those shifts is usually critical. For your monthly fee, you expect an ASP to have done its homework and to have calculated the cost of expedient customer service into the price of the service. By doing things like maintaining records of your behavior over time, ASPs can better predict busy periods to plan adequately for them.

Putting a face on virtual service promotes intimacy, and intimacy usually leads to customer trust and a long-standing business relationship. ASPs should pursue relationships as well as sales. Not only is this a fundamental premise of customer service, but CRM studies have shown that a long relationship with one customer is much more profitable than separate brief relationships with multiple customers. The marketing, administrative, and other costs associated with winning new customers or winning *back* dissatisfied ones can hurt both the ASP's bottom line and—as important for ASPs balancing their own payments to their service providers—its cash flow. The same goes for you. Changing ASPs, although easier than overhauling installed systems, drives up your costs and wastes time.

A related point is also true. In most cases, ASPs will give superior service to the 20% of customers that bring in 80% of their revenues. This is not to say that other customers get *poor* service as a result. Often, to avoid this, ASPs will offer tiered customer service plans—like Silver, Gold, or Platinum—so that customers can purchase different levels of customer service according to their budgets. For instance, Platinum might get a customer a phone response from an IT expert within five minutes of the inquiry and a guarantee that any application problem will be fixed within one hour of the call. Gold and Silver levels might merit a less-prompt response. The ASP may even provide incentive for customers to lease more services by offering Platinum customer service at the cost of Silver if they spend a minimum amount monthly. Neither strategy shortchanges you unless the resulting service proves insufficient to meet your anticipated requirements.

You have to remember, ASPs are in business to make money. If your excessive service demands consistently outweigh the revenues you bring the ASP, it's likely the ASP will pay less attention to them in the hopes you'll sign on with someone else.

You may save yourself a lot of trouble by, in addition to checking the ASP's reference accounts, finding out the number of customers an ASP has had and the length of the relationships. Numerous short engagements usually indicate either customer dissatisfaction or frequent revisions to an ASP's business plan and strategic mission. Neither suggests stability. Relationships, on the other hand, indicate customer satisfaction and intelligent business strategy as well as commitment to a market and financial stability.

Ideally, the ASP should offer such bulletproof hosted applications that you never tax the resources of its customer service personnel. However, it's probably reasonable to assume that the more customers an ASP has, the more likely something will go wrong.

Nevertheless, you should expect customer service commensurate the requirements of your hosted solutions for the duration of your contract. If your ASP fails to understand that customer service is both your *right* and an *ongoing process,* then it does not have your best interests at heart and should not have your business long term.

Key Concepts

- Service provision—The ASP sets up, turns on, or orders network, system platform, application, servers, billing, reporting/monitoring, and security
- Implementation estimate—The ASP estimates the extent of customization and fee
- System sizing—The ASP decides the number, type, and use of computers to be deployed as well as the number of software seats; and the general system architecture
- Platform preparation—The ASP loads operating systems, partitions drives, loads servers and storage devices into data center racks, and deploys firewalls
- Client preparation—The ASP loads communication protocols and client, encryption, and remote management software on customer desktops
- Customization—The ASP makes actual code changes to the hosted software that may involve integration with legacy applications and other value-added integration
- User policies—Network policies grant different types of traffic from different companies or departments greater or lesser availability and bandwidth;

application policies authorize certain users access to certain applications or application resources

- Data conversion—The ASP or a partner converts the formats of customer legacy applications to formats usable by the hosted applications

- Testing and QA—To guarantee SLA performance levels, the ASP maintains a separate testing environment to "test drive" hosted applications loaded with customer data

- Training—The ASP should cover any functionality created by the customized hosted application and often uses train-the-trainer strategies

- Going live—The ASP replicates the customized application from the testing environment to the production environment so the customer can conduct legitimate business

- Maintenance and upgrades—The ASP should include client software, operating systems, patches for software bugs, data backup, restore and archival, and an on-call database administrator

- Monitoring and reporting—Monitoring should be proactive and should cover key components of and equipment integral to the hosted infrastructure; reporting should contain data relevant to the customer's typical production work periods

- Call centers—Customers should be able to contact the ASP call center readily (often in multiple ways like phone, fax, e-mail), and agents should have access to the customer's service history

- Billing and mediation—The ASP should present consolidated, itemized services from multiple providers on one bill; ASP mediation should track *actual* application activity to calculate usage-based fees

- ASP CRM—An ASP's CRM should combine best business practices, optimized work processes, apt technology, and relevant knowledge to service customers better, retain their business, and win new customers

CHAPTER ELEVEN

Enabling Technologies for ASPs

This chapter discusses

- VPNs
- PC-based encryption
- Router-based encryption
- Firewall-based encryption
- VPN-specific box
- Integrated boxes
- SANs
- SAN value proposition
- Network-attached storage (NAS)
- The value of SANs to ASPs
- Portal interfaces
- Digital wireless
- Analog wireless
- WAP
- Third-generation (3G) wireless
- Wireless ASPs (WASPs)

Virtual Private Networks

Until the last few years, if an enterprise needed broadband WAN connectivity for transmitting data, it had to build a private WAN or lease a shared broadband network or dedicated broadband T1 or T3 lines from a network service provider. Building private WANs was expensive and time-consuming. Only G2000 companies could afford the investment. SMBs typically leased shared networks or dedicated lines.

Although dedicated lines provided sufficient bandwidth, they were point-to-point connections. An SMB that needed to connect many sites quickly ran up high fees for multiple leased lines. What's more, because those lines were always on, they had to pay flat fees for 24/7 fixed bandwidth connectivity, although they might only exploit the lines' maximum capacity, for example, from 9 AM to 5 PM, and even then only intermittently according to the vagaries of user traffic. Leased lines were adequate but not elegant.

Both private WANs and leased lines gave enterprises more throughput and fixed infrastructure than they might ever use and at prices that could get exorbitant in a hurry.

Of the three broadband options, leased shared WANs were usually the most cost-effective for SMBs needing pervasive connectivity. Network service providers found they could offer cheaper broadband services to enterprise customers if they leased broadband networks to multiple customers who shared the bandwidth. The network customer saved not only on building costs but also on maintenance, upgraded equipment, and specialized permanent network administrators. Most network service providers offered shared X.25, then Frame Relay, and then ATM WANs.

But then business for Internet service from ISPs and CLECs exploded. After all, the Internet was the world's most pervasive network and the subscription fees for using it were ridiculously cheap compared with leasing fees for shared WANs and dedicated lines. As more people used the Internet, ISPs began creating value-added broadband trunking and tunneling to transmit their customers' data faster and more securely than data sent over the native Internet. Eventually, these technological developments did more than retain customers and differentiate providers. They convinced all network service providers that, with enhancements, the Internet could be exploited as a low-cost, pervasive infrastructure for data transfer between enterprises.

By the late 1990s, most large providers and some large corporations had created their own Internet-based VPNs. Many of the large providers in turn leased use of them not only to their own customers, but also to smaller providers that added some value, and resold the use of the network to their customers.

Internet-based VPNs essentially enhance the native Internet infrastructure with broadband connections and secure data on the value-added networks so it can't be hacked into by unauthorized parties. So, they are high speed but secure. But because much of their physical connectivity is already provided by the public Internet infrastructure, they are much less expensive to build than private WANs and inherently more pervasive than leased lines. They essentially combine the

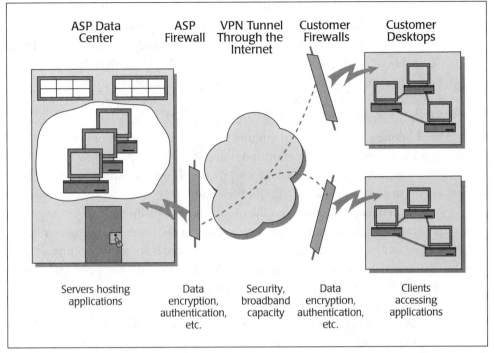

Figure 11–1 A virtual private network transmits data through a secure broadband tunnel

best characteristics of WANs, leased lines, and the Internet into an affordable, robust, and secure wide area infrastructure for data transfer between enterprises (Figure 11–1).

Different Types of VPNs

Each VPN is unique for numerous reasons: they span different geographical regions; connect to different numbers of users; use assorted protocols like Frame Relay, ATM, and IP; use different transmission materials like copper and fiber optics; enhance these materials with superhigh-speed technologies like WDM and DWDM; and feature varying throughput and levels of security. What's more, different providers offer varying SLA levels, depending on things like their customer type and their network capabilities. However, the differentiating characteristic unique to VPNs—as opposed to private WANs and leased lines—is security.

VPN data security is the result of data encryption and user authentication. Encryption involves scrambling the data according to algorithms ("keys") at the sender's location and unscrambling the data by the same algorithm at the recipient's location. However, complex encryption creates proportionately more calculation by the network equipment and, therefore, more network overhead that slows down transmission. Another encryption rule of thumb is that encryption performed in hardware is faster than encryption done in software. So a customer's level of data security is always the result of balancing three factors: complexity of encryption, network speed, and customer cost. A customer that must have hermetic security and premium throughput will pay more than one that requires less complex encryption and slower throughput. According to their SLA, of course, customers can make various trade-offs between speed and security to get the most desirable leasing fee for their budget.

Authentication verifies that the transmission actually came from the person it purports to, not from someone impersonating that sender. Common authentication methods are user names identifying the sender combined with passwords that only the sender knows, and secure ID account codes combined with password codes. This is known as *user-level authentication* because actions by the user verify the authenticity of the data.

To ensure the integrity of transmissions, some VPNs also include a checksum in the header of each data packet that verifies that the exact amount of data sent in the packet is the exact amount received. If it isn't, then someone has tampered with the data.

VPNs differ according to where the administrator locates the encryption. Encryption will always reside in a device near the edge of the network, not in the network cabling. The simplest method is encrypting data in PCs that access the network. Major vendors like Microsoft offer encryption software that can be loaded onto PCs for this purpose.

Some router vendors offer routers that perform encryption. Router-based encryption requires that the involved routers be compatible and offer the same type of encryption. Users who access the network remotely and don't go through a router must have encryption software on their laptop or PC compatible with the encryption in the routers. In general, because encryption slows down router operations, this method should be used only on networks with relatively light traffic so the encryption does not create bottlenecks in the routers.

Encryption can also be located in firewalls, but (like routers) firewalls should have compatible encryption (preferably from the same vendor), and mobile users must use compatible encryption software. Because firewall-based encryption also creates network overhead that slows throughput, this method should also be used only on networks with relatively light traffic.

VPN-specific boxes are stand-alone encryption equipment installed near the firewall that create secure tunneling using encryption and certificates. They can be hardware or software based, but hardware-based ones generally process traffic faster while being more secure because they use proprietary technology generally more difficult to hack than publicly available operating systems. Because they process traffic faster, these devices are best for high-volume networks.

Integrated boxes perform routing, "firewalling," and VPN encryption in the same device and, generally, are best used on networks with lighter traffic volume.

Various factors like packet size, data compression, complexity of the encryption algorithm, and number of simultaneous network users can affect VPN equipment performance. The smaller the packet, the more header information in the network traffic the equipment will need to process. Compressing data also adds overhead, as do more complex encryption algorithms. As the number of simultaneous users increases, the equipment must set up and tear down more simultaneous sessions. This can create delays at common sign-on times and peak traffic periods.

Value-Added Characteristics of Different Providers' VPNs

Not to belabor the obvious, but different customers will require different capabilities from Internet-based ASP VPNs. So before committing to any ASP, you should conduct some basic traffic analysis to determine the key requirements for your hosted network. Try to answer questions like the following: How secure does the VPN need to be? How many total and simultaneous users must the VPN support? When are peak traffic periods? When do most users sign on to the VPN? How reliable does it really have to be (say, at 3 AM *and* 3 PM)?

For example, if competitors are actively trying to hack into your data, then you'll need maximum security measures—things like hardware-based encryption and complex encryption algorithms, as well as multiple levels of firewalling. If the network must also be very fast, then the ASP will have to compensate for the security overhead that slows down traffic with features like OC12 and OC48 connections, fiber-optic network cores, WDM/DWDM, and ATM that ensure especially robust throughput.

Obviously, this is not to say that all applications require, say, ATM-enhanced VPNs, or even VPNs. You must balance your budget and performance requirements and decide on the most cost-effective network solution.

Networked Storage

When most users think of storage, they imagine actual paper files, cabinets of microfilm or microfiche, tape arrays, or optical jukeboxes. Until recently, these were the predominant modes of information storage. However, storage technology has changed at a blinding pace during the last 10 years.

Until the advent of optical disk, film- and tape-based analog storage was the norm. But when Write Once Read Many (WORM) debuted, it quickly became a viable digital alternative because the optical disk format permitted storage of more data in a much smaller space, and its indexing and retrieval schemes gave users almost instant access to data. However, WORM was also more expensive than older technologies.

CD-recordable (CD-R) largely addressed the cost issue of optical. Alhough CD-R access speeds and data capacity weren't equal to those of either 5.25- or 12-inch WORM, they were still acceptable in many cases, especially since CD-R disks and jukeboxes were so much cheaper than their WORM counterparts. Of course, soon digital virtual display (DVD) proved that multimedia data could be stored on disk too.

Although optical storage capacity and performance improved and cost dropped, the same was true of magnetic storage. Traditionally, a direct-access storage device (DASD) technology was so expensive it was used sparingly as buffer storage for on-line data before data was migrated to cheaper media like WORM. Today, DASD is almost as cheap per megabyte as optical, but boasts greater capacity and faster retrieval speeds. Just as optical outmoded film and tape for certain storage applications, so too DASD has outmoded optical in many cases.

This is not to say that any of these technologies are obsolete, or soon will be. Based on price and performance, there are still applications appropriate for them all. Indeed, film, tape, optical, and DASD often coexist in the same enterprise. Typically, frequently retrieved data is stored on faster, more expensive, media like DASD and optical, and infrequently retrieved data is stored on slower, less expensive media like tape and film. Organizations can also migrate data to progressively slower, less expensive media as it ages and is accessed less and less. Known as *hierarchical storage management* (HSM), this practice evolved so users could exploit the unique costs and characteristics of diverse storage technologies.

During the last three years, a new storage technology developed that was as different from optical as optical had been from its analog forebears—different because it was networked independently of the servers accessing it. DASD, optical, and tape are deployed as storage repositories on the same network as their servers. So, although storage media access speeds have dramatically accelerated, overall retrieval speed of data has still been constrained by the amount of traffic on the network. Retrieval speeds of even the fastest storage technologies fall off as more users get on the same network. SANs and NAS are forms of networked storage that operate independently of primary networks and achieve incomparable access speeds because among other reasons, they are not hampered by network congestion.

Storage Area Networks

A SAN is a robust storage network comprised primarily of Redundant Array of Inexpensive Disks (RAID) storage devices typically linked by fiber-channel cable, switches, and hubs to heterogeneous servers. Typically, any server can access any storage device in the SAN. Access is especially fast because the fiber-channel links are broadband. But, because SANs also operate independently of primary computer networks, data can be transferred and backed up between SAN-based devices without ever having to pass over the primary networks, where congestion can slow down transfer times.

Most data in most extended enterprises is dispersed ad hoc over numerous storage devices (like optical jukeboxes) and sources (like multiple databases), so it's often difficult or impossible to access the most recent and complete data. DASD, optical, and tape devices are linked to their own dedicated servers and constitute "islands" of disconnected data. SANs pool storage resources so they can be shared by multiple servers that are not dedicated to any one device and used without impairing the performance of the SAN or the primary network. Thus, SANs comprise "continents" of information that are linked by broadband fiber links. SANs can also be integrated with traditional storage devices so the latter operate as other universally accessible repositories in the storage environment. Such an arrangement permits not only better performance, but also the kind of elegant connectivity that can help eliminate redundant data on decentralized and disconnected storage devices.

The high-bandwidth fiber network is especially critical because previously servers and storage devices transferred data over small computer system interface (SCSI) interfaces that could achieve speeds of only 10 to 20 Mbps and could span physical distances of only a few yards. Configured with appropriate switching technology, a fiber channel can transfer data at speeds of 100 Mbps or faster, and can link servers and storage devices up to ten miles apart. So, applications tapping

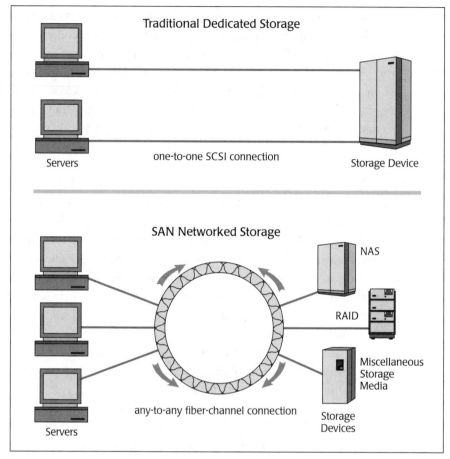

Figure 11–2 SAN networked storage provides any-to-any connectivity between servers and storage devices

a SAN can achieve "local" speed of access even if the data accused is physically located quite far away.

SANs' Value Proposition

SANs' obvious value derives from their many user benefits:

- As mentioned, SANs allow centralized management of storage. Instead of maintaining many individual, disconnected storage devices throughout an enterprise, the administrator can consolidate storage in one or a few locations to save labor time and cost, and to ensure the most recent and accurate data is available.

- SANs make data more accessible to everyone in the enterprise. They let users share storage and servers both within the SAN and across LANs and WANs.
- They also make data 100% available. SANs use automatic data redundancy and backups and permit easy maintenance of nearby disaster recovery copies.
- Because SAN data is more available, the performance of the applications that use it dramatically improves. Data transfer delays are largely eliminated.
- SANs permit more flexible and serviceable storage configurations. SANs not only centralize previously isolated data into one or a few vast repositories, they also let administrators in turn link those "continents" of data with high-speed networks.
- SANs are easier to scale. With network switches and hubs, administrators can add storage capacity within and between SAN configurations completely independent of the servers and without interrupting operations.
- SANs automate data management. SANs come with automated monitoring and management tools that track trends, foresee potential problems like a disk failure, and preempt failures or service degradation by automatically, say, "hot switching" to a replacement disk.
- SANs improve disaster recovery. SANs enable affordable deployment of remote mirrored arrays so data can be automatically backed up, transferred, and recovered at both local and remote sites.
- SANs also improve failover with clustering. By clustering servers to provide automatic failover in the event a server fails, administrators can create a SAN that dynamically switches users and applications to a backup server to improve application availability dramatically.

Network Attached Storage

NAS devices attach to any kind of network for the purpose of superefficiently serving files to users. These devices are comprised of several components: embedded processors that host specialized operating systems, highly optimized file systems that implement the file services, and one or more storage devices like disk and/or tape arrays. They are used to manage storage intelligently on one or more servers for better performance, reliability, and space management, and are typically designed to be easily installed and configured.

In most cases, however, NAS devices serve files to heterogeneous clients over a LAN. NAS devices can be connected to a SAN and can perform local disk-to-tape data movement without even going across the SAN's fiber-channel network for backup and restore or HSM.

NAS devices are ideal for providing shared file access to a number of different clients because they are built on existing LAN and file system protocols. Sometimes NAS devices use SANs for their back-end storage, and some allow for the attachment of external storage. In fact, many NAS systems now have fiber channel ports that allow them to connect to a SAN and enable the NAS file system to reside on a SAN device.

SAN + NAS + HSM

When SANs and NAS devices are integrated into a networked storage environment, both users and administrators benefit. Users get better file access from an optimized file server and better enterprise data accessibility and application performance from the SAN, whereas administrators can more easily and efficiently manage data throughout an extended enterprise on a centralized storage system (Figure 11–2).

However, administrators should also use an HSM strategy for all storage devices in the networked environment to optimize the benefits of both SAN and NAS—as well as attached tape, DASD, and optical disk—while minimizing costs.

Why Lease Networked Storage from an ASP?

Various studies suggest that a storage administrator can manage seven to eight times more data on a SAN than on a traditional decentralized storage system. What's more, networked storage all but eliminates system downtime that, depending on the size of the enterprise, can cost from thousands to even millions of dollars per hour. However, SANs are expensive. Systems average in the hundreds of thousands of dollars. They are also complex. The administrator must integrate and manage fiber-channel-based disk arrays, hubs and switches, host bus adapters, tape devices, bridges, storage management software, and backup software. Needless to say, most mid-size organizations would be hard-pressed to afford such technology, not to mention personnel with the storage expertise to run it.

Offloading data to a networked storage-enabled ASP that can more cheaply and efficiently store it makes eminent sense for SMBs. The SMB is leasing instead of buying the solution, so they conserve up-front costs. Because ASPs can store data cheaper, they can pass on the savings to SMB customers. SMBs get state-of-the-art storage at prices lower than they could ever achieve on their own.

Also, because ASPs are spreading their storage system and personnel costs over multiple customers, ASPs achieve further economies of scale that lower price.

At the same time, the SMB is guaranteed in an ASP's SLA that the data is secure, instantly accessible, and always available—and that's a promise very few IT departments can safely keep.

STORAGE SERVICE PROVIDERS

Each year, the demand for storage doubles while the price of storage hardware falls as much as 30%. Although companies are hard-pressed to keep up with their data archive requirements, the storage industry is certainly doing its part to address the issue. The problem, however, is not the cost of equipment—it's the cost of managing it. Some experts claim the cost of managing storage hardware is seven times the cost of the hardware itself. In large part, that's why IDC predicts the US SSP market may grow to $5.6 billion by 2004.

However, subtler forces are also driving the SSP market. DataQuest, for instance, says that as more companies are adopting virtual business and computing models, they are loathe to invest in additional storage management infrastructure and staff. Also, storage requirements change. An e-tailer, for example, might need massive storage at Christmas when it's receiving lots of e-mail and orders, but that demand will slack off dramatically in January and February. Obviously, it's expensive to deploy equipment and staff to accommodate these peak demands, but it's also wasteful to maintain both infrastructure and staff during off-peak periods. Outsourcing storage to an SSP saves such companies money by cutting these management costs.

Of course, the Internet is the prime generator of new data. Most companies report that they need new storage simply to archive ever-increasing intercompany e-mail. However, with the growing viability of electronic imaging and multimedia, more dense image, audio, and video files must also be transmitted and stored. And, certainly, the boom in enterprise applications hosted by ASPs across broadband networks is becoming a key factor in the outsourced and managed storage equation.

continued

SSPs are a breed of hosted service provider that lease both storage infrastructure and personnel to companies that want to outsource storage equipment management and/or infrastructure. SSPs typically design, implement, and operate the storage solution. This could involve loading customer data onto a storage platform in a data center, periodically backing it up, and creating archive copies of data and storing them in a secure environment like a fireproof safe.

However, SSPs almost always use HSM storage strategies that exploit different types of media like RAID, optical jukeboxes, and tape arrays for frequently or less frequently accessed data. HSM requires management personnel to at least set retention periods, maximum and minimum data levels, and data migration paths from one type of media to another. Most SSPs also own SANs and NAS to serve files more efficiently, manage different data repositories centrally, and transport dense data across storage networks without congesting primary telecom networks.

The SSP market is even younger than the ASP one, so the storage utility model will likely diversify. At this stage, most SSPs tend to offer services in one of several ways. An SSP may own and maintain multiple data centers (sometimes called *storage centers*), which contain its storage equipment. If so, the network connecting each storage center to its customers will likely feature fiber channel and will be linked to a SAN. The customers will be located within the compass of the fiber channel network of each storage center. SSPs may also own a central storage facility and the equipment therein, and lease their network and alternate data centers from network service providers and infrastructure service providers but perform their own storage infrastructure management. They may also lease the network and data centers, and let the infrastructure service provider help them manage the storage infrastructure. Some SSPs do any or all of this as well as manage customers' in-house storage infrastructures as in a traditional outsourcing arrangement. Some offer disaster recovery services. Some even provide warehouses where companies can store hard-copy documents that legally must be retained for fixed periods.

Companies of all sizes can use SSPs, but SMBs and dotcoms may benefit the most. Both tend to have limited funds and a restricted infrastructure, so

continued

outsourcing storage for a manageable monthly fee is appealing. Otherwise, they'd have to lay out a lot of up-front capital to build advanced storage, hire expert personnel, and then spend more money maintaining it. Smaller, virtual companies can also implement storage faster using an SSP, and can scale it easier and more affordably because they don't have to build new infrastructure, just order more storage capacity.

Although G2000 companies tend to have fairly robust in-house storage, with an SSP they can reap savings on primary data and backup and retrieval. Because SSPs are specialists, they tend to optimize their business processes and leverage economies of scale that let them charge the lowest rates and still be profitable. For this reason, alone, most organizations will save money using SSPs while being guaranteed affordable, reliable, 24/7 data access.

Most SSP customers will readily outsource their nonsensitive e-mail archives and other Web-generated data, but they are hesitant as yet to part quickly with mission-critical data like accounting and customer information, or forfeit their legacy storage infrastructure to house the family jewels with an SSP. Once SSPs prove that they are financially viable and have staying power, it's likely those fears will diminish. Until then, many large customers will go with managed storage services from large SSPs (Figure 11–3) with solid financial performance and that offer SLAs.

ASPs, infrastructure service providers, and resellers also comprise an indirect sales channel for SSPs. The first two will use SSPs as the virtual storage component of their hosted solutions, and they will require stringent SLAs to satisfy their end customers. Major storage vendors will team with VARs, integrators, and others to launch ASPs and resell managed storage services based on their products.

continued

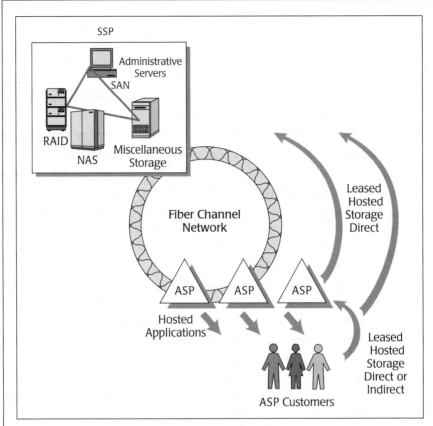

Figure 11–3 Storage service providers (SSPs) lease managed storage services to multiple ASPs

Enterprise Portal Interfaces

Portal interfaces better organize access to data, applications, and people to improve each worker's focus on company goals, make them more efficient in their own jobs, and enable them to collaborate better with coworkers. Users can "personalize" their own version of the portal interface to display only the applications, information, and personnel they deal with in their company role. They can toggle between applications on their desktop without exiting one then opening another, and without having multiple windows open at the same time. They can also simultaneously access multiple data repositories and collaborative tools like chat rooms, e-mail, and workflow to communicate with coworkers.

As important, enterprise portals provide a common interface to shared commerce environments evolving around virtual communities. In B2B environments, enterprise portals unite a defined group of suppliers, business partners, and vendors around a common objective or business need. For example, virtual trade exchanges—"auctionlike," demand-driven B2B virtual commerce venues— let multiple corporate buyers and sellers in a common market like the automotive industry buy and sell products and services quickly and in volume. Portals let the personnel working for buyers, sellers, and the trade exchange itself better communicate, negotiate, and trade proprietary information. Sharing the same portal interface also gives users from different companies the look and feel of a uniform business/IT environment—a metaphor for the *common* ways in which everyone works in the exchange—that promotes interenterprise cooperation. Individual users can also tailor their version of the interface to the specific requirements of their role—a metaphor for the *unique* ways in which each person works in the exchange—that promotes focused personal efficiency.

As extensions of their front ends, ASPs may offer hosted services via their own enterprise portals or link them to your enterprise portal. The first option gives you easier access to applications and data repositories hosted by the ASP; the second offers better access to your installed applications and data stores. In both cases, the portals function as common interfaces to virtual communities, either those comprised of you and other customers using the ASP's services like hosted applications and storage, or those comprised of members of your value chains like business partners and suppliers.

Also, as community-based commerce like trade exchanges becomes more widespread, it will make sense for a few ASPs to host most of the applications used by most corporate members of the same community, and to have those applications accessible via a common portal interface. ASPs then host the IT substructure common to all members of the community that the members, in turn, access via one portal interface. The community members save on application installation, and the ASP can offer lower leasing fees to a captive corporate customer base.

Wireless

Wireless voice and data communications have become increasingly popular during the last few years. Earlier in the book, we discussed the reasons for this phenomenon. Here, let's focus on how data especially is transmitted via wireless and why ASPs see such promise in offering wireless services.

Wireless transmission is based on radio signals that ground-based antennae and communications satellites beam to and from wireless devices like cell phones. Not all wireless networks use satellites, however. Antennae-based networks transmit from antennae to mobile devices via mobile switching centers. Each antennae sends and receives signals to users throughout a geographical service area called a *cell*. When a user—say, in a car—approaches the boundary of a cell, the wireless network detects the weakening of the signal and alerts the antennae in the cell the user is entering, and that antennae assumes the signal. The transition is known as a *handoff*. If that antenna belongs to a different wireless service provider, then that provider also takes over the wireless signal and manages the call. The ability for users to move between cells controlled by different service providers but still maintain a continuous wireless signal is called *roaming*.

Wireless signals are transmitted in the 800-MHz frequency range and are analog. Wireless was initially designed to carry analog voice. Because radio waves weaken as they get farther from their antennae, network equipment amplifies or recreates the signal at different points along its route. To accommodate digital data, providers developed digital wireless that converts the analog voice signal into digital computer code appropriate for sending data.

Analog wireless is an older technology and generally available. For instance, it's available across about 95% of the United States. Digital wireless is newer and has not proliferated as broadly. By contrast, it's available across only about 50% of the United States.

In addition to ground-based antennae, wireless networks can also use geosynchronous earth orbit (GEO) or low earth orbit (LEO) satellites that receive very high frequency (giga-Hertz) signals transmitted from sending earth stations and send them in turn to receiving earth stations, which in turn send them to wireless devices. The transmission system from the sending earth station to the satellite is called the *uplink,* and the one from the satellite to the receiving earth station is called the *downlink*. What's known as the satellite's *footprint* is similar to a ground-based antenna's cell. It's the area on earth that can receive that satellite's signal.

Most satellites are GEOs, which means they orbit 22,300 miles above earth and at the same rate that the earth rotates. Because they appear stationary to transmitting and receiving earth stations, the antennae dishes on earth never have to be moved once aimed at the satellite. But because they orbit so far away, their earth stations must use bulky and sensitive receiving equipment and, even then, there is some delay in their transmission signal. LEOs orbit from 500 to 1,000 miles above earth, so they require little value-added receiving equipment and suffer little transmission delay. Either type of satellite can process lightweight data transmissions like short e-mails.

M-commerce

Whatever the method of wireless transmission, by far most data transmitted in the relatively near future will be short e-mails, not downloaded Web pages and other denser multimedia forms of data. Capacity limitations of the technology prevent dependable transmission of dense data. Other limitations like latency, poor signal quality, and undependable availability prevent transmissions of long duration. What's more, many wireless devices, especially cell phones, have limited battery power and data memory, and fairly simple user interfaces, so they can't handle longer, dense data transmissions.

The good news is the industry is gradually addressing all of these problems with the help of evolving standards that compensate for them. The Wireless Application Protocol (WAP) enables interoperability between WAP-compliant devices. Wireless networks, applications, and devices can be optimized for a common environment so the same applications, for instance, can run on different providers' networks and manufacturers' devices. As importantly for Internet access, WAP devices will interoperate with WAP-compliant servers so they can access data residing on them that's been converted to WAP.

WAP was developed to meet the specific requirements of users accessing data, most of whose wireless behavior has been conditioned by using wireless voice. Therefore, future wireless devices must be made easy to use and affordable. They must also offer a quality of service comparable to wireless voice—less latency, better transmission over longer distances, accommodation of denser data like Web pages, and other changes that allow users to reliably perform short, focused, Internet-oriented tasks. Customers will not use future small-format wireless devices the same way they use laptops now; instead of surfing the Internet on laptops for sustained periods in a hotel room, they'll tend to use PDAs and cell phones to do things like skim their e-mail and access directions to gas stations while driving.

In evaluating wireless standards and technologies for use in your ASP environment, you should also be aware of a few other issues. The hosted wireless service should take advantage of new markup languages that more elegantly format Web page data to be less dense and easier to download. They should also offer security mechanisms adequate to your users' requirements such as encryption, integrity, authentication, and denial-of-service protection. Increasingly, too, features like bookmarking, caching frequently accessed data, and "push" mechanisms that are common wireline Internet access tools will become standard wireless offerings.

Both WAP and 3G are driving what is known as mobile broadband wireless Internet access (or *m-commerce*), an industry that, like the ASP industry, is changing at light speed. You'd be wise to do a thorough evaluation of the status of all pertinent wireless standards used by your ASP before committing to wireless hosted services. For instance, one may be better suited for your geographical location, or customer base, or offer more enhanced e-mail features and functionality. This said, wireless hosted services should precipitate dramatic changes in hosted services and, indeed, drive them into the mainstream consumer market. So make no mistake about it, wireless deserves your attention.

WASPs

In the meantime, certain ASPs are already offering wireless services, but according to different business models than conventional ASPs. As explained earlier, they are known as *WASPs* (wireless ASPs), and in most cases either host custom wireless applications they have developed or wireless-enable existing installed or hosted applications. They rely on infrastructure service providers for data center and network infrastructure (Figure 11–3). Their customers are typically enterprises requiring hosted wireless functionality and software vendors or integrators that need existing or developing applications to be wireless enabled. Although they derive some revenue from leasing fees for their hosted wireless services, most comes from professional service fees for consulting and customization.

Broadly speaking, there are two types of WASP: those that sell general-purpose wireless applications to companies like wireless service providers and portals that then resell them to consumers, and those that develop and lease custom applications to corporations doing e-business so they can better serve their mobile customers or empower their mobile employees.

The first type aggregates content and provides services like messaging to wireless carriers and portals that in turn pay the WASP usage fees, and re-brand the services for their end customers. The second type, if they wireless enable customers, develops custom applications for corporate customers like

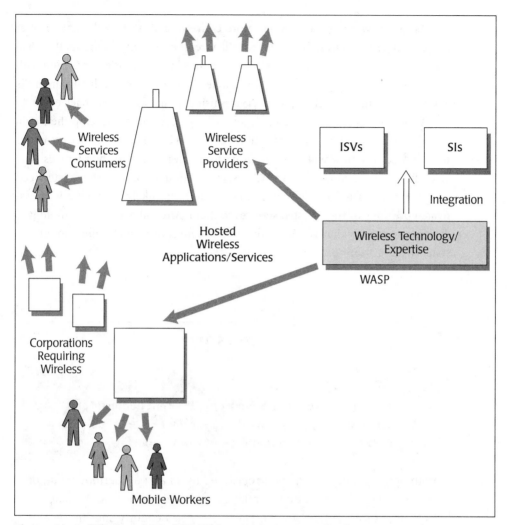

Figure 11–3 Wireless ASPs (WASP) lease wireless applications and services to wireless service providers and corporations

financial organizations that offer wireless virtual banking services to their users. They earn revenues through application development, implementation, and usage fees. If they wireless enable employees, they sell software and customize wireless solutions to corporations for users performing sales and customer service tasks. These earn their revenues through software license and professional service fees.

As use of wireless data grows, more conventional ASPs will want to offer hosted wireless services. However, they'll face competition from smaller Web integrators that are developing their own wireless applications and teaming with infrastructure service providers to host wireless applications. Gradually larger SIs will also move into hosted wireless services using their own or ASP back ends.

Although any large service providers will use large SIs to develop their own portals and custom wireless applications, other large and most smaller providers with limited cash flow will look to WASPs to develop and host their wireless services. Rather than compete with WASPs, conventional ASPs (already challenged with the new hosted virtual computing model) will likely outsource wireless-related portions of their hosted services to them. After all, wireless technology is evolving so rapidly that WASPs with wireless core competence will maintain the state-of-the-art for hosted wireless services.

SUCCESS STORY

WASP: 2Roam
Customer: eBay
Key elements of the solution: Support for different domestic and international wireless platforms, devices, browsers, markup languages and protocols; integration with different wireless portals

With approximately 35 million registered users and a quarterly value of over $2 billion in goods traded, eBay is the world's online marketplace. A truly diverse and global marketplace, eBay has country-specific sites in the US, UK, Canada, France, Germany, Japan, Australia, Italy, and Korea with users representing 150 different countries. The company receives, on average, 3.5 million unique visitors daily and eBay hosts approximately 100 million items per quarter. In mid-2000 eBay identified wireless users as its next growth area and, with the help of wireless ASP, 2Roam, set out to reach and serve this growing global market with an anywhere, anytime service called *eBay Anywhere*.

continued

eBay knew that to maintain customer satisfaction and brand loyalty, as well as to increase its global expansion, it had to offer site access from users' preferred devices. This may be a PC, but it could just as well be a laptop, cell phone, or PDA. Indeed, in countries outside the United States where wireless exceeds PC penetration, it's more likely to be a wireless device. According to Todd Madeiros, director of business development and eBay Anywhere, "We wanted to ensure that the user experience was uniform in all media," so any wireless solution would have to support the dominant, but disparate, wireless platforms.

However, as important, it also had to be scalable, reliable, and universal. With general Internet traffic increasing dramatically, it would have to accommodate ever-increasing transaction volumes. Also, service outages were not an option. At a high-profile site like eBay, a half a day of downtime can equate to serious brand damage. Yes, it could lose business during that period, but its stock valuation could also suffer, and possible long-term customer attrition was incalculable. Of course, to enable eBay's aggressive international expansion, any wireless solution also had to support both domestic and international browsers, markup languages, and protocols.

That's a lot to ask from a company whose core competency is e-auctions, not ubiquitous wireless access. And, as eBay found out in its vendor research, wireless technology was changing at light speed. So who could say an installed in-house solution would be adequate in three years?

Ultimately, eBay settled on 2Roam because, says Madeiros, "it was 'best of breed'—the only provider that offered a complete end-to-end solution that met our technology requirements and met our business objectives. . . ."

First, eBay engaged Sprint PCS and AT&T Wireless as wireless portals. eBay customers would access the auction site wirelessly via these venues. 2Roam then integrated eBay functionality and content to work wirelessly according to the different design requirements of both portal carriers. Leveraging 2Roam's XML architecture, eBay site producers then

continued

defined suitable content, organization, and navigation for the different platforms of supported wireless devices.

Now users can register wirelessly with eBay, check My eBay personalized content, access featured items, and browse the site. And, of course, customers can access current bidding data as well as submit bids.

The eBay Anywhere launch was so successful, 2Roam is now duplicating wireless sites for eBay in Japan, Germany, the United Kingdom, and Australia. This uniform look and feel will let eBay maintain a consistent brand identity while extending its world-class service across numerous countries, technologies, and devices.

Key Concepts

- VPN—An Internet-based native Internet infrastructure enhanced with broadband connections and security mechanisms
- PC-based encryption—Encrypting data in PCs that access the network
- Router-based encryption—Encrypting data in routers that link network sections; slows down router operations and should be used on light-volume networks
- Firewall-based encryption—Encrypting data in firewalls at the edges of networks; creates network overhead that slows throughput so should be used on light-volume networks
- VPN-specific box—Stand-alone encryption equipment installed near the firewall, creating secure tunneling using encryption and certificates; processes traffic fast so it is best used for high-volume networks
- Integrated boxes—Performing routing, firewalling, and encryption in the same device; create network overhead so best used on light-volume networks
- SAN—Robust storage network of RAID devices linked by broadband fiber channel; transfer data independent of primary networks so congestion doesn't slow transfer times
- SAN value proposition—Making data and applications more accessible and available to improve system performance; also centralizes data so it's more manageable by administrators and accessible to users
- NAS—Attaches to networks to serve files superefficiently to users; used to manage storage intelligently on servers for better performance, reliability, and space management
- Portal interfaces—Organize and display applications, information, and personnel that workers deal with in their company roles; unite a defined group

of suppliers, business partners, and vendors around a common objective or business need

- Digital wireless—Converts an analog voice signal to digital computer code appropriate for sending data
- Analog wireless—Used for voice transmission and is older and more generally available than digital wireless
- WAP—Enables wireless interoperability between WAP-compliant networks, applications, and devices, notably WAP-compliant servers so wireless devices can access Internet data
- WASPs—Hosting custom wireless applications they have developed or wireless enable existing installed or hosted applications

CHAPTER TWELVE

The ASP Channel

This chapter discusses

- Direct ship
- Channel consolidation
- The double channel
- Tech/touch dilemma
- High-margin/recurring revenue dilemma
- SI ASP strategies
- ISV ASP strategies
- The ASP brand
- The first-string ASP channel
- Big losers in the new ASP channel
- Big winners in the new ASP channel

Early on, some experts predicted that the advent of the ASP would do nothing less than destroy the traditional IT channel. At the time, the view was certainly justified. After all, if hardware/network, software, and vertical market players could launch ASPs, didn't they largely eliminate the roles of traditional resellers and integrators? For instance, if IBM, AT&T, and Ernst and Young combined their hardware/software, network, and accounting vertical market experience to offer hosted accounting solutions, why would they need a channel? The ASP became the reseller and the integrator—at least for hosted solutions.

This argument alone was sufficiently compelling, but other channel changes had already happened to lend it even greater credibility. The most dramatic was the "direct-ship" phenomenon initiated by Dell Computers. By shipping preconfigured computers direct to end users, Dell—and later Compaq, Gateway, and others—undercut the retail prices of other manufacturers like IBM still using the channel to sell, configure, and ship their PCs. By eliminating these activities and their added costs, Dell could cut price, pass on the savings to customers, and still make nice margins. In fact, direct-ship vendors could afford to keep shrinking margins to be even more competitive as they won more volume business away from traditional vendors (Figure 12–1). Also, by guaranteeing faster delivery, simplifying the ordering process using e-commerce, and offering generous return policies, direct-ship vendors hit on an unbeatable formula for customer satisfaction: lower price, better service, and less hassle.

To compete with the new breed, traditional vendors and channel players eventually made changes. Vendors started shipping some product direct while still maintaining their channel relationships. In this way, they could stem their losses but not alienate their channels and sabotage legacy revenue streams from integration and other traditional channel services. In turn, distributors, VARs, and integrators assumed more configuration, assembly, and other responsibilities. Distributors assembled and configured PCs so VARs could more quickly integrate them. VARs and integrators evolved regional integration centers where much of the integration could be done before ever stepping on the customer's site. And all channel players adopted e-commerce practices like virtual ordering

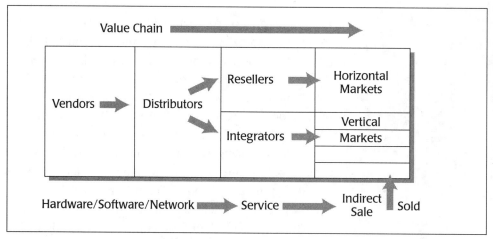

Figure 12–1 In the traditional channel, vendors sell products to customers through various types of resellers

and billing, just-in-time delivery, and Internet-based customer service to accelerate procurement and other channel processes.

In delivering value virtually, however, the channel endangered more traditional VARs. Those that merely marked up and passed on products had less of a role in the new scheme of things. Many of these players merged to achieve a size sufficient to survive on thinner margins by selling in volume. Others specialized on a market, application, or technology so that, despite the increased preparatory work done by the channel at large, they would still control each customer's on-site integration. At the same time, the vendors themselves began teaming with select distributors, VARs, and integrators to push more product through a leaner, more efficient channel and conserve co-op, marketing, and other channel support costs. Larger distributors and VARs merged so they could distribute their costs over more customers, thin margins, and negotiate better with large vendors by controlling more of their end market. The result of these forces was dramatic channel consolidation.

Virtual computing was catalyzing this type of disintermediation-and-reintermediation process on many fronts. The premise of e-market models like virtual communities and trade exchanges was that, if relevant buyers and sellers could reach each other easily and as opportunities dictated, both would be much less dependent on middlemen that drove up price. Similarly, the rise of dotcom companies that bought and sold traditional products over the Internet threatened more than their BAM forebears. They threatened the entire reseller structure on which BAMs depended for sales, distribution, customer service, and customer feedback. In a very real way, the Internet was changing everything, and anyone in business who made their living by mitigating the effects of time and distance on buying, selling, distribution, service, and support had to reevaluate their viability. Such a global infrastructure would increasingly deprive them of their mediating value. As ASPs proliferated, then, they heralded a new opportunity as well as a serious threat to channel players already scrambling to redefine themselves.

Figure 12–2 illustrates the evolution of ASPs as an alternate, more direct channel for leasing IT services. If ASPs developed in a vacuum, this illustration would accurately model a still-viable dynamic. But they didn't. Often, to create an ASP, hardware, network, and software players would team with existing channel players, not instead of but as well as, independent vertical market TBAs. The result turned out to be not an alternate channel for hosted services that operates independently of the traditional channel but rather an amalgam of the channels for installed systems and hosted services. Just as the traditional channel reacted

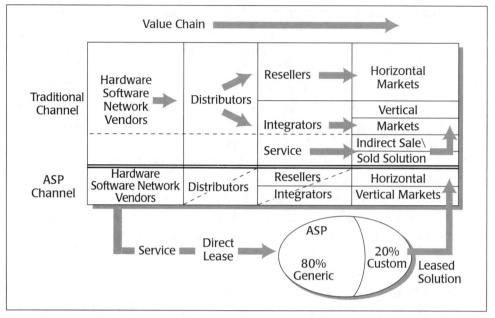

Figure 12–2 In the alternate ASP channel, vendors sell or lease products to ASPs that then lease them to customers

to new competition from direct sales and other market forces, so too did they co-opt the ASP secession from the old market model. Channel players saw that virtual services were inevitable and started spinning off ASPs themselves.

The Double Channel

Several factors drew traditional channel players into the ASP movement. First, their profits were threatened by an alternate direct-sales channel, so they had to modify their identity to this new reality. Second, to succeed, ASPs would have to build a customer base fast. This entailed introducing generic solutions into vertical markets and tailoring them to specialized applications. This meant that, third, they would have to team with select traditional channel players that understood these market niches, had the customer contacts, and could implement solutions cost-effectively and fast. Fourth, offering generic applications was good for the customer: They were cheaper, faster, and less risky. But, to make money on them, ASPs had to differentiate themselves on more than price. If 100 ASPs sold hosted ERP to a common market, a few would win big if they captured lots of volume fast, and the rest would end up in price wars that would eventually kill margins and profitability. Even those that won would sacrifice profits in the process. A better course was to compete on other criteria like value-added services, and market and application focus. In this way, more ASPs would prosper by addressing a niche they had mastered while at the same time uniquely defining themselves. Fifth, the target audience for ASPs was SMBs, but this was a customer type largely unfamiliar with the direct sales model and about which direct sales vendors and new ASP entrepreneurs knew little. The experts on SMBs were traditional channel players.

So, while software and hardware vendors teamed with network providers and TBAs, channel players sought out infrastructure service providers to complement their vertical expertise with hardware and network capabilities. Meanwhile, infrastructure service providers themselves were under extreme pressure to build a customer base fast. Offering favorable terms to both vendors and their VARs was in their interest.

Currently, both vendors and VARs benefit little by committing to either installed systems or hosted services. The safe play is to offer both. Most vendors will offer their channel the option of selling both. Most VARs will sell both until the general market tide turns in favor of hosted services. The result will be a double channel of sorts for the duration of the transition to a new computing model (Figure 12–3). Vendors and VARs will have more time to learn the new model, consolidate their power, and then choose to go their own ways or not.

However, there are several ironies operating in the channel dilemma. To begin with, the majority of hosted service providers will pursue the SMB market with lower priced, easier-to-implement services—essentially generic technological solutions—whereas most SMBs are used to getting customized ones that require more people skills to implement. There has never been a greater shortage of qualified IT personnel, so even if they request custom solutions, SMBs will pay dearly for them and have to wait until the existing personnel are available to implement them. Thus many mid-size companies are facing a "tech/touch" dilemma.

Also, although VARs make most of their revenues from high-margin custom integration services (not reselling technology), the idea of predictable, recurring revenues from subscription-based services is very appealing to them. As SMBs themselves in many cases, cash flow is their biggest problem, and subscription revenues nicely address that issue. Most VARs are dealing with a high-margin/recurring revenue dilemma.

Of course, although hosted services threaten traditional resale and integration revenues, they also open up new markets and opportunities for channel players, as well as provide a means of augmenting existing services to their current customers.

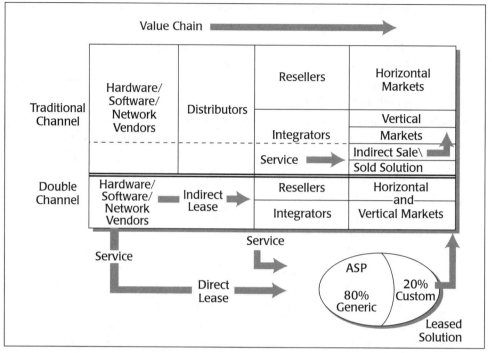

Figure 12–3 In the Double ASP channel, vendors sell or lease products to resellers that have launched ASPs and to conventional ASPs, both of which then lease them to customers

These conflicts notwithstanding, the dominant issue is not whether the channel will adopt hosted services, but *how* they will do so.

SUCCESS STORY

VAR ASP: netASPx
Customer: HomeBanc
Key elements of the solution: Accelerated deployment, legacy/hosted application integration

HomeBanc is Atlanta's largest residential mortgage lender and the fastest-growing mortgage lender in South and Central Florida. It was

continued

founded in Atlanta in 1929 as a building and loan association. In the early 1990s, HomeBanc sold its banking division to concentrate on home mortgages. But when it spun off from its parent company, First Tennessee, it forfeited access to First Tennessee's financial software package. Independence came at a steep price—HomeBanc would need to acquire and deploy a new enterprise-wide financial system within six weeks.

HomeBanc was quick to realize that, given its time frame, a traditional, installed solution was out of the question. However, any ASP solution would have to meet some basic requirements. Obviously, it would have to be implemented rapidly, but it also had to be flexible enough to accommodate the company's future growth. More specifically, though, the resulting integrated financial solution would have to handle loan-accounting needs and readily integrate with HomeBanc's legacy applications.

After comparing several ASPs, HomeBanc selected netASPx and, a month and a half after signing the contract, netASPx completed implementing a hosted Lawson Financials package. All told, the Lawson application included several financial modules: General Ledger, Accounts Payable, Cash Ledger, Activity Management, and Asset Management. NetASPx supported them on its Sun Solaris software platform, while HomeBanc accessed them via the ASP's Virtual Private Network.

A major part of the deployment was integrating the hosted application with legacy applications like HomeBanc's loan origination system. For example, netASPx linked the loan origination system with Lawson activity management to account for and report on loan activity. Then the ASP performed rigorous development and testing procedures to ensure the applications inter-operated as planned.

With netASPx's help, HomeBanc launched a fully integrated financial system less than two months from the day it became an independent company. And, because netASPx fully maintains and supports the application from its data center, HomeBanc eliminated the added cost and burden of maintaining a state-of-the-art ERP system internally. In fact, HomeBanc found that because netASPx's help desk experts are trained specifically to troubleshoot Lawson software, they resolve problems faster than its own IT department ever could.

continued

> Now HomeBanc can focus on doing what it does best: delivering superb residential mortgage service from application to closing. And the financials package proved to be the first phase in what promises to be a multi-module implementation. HomeBanc is now evaluating two other net-ASPx-hosted ERP modules: Lawson Procurement and Human Resources.
>
> Permission courtesy of netASPx

SI ASP Strategies

Although it is still too early in the channel's evolution to make hard-and-fast predictions, some general trends are emerging that indicate how SIs will adopt the ASP model. Although many VARs, particularly larger ones, perform integration services, they tend to be more dependent on ISV partners for funding, education, marketing, and other services, and thus less autonomous in their market strategies than larger SIs. Larger SIs tend to maintain relationships with multiple ISVs and hardware vendors, wield them as needed for better leverage with each partner, and command more revenues and a broader customer base than smaller VARs. Thus they are less vulnerable to vendors' whims and tend to chart their courses more according to their own core competencies.

Most large SIs have chosen one of four strategies for moving into hosted services. They can lease their own hosted services from their own data centers and network. They can lease them over an infrastructure service provider's data center and network. They can host their own applications but resell them through various channels. Or they can integrate various hosted applications into a unique turnkey solution that they host in turn to a very focused market. In all four scenarios, the large SI still performs the value-added services like consulting, on-site integration, and technical support.

The lease-your-own approach lets large SIs easily pitch hosted services to the existing customer base by working with them to develop, refine, then service and support relevant hosted applications. Instead of leasing a generic solution from an ASP, the customers work hand-in-hand with the SI (just as they did in developing installed systems) to evolve a hosted solution that more exactly meets their unique requirements. Once the SI has created a stable of hosted services, it can generalize them and sell them downmarket to new SMB customers. This approach leverages large SIs' legacy integration skills and customer relationships but challenges them to learn the skills needed to run a data center and network, and to deliver SLA guarantees—traditionally not SI core competencies.

The infrastructure partner approach is the most appealing to SIs. By contracting out the data center and network to infrastructure service providers, they are better assured of success in that area, can get into business faster, and are liable for less up-front costs. In addition, they can emphasize their core consulting and integration skills and market them as value-added services that help differentiate their ASP offering from others hosting similar applications. However, the arrangement requires SIs to share revenues with infrastructure service providers and may lead to finger-pointing between the SI and infrastructure partner on SLA issues. However, these are minor liabilities because any performance failures should be covered by the SI's SLA with the infrastructure service provider.

The channel approach lets SIs quickly disseminate hosted applications to mid-size customers, but it requires that they learn and develop the infrastructure component of the business and move to a more volume-based services model rather than the high-margin custom services model they are used to. This approach wins by offering select and standardized generic applications that the SI can easily develop and manage for many SMBs for a new customer set and new revenues. It may best succeed in cases in which the SI will still primarily sell its traditional integration services directly.

The aggregated service approach lets large SIs develop specialized applications hand-in-hand with large clients with very focused application- and market-dictated requirements, and then use the client to lease the services to its customers. The client becomes a TBA through which the SI penetrates a very specialized market with a custom service but in a hosted model. This resembles the old SI practice of creating a custom, installed solution for, say, a large insurance company, then productizing it for similar companies. The approach involves revenue sharing and cobranding, but it gets the SI quickly into a captive customer base and reduces customer objections by leveraging the client's existing relationship with them.

Smaller SIs and VARs may adopt any of these approaches, but the formality of their ASP partnerships varies greatly. They range from very loose, deal-by-deal arrangements with no financial or contractual commitment from partners beyond each deal to a long-term equity relationship between the partners that may even involve mutually developing proprietary data centers and networks. Depending on the deal, both larger and smaller SIs and VARs may provide any or all of their traditional services like application development and customization, business process reengineering, technical support, customer service, and outsourced IT management. Channel players will use all of these approaches to expand current customer engagements or cultivate new customers via hosted services.

SUCCESS STORY

SI ASP: World Technology Services (WTS)
Customer: J.R. Abbott Construction
Key elements of the solution: Rapid deployment, huge cost savings, industry-specific hosted solution

Having grown to a $75 million-a-year construction firm, J.R. Abbott Construction was pushing the limits of its in-house job cost and accounting system. Certainly it could install new ERP modules or upgrade the existing ones, but it also wanted to avoid ongoing capital expenditures over the long term. With its rapid growth, J.R. Abbott really did not have the time or manpower to devote to a protracted IT installation. Critical, too, was this: The new system had to deliver real-time information from its Seattle, WA, headquarters to any of its US job sites.

After evaluating four vendors, J.R. Abbott decided on a hosted J.D. Edwards solution from SI and ASP World Technology Services (WTS). According to Art Solbakken, executive vice president at J.R. Abbott, WTS sold the firm on an ASP solution with compelling evidence, "We didn't have to advance one to two million dollars in hardware and software; . . . we didn't have to hire staff, or worry about maintaining the system; . . . it's a huge cost savings." What's more, the firm was worried that building an installed system would commit it to technology that might soon be outmoded. As Solbakken puts it, "Do you really want to own something that's changing so fast?"

J.R. Abbott went live with the payroll and job costs hosted applications three months from start of deployment. According to Solbakken, "The J.D. Edwards system was already set up for a contractor, so we

continued

didn't have to do a lot of custom design . . . That saved us money we would have had to spend on another system, and helped us get up and running in a hurry."

Equally helpful was the fact that, as an integrator and then as an ASP, WTS had long specialized in deploying applications for the construction industry. "WTS understands our business, because they've been in the construction business for years," says Solbakken. "They solved many of the problems we were facing with how to use accounting data and interface accounting data with the needs of the project manager, a superintendent, and a foreman," he adds. In short, because WTS had customized the ERP package into a generic solution for construction, it already contained the application functionality the firm needed.

Now J.R. Abbott personnel have access to all the data they need on any job site in the nation. And the company got bonus functionality in the bargain. The old system, for instance, could create one type of labor cost report whereas the hosted application provides the firm reports in any form it requires. In fact, says Solbakken, "Our biggest concern [is] learning how to use [a system] that [can] do so much."

Hardware Vendor ASP Strategies

Major hardware vendors, especially those with large service organizations, are launching ASP programs as well. Those that don't may lose big if ASPs and infrastructure service providers standardize on competitors' hardware platforms. In doing so, they face three major challenges: Develop a robust sales conduit to infrastructure service providers and ASPs before their competition does; enable select players in their respective channels to move to the ASP model using their equipment, not another vendor's; and partner with select infrastructure service providers and ASPs to accelerate the ASP state-of-the-art and thereby differentiate themselves.

To what extent the first and last initiatives conflict remains to be seen. Preferred partnerships with certain infrastructure service providers and ASPs may undermine vendors' relationships with other channel players that suspect the partners are getting sales leads, price breaks, and other advantages. If the R&D alliances yield better solutions, then the channel at large will adopt them to remain competitive, and the strategy will produce increased sales. Doubtless, some big vendors are pursuing this strategy just to cover their bets now, and later will switch allegiance to those players who succeed early.

As with SIs, each hardware vendor's ASP strategy is influenced by its market pedigree: existing partners, core competencies, traditional customer base, and IT service heritage. Each is also differentiated by the way they balance the four alternatives in their overall strategy. Will they sell mostly products or services to the channel, and will they partner with certain channel players or deal equally with all?

Sun Microsystems espouses a software/hardware "arms merchant" strategy whereby it optimizes its Java/Solaris platform for the hosting model and sells equipment, not services, to all channel players equally. Sun itself will not actually host any applications. This is an apt strategy for Sun. Historically, it's never placed a premium on its service business, and recently it has aggressively strengthened its Java application development to compete with Windows, and its server robustness and scalability to handle intense Web activity in e-business environments.

Compaq is also pursuing an "arms merchant" approach whereby it will supply servers to all of the channel, but it has also invested in select ASPs and infrastructure service providers. Compaq will not offer hosted services, but instead will leverage its partnerships to develop more competitive ASP solutions to then sell to the channel at large. Compaq is also providing select services like help desk support to its partners to help them succeed in the ASP space. Traditionally a high-volume server wholesaler, Compaq has chosen an ASP strategy that's consistent with its core expertise.

For several reasons, IBM has gradually been migrating toward becoming a services-oriented vendor. The mainframe market seems to have plateaued. Beaten to the punch with direct sales, IBM forfeited PC sales leadership to Dell and Compaq. To dominate in e-business, it's undertaken a massive initiative to integrate its existing customers' high-end back ends with Web-enabled front ends. To create a more truly open application development environment than the prevailing Windows one, it has partnered with Sun Microsystems to establish Enterprise JavaBeans as standard middleware for enterprise computing environments. Consistent with its service thrust, IBM has moved on many fronts with service-oriented ASP initiatives. It's established worldwide data centers from which customers can lease its own, as well as other vendors', hosted services; it's launched extensive ASP enablement programs for its channel; it's created innovative financing programs for acquiring its hardware; and it's developed ASP-enabling software platforms at Lotus. IBM will pitch services, hardware, and software directly to end users, as well as wholesale them to infrastructure service providers. But, it's also committed to building and hosting virtual trading networks in vertical markets to which participants can subscribe. Generally, IBM deals equally with its channel players on these initiatives.

Hewlett-Packard is also pursuing a multifaceted service model but with strategic ASP and infrastructure service provider partners. Generally, Hewlett-Packard wants to migrate aggressively to an "apps on tap" stance in the industry by creating a business and IT environment in which customers can lease HP-UX and NT-based services via ASPs and portals. Although Hewlett-Packard will create and host some of its own hosted services like messaging, its ASP partners will provide the broadest range of hosted enterprise applications like ERP and portals to cater to vertical markets like health care. But Hewlett-Packard is also committed to brokering virtual functionality and services dynamically over the Internet to customers as they need them. Imagine application developers and customers ordering and downloading, say, Web server functionality right off an Internet-based menu. To this end, Hewlett-Packard is offering innovative financing, preintegrated components, marketing, training, and technical support help to partners offering its services in exchange for a share of their subscription and transaction revenues. But, as opportunities dictate, Hewlett-Packard will also sell servers direct to infrastructure service providers. Unlike any of the other hardware vendors, Hewlett-Packard is really trying to be its own channel for hosted services.

ISV ASP Strategies

Aside from partnering with hardware, network, and vertical market players in a conventional ASP coalition, software vendors may pursue any number of strategies to maintain their leverage with the channel. Generally, these will resemble a combination of the four hardware vendor ASP strategies. For instance, Oracle has teamed with Qwest to set up its own data centers and network from which it can host Oracle ERP applications and act as its own ASP channel. Microsoft, on the other hand, has struck up strategic partnerships with numerous players and is actually invested in several ASPs that host Microsoft Office applications. It has also launched its own ".NET" ASP program.

Other ISVs like Documentum and Open Text have pursued hybrid strategies that either leverage current channel relationships, or have ambitiously launched equity partnerships with new and complementary players. Documentum, for instance, is working with resellers like Technology Services Group, an integrator specializing in customizing Documentum for engineering applications deployed over intranets. The two companies have launched ConnectSite.com, a document management ASP, and are using a data center and network from an infrastructure service provider, Level3. Documentum believes VARs are the best-qualified companies to offer hosted services, and will now also lease its previously very high-end software downmarket to SMBs. It's likely Documentum will team with only certain of its channel members to offer hosted services and to continue pitching installed solutions to the G2000 through others. Open Text, on the other hand, has teamed with KPMG and Qwest to launch multiple, new state-of-the-art data centers as well as a value-added fiber-optic network infrastructure to host its portal-enabled knowledge management software to G2000 customers in Europe. It's also launched a reseller program for hosted services that requires some financial investment from its channel players to participate.

In general, ISVs must balance several conflicting market impulses. Probably the most dominant factor affecting an ISVs' ASP strategies is getting into hosted services without cannibalizing installed software sales. This is a difficult balancing act. If they don't offer hosted services, they risk losing customers to competing ISVs that do. So many are launching ASP programs defensively, as it were, to retain existing customers. But as they get better at hosting applications, more of their existing customers may want them, and this will hurt installed software sales. If they do not have a very high-end customer base that will always want installed solutions, then they must gradually build their volume hosted business to compensate for declining high-margin installed system sales. But this is tricky. Most VARs have seen the light and either want to resell an ISV's hosted services or launch ASPs themselves. It's likely that most ISVs will protect themselves by teaming with larger channel players to lease their software through the player's ASP, team with infrastructure service providers to sell hosted services direct, or resell them through smaller VARs who can't afford to invest in hosting infrastructure themselves.

One great irony of the ASP channel evolution is that, although vendors initially stood to capture greater margins by cutting out channel members in the direct-ship model, they now may have to settle for smaller margins from VARs operating as ASPs. Some ISVs will renegotiate licensing fees for software that will be hosted to preserve margins for the short term, but they might find this to be a dangerous tactic. Inflating VARs' costs will make their channel more vulnerable to competition on price, and will undermine a key goal of ASPs—to make enterprise applications affordable to SMBs. A better strategy is probably to assist VARs in growing their SMB customer base with reasonable licensing fees, co-op dollars, and marketing help. In the long run, this will compensate vendors' falling margins with greater overall volume of licenses sold.

Rebranding and the Value-Added Channel

The ASP movement has also spawned a new species of market player, the infrastructure service provider, whose indispensability as an ASP partner and considerable clout as a customer for servers, operating systems, and middleware makes it a formidable channel force. AAAs may even emerge as influential channel players. AAAs bundle hosted applications from multiple ASPs and related providers behind one interface and then resell them to end customers. But these players, as well as pure-play ASPs, have won more than just market leverage. They are also assuming greater branding influence and customer control. In essence, the new brand is the ASP brand, not the hardware or software one. And the new customer is the ASP's customer, not the customer of the vendors supporting the ASP. In the hosted services channel, the ASP operates as the interface to the customer much the way the VAR does in the installed systems channel.

Consider the following scenario: VAR A teams with infrastructure service provider B to host ISV C's software application. Although in a very real way A's credibility depends on its partnerships with B and C, A is the ASP, A's name is on the service, so A is the brand. Even though B might provide SLA guarantees and C might perform some technical support, the customer will go to A with any problems. In essence, the ASP sells, services, and supports the customer. So it—not its "under-the-covers" partners—controls the account.

Vendors, of course, can take steps to limit the ASP's influence on customers. For instance, in trade for a later share in revenues, they can give certain resellers co-op funding and marketing resources to host its software in vertical markets the vendor wants to penetrate better. They might also select top revenue-generating resellers to be their preferred ASPs, and provide incentives accordingly. Players like these will come to comprise a vendor's "first-string" ASP channel. If an ISV alienates some of its resellers with its choices for value-added channel partners, it's probably willing to risk, for instance, forfeiting a low-performing reseller to provide incentive to a peak performer to develop another, or better, revenue stream in hosted services. Or it may relegate second-string channel partners to different supporting roles like providing technical support for new hosted services.

ASP Channel Winners and Losers

Although for the foreseeable future all of the players in the ASP space will be jockeying for market leverage, it's instructive to identify which players have the most to win and lose in the new virtual computing paradigm. The big losers will tend to be small VARs and channel players that offer little added value, as well as those who are slow to adopt the ASP model. These players risk elimination or consolidation. Hardware and software vendors that refuse to cannibalize their installed sales by merely giving lip service to the model will eventually lose business anyway to competitors offering lower priced hosted services.

By comparison, large VARs and SIs that can afford to lease or build their own hosting infrastructure can better bargain with the vendors whose products they resell and use in their data centers. Infrastructure service providers have little to lose and everything to win. Many will struggle as new companies in the inevitable uphill effort to get brand visibility, but winning business should not be difficult. Most software will eventually be hosted, and an entire new SMB market segment will open up to take advantage of those services. These players will tend to be the big winners in the new ASP channel.

Many experts are predicting an eventual consolidation in the ASP market. After all, few markets have grown this fast without some later fallout. Venture capital will dry up for slow-growing ASP ventures, bad business plans will undermine amateurs' efforts in a new industry, and larger, slower companies behind the ASP curve will buy smaller more visionary ones that demonstrate early success. These kinds of factors winnowed the glut of CLECS and ISPs after telecom deregulation and the postbrowser Internet boom. As explained earlier, the most vulnerable channel players will be the first to fall. But just as CLECs prospered by focusing on customers with special needs that the incumbent providers could not affordably address, and just as ISPs captured a new consumer customer base with low monthly Internet service fees, the majority of ASPs will succeed by offering unique or cheaper applications. What's less easy to predict is which players will dominate the high-margin value-added services that will most differentiate ASPs in the long run. This arena may be the saving grace for near-certain casualties, and a nice source of professional service revenues for formally powerful players whose markets and margins will shift to a new breed of virtual service provider.

Key Concepts

- Direct ship—Vendors shipping preconfigured computers direct to end users to undercut prices of competitors using channel players that marked up such services
- Channel consolidation—Distributors, VARs, and integrators merging to compete better with the direct-ship tactics of vendors
- Double channel—A transitional phase of channel development in which resellers offer both installed and hosted solutions
- Tech/touch dilemma—SMBs like hands-off hosted solutions because they are cheaper than installed ones but are used to installed solutions with custom hands-on deployment
- High-margin/recurring revenue dilemma—Channel players like the high margins on custom integration but need the recurring revenues from subscription-based services
- SI ASP Strategies—Own the hosting infrastructure/lease direct, team with infrastructure service provider/lease direct, own the hosting infrastructure/resell, and aggregate applications/lease to focused markets.
- Vendor ASP strategies—Sell mostly products or services? Partner with select channel players or deal equally with all?
- The ASP brand—In the ASP model, ASPs (not vendors or traditional channel players) have the most brand influence and customer control.
- The first-string ASP channel—A value-added channel comprised of resellers like peak performers that the vendor selects to offer hosted applications while abandoning or relegating other resellers to more traditional channel roles
- Big losers in the new ASP channel—Small VARs, channel players that offer little added value or are slow to adopt the ASP model, hardware and software vendors that refuse to cannibalize their installed sales with lower margin hosted services
- Big winners in the new ASP channel—Large VARs and SIs that can afford to lease or build their own hosting infrastructure, infrastructure service providers

CHAPTER THIRTEEN

What's Ahead for ASPs?

This chapter discusses

- The maturation dynamic of the ASP industry
- The data center of the future
- Wide area storage
- The coming value-added Internet
- Microsoft's impact on the ASP industry
- Tribal commerce in ASP conglomerate communities
- Winning and losing ASP strategies

Young IT industries like the one for ASPs typically experience a maturation dynamic distinguished by several phases. They are often kicked off by "disruptive" technology breakthroughs that outmode old IT paradigms. These become revolutionary products like the Web browser that are so advanced or add so much value to existing technologies that they relegate their nearest precursors to sunset markets with flattening revenues. Because the new product offers such broad value to mass markets, many vendors duplicate it or plug into the standards on which it is based. Both trends grow the product's popularity until that vendor "owns the industry platform"—the product becomes the "Windows" of its market niche.

New markets are high risk and high growth. Entrepreneurs and venture capitalists love them. So technology breakthroughs and their new markets usually attract hordes of IT prospectors, usually more than the incipient market can support. Because few entrepreneurs and VCs are created equal, not all of the companies they create survive even their various rounds of VC funding. Those that do, of course, can continue on course, go public, and get acquired by other companies.

The late 1990s saw an amazing number of new telecom companies launch, make it through funding rounds, and then earn almost laughably high Initial Public Offering (IPO) valuations. If, in the long term, the company's product lived up to the stock market's expectations, then everyone won. VCs earned huge returns on their investments, entrepreneurs got rich on stock options overnight, and stockholders got in on the ground floor of a stock, the value of which would steadily increase. However, if Wall Street guessed wrong and a year or two after IPO the stock value fell, a lot of folks lost. Usually the entrepreneurs cashed out quickly and made nice profits, the VCs made early returns and then took a beating, and the stockholders were left holding a dog and losing lots of money. Entirely too many new telecom companies suffered this fate.

After awhile, instead of risking post-IPO devaluation, entrepreneurs built dotcom telecoms for the express purpose of selling them to larger established companies instead of going public. Large telecom vendors like Cisco actually built a business model based on rapidly acquiring companies with promising technology instead of building it themselves. "Innovation through acquisition" became cheaper and faster than internal R&D. But even the masters of this method like Cisco were surprised at how fast those acquisitions also delivered incredible revenue returns.

So, if dotcoms did it right, either going public or getting acquired could create substantial wealth for the owners, VCs, stockholders, and acquiring companies. The wildcard, of course, was how Wall Street perceived a company's potential value.

Many new industries thrive for awhile in this kind of heady atmosphere, but eventually the wild proliferation of new companies stabilizes, and the market begins to segment. Dominant players emerge in different segments; for example, in vertical markets or at the high or low ends of those markets. Smaller companies may specialize; larger ones may focus on broader markets with products with wider appeal. It doesn't take too long to discern which companies will soon run out of capital or market share. This is when the number of companies stops expanding.

This phase is characterized by consolidation. The successful companies acquire the less successful ones that still have promising technology or customer base. The less successful companies merge to combine capital, market share, and customers. During consolidation, unless a company is very large (and doesn't need acquisitions) or very specialized (and doesn't fit into a larger company's strategic product/market portfolio), they eat or get eaten.

During the last phase, markets stratify. The dominant two or three vendors control the bulk of market share and many smaller vendors subsist on their percentage of what's left. Sometimes called "the walking dead," these smaller companies are not valuable enough to be acquired by the dominant players but are too moribund to bring in big profits.

That's the way markets shake out. All the vendors will make evolutionary changes to their product lines to profit from the growing market as long as they can, until the next disruptive technology breakthrough starts the cycle over again in a new market.

So as of 2001, at which phase of maturation is the ASP market? How long will it take to reach its full potential? And what developments will drive that growth?

These questions are unanswerable, but here are some educated speculations. The ASP market is approximately 70% proliferated. Every conceivable type of IT player, from integrators and VARs to hardware and software vendors, has thrown its hat in the ASP ring. So the *number* of ASP players will increase by 30% or so during the next decade. New ASPs and related players like infrastructure service providers will continue to emerge, but they will be specialists in focused markets managing dense multimedia files like X-rays for the health care market. It's likely that new fauna in the ASP ecosystem will also emerge. Just as we've seen AAAs and WASPs evolve during the last year, so too it's probable that the future might produce ASPs hosting virtual trade exchanges, knowledge exchanges, and other new IT environments.

These new players, of course, will be somewhat offset during the industry consolidation phase, when a certain percentage of ASPs will fail because of poor business plans, faulty execution, cash flow crises, and so on.

This said, though, *70% proliferated does not mean 70% mature.* Whereas proliferation is gauged by the *number* of players in an industry, maturity will be measured *by customers acquired and revenues earned.* Usually, maturity does not occur until the consolidation phase, when the weaker players have gone out of business or been acquired by stronger ones. Then, even though the *number* of players is fewer, *the market for those players is bigger* because it is comprised of companies that are more conservative and mainstream, not of risk-taking early adopters. The ASP industry will grow at a high rate through the middle of this decade and will eventually settle down between 2010 and 2015. In Internet time, 15 years is an absolute eternity. But the reason the ASP industry will crest this far out is not a negative one. On the contrary, hosted applications may be the biggest change in IT since the advent of mass-marketed software. Just as all previous computing models still exist in one form or another, so too all installed applications will not simply disappear and be replaced by hosted ones. This kind of high-powered virtual computing requires time before the mass market can culturally absorb it. However the eventual scope of this change will probably be unprecedented.

At this point there is probably no way to predict accurately the worth of the ASP market in 10 or 15 years. More to the point, market predictions are not a major aim of this book. By now, you should understand all facets of the ASP model sufficiently to start evaluating ASPs with which you may do business. Whether you'll want to do business with the same ones five years from now will depend on how well they address changing technologies and business models. Therefore, pending technology developments as well as macro trends in virtual business likely to affect ASPs merit passing mention.

The Data Center of the Future

The data center of the next decade probably will not look a lot different than those of today. Short of floating the facility on a bed of silicon and implementing Alcatraz–like physical security, data centers could get only nominally more disasterproof and physically secure. Obviously, as in all areas of IT, the dramatic changes will take place in the computing infrastructure: servers, operating systems, middleware, and storage.

At the Comdex/Fall '99 trade show, Unisys and a consortium of industry partners implemented a Windows 2000 scalability proof-of-concept as part of The Data Center of the Next Millennium demonstration. Partners included Microsoft, EMC, Cisco, StorageTek, and several other companies. The consortium created a Web site in a "glass house" for a fictional e-commerce company called Interstellar Outfitters, a supply station for spaceships and spacestations.

Unisys used massively parallel 4-way and 8-way servers as the hardware platform. EMC provided a 9-TB data warehouse for analysis of a 43-TB Symmetrix Enterprise SAN. All the interconnect technology was high-speed LAN, with the exception of a fiber-channel connection to the EMC SAN. EMC hardware and software backed up the system to tape at the rate of more than 1TB/hour. And administrators managed servers in the data center from a single sign-on using any of the desktops linked to the Microsoft management console. The project used public key data security, and all networking equipment was redundant and backed up by UPS.

When you get past the tech-speak, the bottom-line importance of the project is this: It proved, pretty convincingly, that such an infrastructure could manage 4,000 transactions per second, or about 5 billion Web hits and 300 million page requests per day. Over the five-day demonstration, the infrastructure sustained a continuous data transfer rate of 100 Mbps. The consortium estimated that, at that rate, the site could accommodate $187 billion in transactions per year— roughly the total value of the world's current annual e-commerce. What's more, the system was built in five months, and during stress testing encountered infinitesimal unscheduled downtime. Most impressive, possibly, was the price— around $12 million for hardware and software *to host all the world's e-commerce transactions for a year.*

This level of reliability, scalability, manageability, security, and interoperability was the state-of-the-art for a Windows Operating System/Intel chip platform in 1999. If the Comdex demonstration was even half as robust as its supporters claimed, the results would still be awe-inspiring. Imagine what benchmarks superpowerful UNIX-based server vendors like Sun Microsystems and Hewlett-Packard, as well as mainframe vendors like IBM, are establishing in 2001. Imagine the hardware/software capabilities of infrastructure service providers in 2010. Computing power in the data center will not be a limiting factor for ASPs going forward.

Wide Area Storage

SANs are right on the cusp of going long distance. For example, a recent StorageNetworks project in New York City extended some financial institutions' fiber channel network range to approximately 120 miles to back up sensitive data on storage repositories in New Jersey. The customers especially feared power outages in the big metropolis, so they wanted to get copies of data off any power grids that might be affected by blackouts or other disasters. Previously, the companies copied all data to tape each day and physically transported the tapes to the New Jersey sites.

The "WAN-ing" of SANs is accomplished by enhancing fiber channel using two methods—DWDM and optical repeaters. DWDM gets very dense data off the fiber-channel network onto network service providers' optical network backbones, where optical repeaters boost it periodically to its destination.

To transport SAN data over the IP edge of the network, various vendors are working on alternate and complementary wide area SAN solutions. SCSI over IP encapsulates SCSI data in IP packets and tunnels it through IP networks, storage over IP converts fiber channel to IP, and fiber channel over IP encapsulates fiber channel data in IP packets and tunnels it over IP networks. Other vendors are at work on fiber channel over ATM solutions. Supporting dense data over new long-distance networks will not be a limiting factor for ASPs going forward.

The Coming Value-Added Internet

AboveNet is an infrastructure service provider with a value-added network that may prove to be the standard by which others are measured in years to come. Leveraging Metromedia Fiber Network's (its parent company) international fiber-optic network, AboveNet's infrastructure spans Europe, North America, and the Pacific Rim. Its main business is leasing server and storage space in its Internet Service Exchanges to ISPs and Web-content providers, as well reselling network bandwidth to ASPs and others. With its mammoth 122.4-Gbps network capacity, it's also able to specialize in transporting dense multimedia content. Real Networks, for example, leases the AboveNet network so customers can speedily download multimedia files to its RealPlayer PC device.

AboveNet uses peering and various traffic management methods to create a superefficient, high-speed data expressway over which its ISP customers can better serve their customers without routing all their data exclusively over the Internet. Unlike a plain vanilla VPN, which encrypts data and transports it via a secure tunnel through the Internet, one with extensive peering actually links servers of companies using it directly so they can access each other's content about as fast as possible. With 457 peering agreements, AboveNet has opened a broadband umbrella network over the Internet with virtually instantaneous throughput. Customer transmission's essentially travel "one hop" from origination to the AboveNet network to destination, instead of having to negotiate whatever number of public Internet routers and routes that can accommodate them at the time. AboveNet excels at minimizing congestion to high-traffic sites like public portals or to one-time Net events like a music CD debut.

Of course, other network service providers like AT&T, WorldCom, and Qwest are likely to start adding comparable but unique architectural value to their infrastructures. But it's doubtful that in the next few years a new breakthrough networking technology will come along and be implemented on a wide scale. Most experts think the telecom merger and acquisition frenzy is over, the economy has slowed down, and venture capital is a little tight for dotcom start-ups working on the leading edge. So most vendors will focus on incrementally improving existing product lines to improve base problems like throughput and traffic management.

In the long term, though, the networking technique called *multiprotocol label switching* (MPLS) holds great promise. Label-based switching lets routers make routing decisions based on the contents of a simple label that accompanies the data packets instead of by performing a complex route lookup in a router's table of destination IP addresses. This process speeds throughput because data is handled more elegantly than most other methods. As a result, network administrators can more easily route different types of data as well as determine the quality of service they require. So at some point MPLS may viably compete with ATM for carrying multimedia traffic. MPLS also lets service providers create VPNs using IP tunnels throughout networks instead of encryption and other techniques. Generally, MPLS may vastly simplify network architectures and management because, with it, data can run on an all-IP WAN infrastructure.

Thus, elegant, affordable, and global transmission of all data types will be increasingly viable for ASPs as we near 2010.

The Microsoft Factor

As mentioned earlier, Sun Microsystems, Oracle, IBM, and others aggressively migrated toward a thin client computing model that supported subscription application services with a common goal—to unseat Microsoft as the reigning king of purchased software. If PC environments were no longer the main forum for widespread application development, and these vendors could change the computing paradigm to a largely hosted one, then they had a shot at reclaiming "ownership of the architecture"—and the vast majority of application developers and customers would no longer have to devote most of their IT resources to playing in a Windows environment. Microsoft seemed slow to heed this threat, but after its protracted legal battle with the federal government, weak reception of Windows 2000, and the explosion of the ASP market, about midway through 2000 it announced it would move toward a more subscription-based software model in the next several years. This may be an attempt to freeze the ASP market by getting potential customers to wait for Microsoft offerings before committing to an ASP solution, or it may be a legitimate attempt to migrate out of necessity to a hosted paradigm. In either case, Microsoft may have an impact on the ASP industry that is worth discussing.

Although hosted services are antithetical to Microsoft's real strengths as a mass market software retail juggernaut, if it can dispassionately wean itself from the PC-centric mind-set, several facts make it the logical candidate for bringing hosted services to the mass market. First, no vendor has a better understanding of the SMB market. The company's bottom-up customer acquisition strategy of winning lower end users first then migrating to the higher end ones over time has led it to focus its marketing and application development efforts on SMBs more than any other vendor. Second, no brand is better recognized by more low- and mid-range users. If Microsoft successfully migrates to hosted services from installed applications, its legions of customers may find that following that path, rather than switching vendors, is the migration strategy of least resistance. The fact that 90% or more of all computers connected to the Web use a Windows operating system will reinforce this trend. Microsoft can quite easily build the most accommodating bridge to widespread business use of the Internet. What's more, 85% or more computers connected to the Internet use Microsoft Internet Explorer as their browser of choice. So even if the PC becomes outmoded as the de facto user interface, Microsoft still controls the interface for the new subscription model. This by no means makes Microsoft the default winner in the race to commercialize the Internet, but it is still the vendor to beat in this contest.

Microsoft calls its Internet-based computing strategy *Windows.NET* because down the road it will migrate its Windows 2000 operating system to one by that name, which is tailored to providing an Internet-friendly architecture, services, and features. The goal of .NET is to transition Microsoft—and the rest of the industry—to a new model for software development, software deployment, and revenue growth. However, because it will not complete that operating system conversion until 2003, in the interim it's migrating to .NET other less complex products like Microsoft Network (MSN) Explorer, which is integrated with MSN Web services such as Hotmail, Money Central, and MSN Calendar, and which boasts seamless, one-window design. During the next two years, Microsoft's .NET strategy will focus on creating development tools, such as the upcoming Microsoft Visual Studio.NET. Microsoft will also give developers tools to create Web-based applications that have all the functionality and flexibility of current Win32 applications so Web-based .NET versions of Word, Excel, and Outlook will be as robust as their Win32 counterparts.

.NET services will be based on the Simple Object Access Protocol (SOAP), which enables users to pass data through XML-based messages in a distributed and decentralized environment among potentially dissimilar networks and operating systems. It lets developers use any programming language on any operating system, so they no longer have to commit to either the Microsoft-oriented Distributed Component Object Model (DCOM) or the multi-vender oriented Common Object Request Broker Architecture (CORBA) architecture. What's more, it lets them combine Web services in different ways to create new hosted applications instead of having to spend a lot more time creating a large application by reusing low-level components. Because SOAP-based communication permits transactions to go from vendor to customer, customer to supplier, parent company to subsidiary, and so forth, it could create the basis of a completely open cross-platform e-business environment.

.NET will also enable users to store personal, application, security, and financial data centrally so they can move from one device to the next without having to reconfigure them. Imagine a salesperson losing his PDA and all the contact and other data on it. With centralized storage, this data is stored on a server instead of each device, so he can simply replace the PDA and synchronize the data from the database.

.NET services, of course, will be subscription based so that, for example, the next Microsoft Office release will offer a subscription model for consumers whereby they can purchase a one-year license at a reduced cost from the installed version.

It's uncertain whether Microsoft will play the ASP software "arms supplier" role to its solution provider partners that become ASPs. That would be the logical strategy. But Microsoft has made some acquisitions that indicate it may move down the food chain with its .NET initiative in some cases. For instance, it has acquired Great Plains Software, an ERP and e-business vendor with an established ASP program and partners. It's also established partnerships with ASPs like Corio and USi that host Microsoft applications. At this point, however, Microsoft appears to be pursuing an "enabler" role by offering what it's calling the *Hosted Applications Development Community and ASP Certification Program* to support its ASP channel with appropriate knowledge and training resources.

However, although .NET computing sounds admirable and revolutionary, it goes against every business instinct for "owning the architecture" that has enabled Microsoft to succeed thusfar. After all, subscription services are another way for Microsoft to sell its applications downmarket at reduced rates while not really forfeiting installed application sales until absolutely necessary. Therefore, .NET may simply give lip service to cross-platform computing while serving to extend Microsoft's customer base into the ranks of those who don't want to spend $500-plus for applications like Office. Although the company is certainly capable of creating such a technology platform, it must overcome it's ingrained cultural behavior of coaxing customers into the fold with affordable and pervasive solutions only later to lock them into a platform from which it's almost impossible to disengage. At any rate, the migration to .NET will take many years and, in the interim, most SMB users who are current Microsoft customers will have to support both Win32 and .NET versions of their applications—a costly proposition.

Tribal Commerce within ASP Conglomerate Communities

With massively powerful and scalable ASP hardware/software platforms, rapid improvements in wide area storage, steadily increasing network capacity and reach, and more imaginative and elegant network architectures, individual ASPs should be able to serve numerous enterprise applications and handle more customers per application. They will also host functionality over increasingly longer distances with minimal network latency and better data repository security. These incremental, linear improvements will, at some point, enable strategic changes in how ASPs, supporting service providers like infrastructure service providers, and end customers do business. Such strategies could lead to exponential improvements in service and new virtual business models. Some new macro model for e-business will probably emerge that combines the synergies of previously unrelated new or existing technologies into a unique technology base, overlapping business processes, and a more holistic, yet improvisational, commerce dynamic. Most of the indicators point toward a phenomenon like virtual trading within a "tribe" of vendors, partners, and customers sharing a common technology infrastructure and product or market focus.

The dominant e-business technology breakthroughs of the last few years can be named on one hand: virtual communities, virtual trade exchanges, enterprise information portals, and ASPs. Over time, alliances among vendors of the different products will render select product lines increasingly plug-and-play. Of course, customers doing business with each other—along a supply chain, for instance—will benefit by implementing common products to maintain a relatively homogenous "interprise" IT platform. At least, that's the strategy they'd use five years ago. As ASPs become a staple of the computing environment, though, it will become much cheaper and easier simply to outsource the needed combinations of applications from common ASPs serving, say, one extended supply chain. That is certainly a reasonable extrapolation to make from current evidence. What can't be predicted or measured, however, is the ways in which that development will ramify into a new virtual business model. At best, we can posit a few probabilities. To do so, let's briefly look at the salient elements of the technologies mentioned earlier to see how they relate.

Virtual communities are groups of customers with a dominant passionate interest in certain products—say, laptop computers—that do virtual business with a stable of vendors via a common e-business infrastructure. Membership in the community essentially "qualifies" the customer as a good sales prospect for vendors serving the community. So vendors essentially trade certain customer benefits—say, group discounts or fast fixes to faulty products—for the opportunity to sell them products in bulk. The vendors save marketing costs, sell the majority of their goods to a demographic that wants what they sell, and can more easily provide focused customer service to keep customers happy and customer profiling to tailor future products to customer preferences. Customers, in turn, get cheaper products purchased en masse and better products built according to their feedback.

Virtual trade exchanges work similarly, but in a B2B context. They are complex e-business infrastructures that permit accelerated auction-based trading between members of an existing supply chain. Say a car manufacturer needs scrap iron with which to build bumpers. Using a trade exchange, it puts out a request for bids on the amount of scrap iron it needs. Its supply partners, in turn, submit price bids, and the lowest price gets the job of supplying the material. Everybody wins: The manufacturer gets the best price, the supplier gets the job it knows it can make a profit on, and the trade exchange takes a percentage of the whole deal as its service fee.

Enterprise portals are essentially interfaces to a user's relevant data, applications, and colleagues in their extended enterprise and on the public Internet. However, they are more than the interface. That's the tip of the iceberg. They are also all of the integration links to the data and applications, the indexing methods used to search those sources, the taxonomies of all the information in the portal's extended information base, and much more. Their great benefit is that they let users "personalize" one interface for their specific organizational role so that only data, applications, and people relevant to their requirements are accessed by the interface. Many portals also automatically "push" relevant data to users so they don't even have to look for it. Portals, therefore, provide users a personal context for accomplishing work amid the blizzard of information that routinely bombards them from cyberspace. They are the relevance lenses through which users view their virtual world.

All of these infrastructures accelerate e-business processes and user productivity. They also encourage fidelity to a group of fellow users, workers, or companies with which members carry on work or trade. At the same time, they discourage working or doing business with parties not part of the existing network. Why? Because the price of changing is too great. It means community members, for instance, have to get to trust new vendors, manufacturers forfeit existing supply chains by moving to a different trade exchange, and portal users must integrate with new data sources and applications.

However, just as important, these infrastructures are also very complex, time-consuming, and expensive to build initially. Why, for instance, would a small supply chain partner of a major PC vendor want to build its own enterprise portal if it could simply plug into the software vendor's portal infrastructure? If that were the ante for continuing to do business in that very lucrative trading environment, it's cheaper and faster to plug into an existing environment. The competitive dynamic at work is similar to the "innovation-through-acquisition" one explained earlier. Only, here, companies don't acquire or merge with a company to get new technology. They plug into its environment in exchange for loyalty to that virtual economy.

Big companies will likely offer incentives for smaller companies to do just this. To grow a more profitable value chain of suppliers, partners, and resellers, a major player may give away entry to the environment as well as integrate new members into it. After all, their construction costs are already largely covered. Giving away services up front is basically an investment to net bigger long-term revenues. By the same token, if that vendor, and possibly its partners, built a virtual trade exchange by which supply chain trade were accomplished, it would keep its supply prices down over the long term. Through the auction process, for example, a PC manufacturer might obtain hard drives 20% cheaper, pass along the savings to customers, and win bigger market share. If the vendor's potential customers were able to plug into its virtual community infrastructure, virtual word-of-mouth testimonials in the community would drive sales of cheaper PCs faster. Similarly, if the cheaper hard drives turned out to have bugs that community members detected after sales, they could pressure the vendor to change suppliers or fix the bugs.

Such a virtual trading cycle not only streamlines the supply chain so products are developed faster and cheaper, but it also cuts costs of raw goods and ensures quality via customer feedback. So the tribal partnering and trading dynamic of such virtual economies works to every member's benefit—from one end of the value chain to the other, everyone wins. There is probably only one improvement we could make, and that is to have the combined infrastructures hosted by an ASP.

This should be a tenable undertaking for the super-ASP of the future (Figure 13–1). It could specialize in just those applications needed by the vendor's value

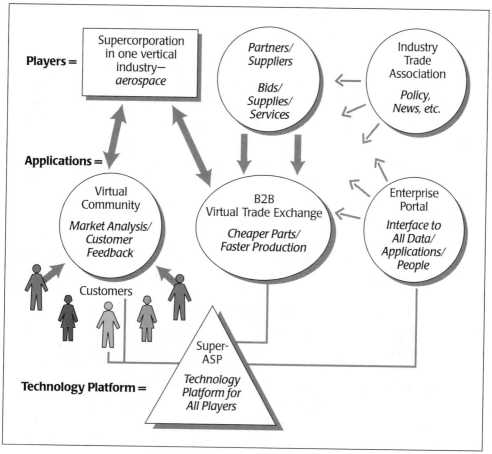

Figure 13–1 A super-ASP leases technology infrastructure to a conglomerate community so that it can carry out "tribal commerce"

chain; become the IT hub for all suppliers, partners, and customers; and offer discounted services to all members because they pledge their IT platform loyalty to that ASP. The vendor saves development and upkeep costs, all members of the value chain get cheaper leasing fees, the ASP is guaranteed hosting business as long as the value chain is viable, and customers can offer feedback not only on the vendor's products but also on the ASP's services, so quality pervades the IT infrastructure as well as the end products. Various vendors might also virtually advertise on various sites and interfaces to bring in additional revenues to the ASP and sales leads to themselves, and the ASP could sell business intelligence services that would help vendors better predict customer's needs, even before the customer knows they have those needs. Such a win/win dynamic would breed in members the kind of long-term loyalty to their trading "tribe" that is all too rare in these days of rapid staff turnover, company merger and acquisition, and accelerated technology change.

This competitive scenario makes sense for G2000 vendor-sponsored conglomerate communities. Need it be said that the vendor could be a major non-IT conglomerate like a car manufacturer, aerospace firm, or oil company? In this case, of course, aligning with the appropriate industry association for policy and news about the conglomerate's industry might be a good idea. Also, the prime mover of such a commercial community would be the G2000. It's likely that it would promote the idea among its customers and partners, and engage the appropriate ASP. Indeed, if the community is large enough, it need be the ASP's only customer. So ASP as well as customers and the supply chain pledge allegiance to the vendor. Eventually, the community would key on its sponsoring supercorporation's target vertical markets, computing platform, standards, and development environment, geographical footprint, and regional ASP or international ASP with multiple data centers.

It stands to reason that members of conglomerate communities will also trade along lines not in the original mandate. For instance, banks and insurance companies using the same hosted ERP package in that vendor's sponsored community might become acquainted in IT user group meetings and eventually swing deals. The insurance company might sell health insurance to bank employees in bulk at a discount. In this way, the market synergies of the basic model get perpetuated ad hoc throughout the community. The denser the web of relationships, the more value is created for members, until the community reaches a critical mass of members, relationships, and accrued value such that getting comparable value in any other community is impossible.

Other ASPs will always want to maintain their independence and serve multiple customers, typically in a vertical niche like banking (pure-play ASPs may have a generic application for that industry) or on a common IT platform like Lotus Notes (FSPs may do integration as well as offer 50% applications, outsourced staff, and so on). But SMBs that want to compete with G2000 conglomerate communities must either form ones of their own or specialize so they aren't a competitive threat to high-end conglomerates.

Winning and Losing ASP Strategies

If you accept these premises, then it becomes apparent that certain ASP strategies are doomed in the long term, and ASPs embracing some of them are already showing symptoms of strain. The following are a few examples:

- ASPs hosting single horizontal productivity applications like e-mail or groupware to consumers for low fees per month—they compete on cost, have no differentiating value, and will lose their consumer customer base to larger operations like popular on-line services or to AAAs that will bundle these applications into more inclusive packages for less cost per application.
- ASPs hosting common enterprise applications in popular vertical markets without further differentiating value—competition will be most intense in these markets, and competing on cost alone is a dangerous strategy.
- ASPs that differentiate themselves only with soon-to-be commodity offerings like value-added storage, security, and network bandwidth—SSPs, MSecPs, infrastructure service providers, and network service providers are best qualified to provide these services most cost-effectively, so ASPs should work the model and resell those services, not build their own.
- Regional ASPs without further differentiation—within several years the industrialized world will have a common broadband infrastructure that will let large ASPs host applications (and virtually monitor and maintain them) to customers just about anywhere, so many regional players will lack the economies of scale to compete on price alone.
- Independent ASPs supporting multiple customers at healthy margins with no affinity programs in place to maintain customer loyalty—conglomerate communities will "cherrypick" their customers with lower prices and better value.
- Ironically, ASPs supporting one conglomerate community that takes forever to assemble a critical mass of members—community market synergies don't produce huge value until they have a solid member base, so the ASP forfeits other customers for a slow-building anemic community market during the first several years.

Likewise, certain ASP strategies look like they can't fail:

- ASPs rapidly deploying e-business infrastructures for dotcoms—dotcoms are not going away, will always be pressed for cash and personnel, but their business model demands speed to market, and hosted solutions are the fastest and most cost-effective for them.
- FSPs offering accelerated e-business applications with integration services at competitive rates to SMBs—to compete during the next 10 years, every SMB will need e-commerce, and they will need it integrated with their legacy back-end systems like accounting, billing, warehousing, and so forth.
- Small SI ASPs offering similar services to SMBs—they have the integration and implementation techniques, and are priced right (but they'll have to fund hosted jobs with installed ones to handle cash flow at first).
- The best infrastructure service providers—in most mature IT markets, unique functionality gets absorbed upstream into larger players' offerings, so it's likely the best ISPs will eventually offer security, storage, and IT management but will also have accrued a solid installed base of server/network users that can't survive without an ISP back end and will provide these players with an ongoing cash flow.
- Ironically, MSecPs and MSPs—customers will rely on these players to keep ASPs and ISPs honest, so until ISPs build up sufficient security and application monitoring credibility, these will be key role players.
- Conglomerate community ASPs that do it right and fast—if they team with a large vendor and supply chain that are largely in sync, can act fast, and have a loyal customer base, then the community reaches critical mass fast, and all its market synergies are activated for everyone's long-term success.

The Human Factor

This said, one wildcard could reroute ASP progress in alternate directions—it's culture, the human factor that always undermines the best IT intentions. Conglomerate communities are really only logical extensions of ASP coalitions. Both require "coopetition." However, there is no more competitive environment than big business and contemporary IT. If the kind of mutual leeriness between vendors and resellers that, for instance, characterized the old IT channel is carried over into these larger coopetition market models, then old model behavior will undermine new model alliances and markets. Similarly, customers have to trust the new virtual models and buy into them. If too many get burned as the ASP industry consolidates and stratifies, they'll be stuck between a rock and a hard place—gun-shy from pulling the plug on previous hosted applications or watching their ASP go broke, yet anxious because they know someone might outcompete them using a successful ASP solution.

The ASP business model offers a wonderfully elegant way of bringing the best computing has to offer to the greatest mass of people who can benefit from it. In business, of course, it should be the great leveler that will permit SMBs to achieve competitive parity with G2000s. Whereas the Internet "democratized" access to global information, ASPs will do so for enterprise computing. This is a fairly prosaic prediction, but it has profound implications. Approximately 80% of the world's wealth resides in 20% of the population, largely in the West. As ASPs penetrate new third-world markets, this wealth will be redistributed and new local wealth will be created. Also, people everywhere who never imagined going into business for themselves will suddenly be able to afford a hosted and leased IT infrastructure. Over time, the dominant market for hosted services will move from B2B to B2C. This is probably where the greatest daily cultural change will occur.

Ten years ago, people could still go to work for the corporation at which their parents worked and expect to spend their life in relative security there. It was a little like being in the armed services. Generation after generation became corporate soldiers for the same company. They exchanged their long-term company loyalty for the corporation's financial protection. Similarly, with proprietary computing platforms, customers often dealt with a single vendor indefinitely. They purchased a relative competitive advantage at the price of long-term loyalty to that vendor. However, these proved to be flawed and sometimes exploitative models. Both could imprison workers and customers for a company's benefit and then abandon them in the form of layoffs when the company's profits fell or in the form of customer service when an IT implementation offered no promise of new revenues for its vendor.

ASP-supported conglomerate communities offer a benefit-driven alternative to these command-and-control practices, but they have to be entered into with philosophies as different as their business strategies. Throughout civilization, most commercial and cultural dynasties proliferated from some central site that had great symbolic significance for its founding people. For instance, when Rome was built, Romulus had a pit dug on the future site of the Court of Assembly. Then into it the founders threw local fruits as well as handfuls of dirt from their native lands. The tribe named the pit *mundus*—or *cosmos*—and then laid a huge stone called a "soul" stone over the opening. That site symbolized a connection with the inhabitants' past, their ancestors, as well as the pact they struck with each other to prosper in harmony in this new location. As they built Rome, the inhabitants made sure the main thoroughfares intersected at that site. The ongoing practice kept Romans in touch with the original spirit of cooperative enterprise symbolically preserved there.

In the IT arena, which is increasingly influencing the cultural arena, ASPs offer the potential for just such enriching flexibility, continuity, and connectedness. However, the prerequisite for prospering in such hosted communities is that all players plug into them with the same spirit.

Key Concepts

- Industry maturation dynamic—Disruptive technology breakthrough, new players proliferate, then consolidate, then stratify
- Data center of the future—Exponentially improved reliability, scalability, manageability, security, and interoperability
- Wide area storage—Using SANs and WANs to transmit dense data over fiber-enhanced long-distance networks
- MPLS—Label-based network switching that lets routers make routing decisions based on the contents of a simple label that accompanies data packets instead of by performing a complex route lookup in a router's table of destination IP addresses; handles different data types elegantly with qualities of service and may vie with ATM in the future
- The Microsoft factor—Using .NET subscription-based application services to enter and dominate the ASP market for SMBs
- Tribal commerce in conglomerate communities—Future super-ASPs specializing in applications for one vendor's value chain so they become the IT hub for all suppliers, partners, and customers, and offer discounted services to all members in exchange for IT platform loyalty to that ASP

Guide to Location
of ASP Case Studies
in Different Chapters

In Chapter 2

Pure-play ASP: Corio
Customer: Vertical Networks, Inc.
Key elements of the solution: Multiple hosted applications, accelerated deployment

Infrastructure Service Provider: Digex, Inc.
Customer: Continuity, Inc.
Key elements of the solution: Turnkey deployment, advanced hardware/software platform, world-class data centers and network, proactive customer service, impressive capitalization

In Chapter 4

MSP: Lucent Technologies Worldwide Services
Customer: NaviSite
Key elements of the solution: Outsourced staff, VPN performance and security optimization, ongoing performance monitoring, resold MSP services

In Chapter 6

ASP Enabler: Agiliti
Customer: Achieve Online Services
Key elements of the solution: multiple hosted applications accessed with one login, extensive technical consulting and service, virtual platform, and performance monitoring

Service Bureau ASP: Critical Technologies/FilesOnTheNet.com
Customer: Loyola University
Key elements of the solution: Accelerated deployment, reduced processing costs, central storage, and simultaneens remote access of documents

In Chapter 7

MSecP: Netegrity, Inc.
Customer: Corio, an ASP
Key elements of the solution: Simplified, one-point access across multiple hosted applications, extensive customization of security software, scalability

In Chapter 8

ISV ASP: DataCert.com, Inc. and Interliant, Inc.
Customers: Law firms and Fortune 100 corporate legal departments
Key elements of the solution: Proven ASP infrastructure to win credibility with Fortune 100 customers, bulletproof 24/7 support, cost-effective data security

In Chapter 10

FSP: IBM Global Services
Customer: CareTouch, Inc.
Key elements of the solution: Accelerated deployment, extensive application development and integration, one-stop shopping for the complete solution

In Chapter 11

WASP: 2Roam
Customer: eBay
Key elements of the solution: Support for different domestic and international wireless platforms, devices, browsers, markup languages and protocols, integration with different wireless portals

In Chapter 12

SI ASP: World Technology Services
Customer: J.R. Abbott Construction
Key elements of the solution: Rapid deployment, huge cost savings, industry-specific hosted solution

VAR ASP: netASPx
Customer: HomeBanc
Key elements of the solution: Accelerated deployment, legacy/hosted application integration

xSPs (ASP-Enabling Companies)

Company Type	Company Name	Address	City	State	Zip Code	Phone	URL
ISP	Exodus Communications	2831 Mission College Blvd.	Santa Clara	CA	95054	408-346-2200	www.exodus.com
ISP	Digex	14400 Sweitzer Ln.	Laurel	MD	20707	240-264-2000	www.Digex.com
ISP	NaviSite	400 Minuteman Rd.	Andover	MA	01810	978-682-8300	www.navisite.com
ISP	Verio	8005 S. Chester St., Suite 200	Englewood	CO	80112	303-645-1900	www.verio.com
MSP	2nd Wave, Inc.	14881 Quorum Dr., Suite 825	Dallas	TX	75240	972-661-2300	www.2wi.com
MSP	Manage.Com, Inc.	2345 North First St. First Floor, Suite 100	San Jose	CA	95131	408-944-1500	www.manage.com
MSP	SilverBack Technologies, Inc.	85 Rangeway Rd.	Billerica	MA	01862	978-670-9944	www.silverbacktech.com
MSP	StrataSource	42701 Lawrence Pl.	Fremont	CA	94538	510-979-9911	www.stratasource.com
MSP	InteQ Corporation	100 Crosby Dr.	Bedford	MA	01730	781-275-3400	www.Inteqnet.com
MSecP	Guardent (was DefendNet Solutions)	75 Third Ave.	Waltham	MA	02451	781-577-6500	www.guardent.com
MSecP	eSecurityOnline, LLC	120 West 12th St., Suite 310	Kansas City	MO	64105	877-373-2874	www.eSecurityOnline.com
MSecP	Riptech, Inc.	2800 Eisenhower Ave.	Alexandria	VA	22314	703-373-5100	www.Riptech.com
MSecP	Telenisus	1701 Golf Rd. Tower 3, Suite 600	Rolling Meadows	IL	60008	847-871-5005	www.Telenisus.com
SSP	StorageNetworks, Inc.	225 Wyman St.	Waltham	MA	02451	781-622-6700	www.Storagenetworks.com
SSP	Storability	118 Turnpike Rd.	South-borough	MA	01772	508-229-1700	www.storability.com
SSP	ManagedStorage International	10075 Westmoor Dr., Suite 100	Broomfield	CO	80021	720-566-5000	www.managedstorage.com

Company Type	Company Name	Address	City	State	Zip Code	Phone	URL
AAA	Jamcracker Inc.	19000 Homestead Rd.	Cupertino	CA	95014-0712	408-725-4300	www.jamcracker.com
AAA	vJungle, Inc.	4104 148th Ave. NE, Bldg G	Redmond	WA	98052	866-858-6453	www.vjungle.com
WASP	2Roam, Inc.	2688 Middlefield Rd.	Redwood City	CA	94063-3481	650-480-1100	www.2Roam.com
WASP	AirFlash, Inc.	12900 Saratoga Ave.	Saratoga	CA	95070	408-517-2200	www.Airflash.com
WASP	Everypath	2211 North First St., Suite 200	San Jose	CA	95131	408-562-8000	www.Everypath.com

Selected ASPs in Major Vertical Markets

Market	Hosted Service	Company Name	Address	City	State	Zip Code	Phone	URL
Health care	Host information systems to Integrated Delivery Networks, physician practices, and physician billing services.	CPU Medical Management Systems	9235 Activity Rd., Suite 104	San Diego	CA	92126-4440	800-597-0875	www.cpumms.com
Health care	Hosts cardiology image and data management.	CardioNow	Gellert Blvd., Suite 229	Daly City	CA	94015	888-225-2560	www.cardionow.com
Health care	Hosts a physician practice management system.	CureMD	246 5th Ave.	New York	NY	10001	212-213-6230	www.curemd.com/
Health care	Hosts administrative processes, claims adjudication, financial transactions, etc., for purchasers, payers, providers, and health plan members.	eHealthDirect	One Cranberry Hill Rd., Suite 203	Lexington	MA	02421	781-372-3800	www.ehealthdirect.com
Health care	Hosts software for asset management and the resale of preowned medical equipment.	Health Asset Management	8381 Dix Ellis Tr., Suite 110	Jacksonville	FL	32256	904-538-9998	www.drused.com
Health care	Delivers, presents, and archives laboratory test results to clinical laboratories, physicians, and patients.	Labtest.com	140 Greenwood Ave.	Midland Park	NJ	07432	201-447-9991	www.info@labtest.com

Market	Hosted Service	Company Name	Address	City	State	Zip Code	Phone	URL
Health care	Hosts physician practice management software, managed care software system modules for managed care organizations, handheld technology for point-of-care transactions, and physician practice management software.	MDserve.com	4800 Sugar Grove Blvd., Suite 320	Stafford	TX	77477	877-MDSERVE	www.Mdserve.com
Health care	Hosts health applications for more than 1,000 health providers.	Shared Medical Systems (SMS)	51 Valley Stream Pkwy.	Malvern	PA	19355	610-219-6300	www.smed.com
Health care	Hosts HealthWeb Internet portal.	The TriZetto Group	567 San Nicolas Dr., Suite 360	Newport Beach	CA	92660	949-719-2200	www.trizetto.com
Engineering	Hosts collaboration and content management based on Documentum software.	Connectsite. com (ASP of Technology Services Group, Inc.)	200 W. Adams, Suite 1450	Chicago	IL	60606	312-372-6797	www.connectsite. com
Engineering	ASP Spatial Corp. offers a complete solution for the translation and repair of three-dimensional CAD models.	3Dshare.com	2425 55th St., Suite 100	Boulder	CO	80301	303-544-2900	www.spacial.com
Engineering	Design chain management infrastructure for on-line electronics design.	Toolwire, Inc.	1533 California Cr., Suite 110	Milpitas	CA	95035	408-935-6000	www.toolwire.com
Engineering	Virtually manages discrete manufacturing CAD databases.	Innova Engineering, Inc.	5 Park Plaza, Suite 150	Irvine	CA	92614	949-975-9965	www.Innova Engineering.com

Market	Hosted Service	Company Name	Address	City	State	Zip Code	Phone	URL
Engineering	Hosts integrated team environment for collaborative mechanical design and data management.	Alibre, Inc.	1701 N. Greenville Ave., Suite 702	Richardson	TX	75081	972-671-8492	www.Alibre.com
Manufacturing	Hosts order entry and tracking, inventory control and resource planning applications.	Automated Graphic Systems, Inc. (AGS)	4590 Graphics Dr.	White Plains	MD	20695	800-678-8760	www.ags.com
Manufacturing	Hosts Streamline application for managing factory operations and synchronizing with suppliers.	Factory Logic Software, Inc.	6850 Austin Center Blvd., Suite 320	Austin	TX	78731	512-502-0110	www.factorylogic.com
Manufacturing	ASP for mid-market manufacturers and distributors.	HotSamba	2355 S. Arlington Heights Rd., Suite 101	Arlington Heights	IL	60005	847-758-9202	www.hotsamba.com
Manufacturing	Hosts ICEPak solution based on Windchill from Parametric Technology Corporation.	NetIDEAS, Inc.	309 Fellowship Rd., Suite 104	Mt. Laurel	NJ	80540	800-859-4995	www.netideasinc.com
Finance	Hosts financial transactions on-line (e.g., for financial institutions originating and transacting home loans).	Dorado Corp.	1900 O'Farrell St., Suite 200	San Mateo	CA	94403	650-227-7300	www.dorado.com
Finance	Hosts financial data and content to Web portals and financial institutions.	Goinvest.com	30851 Agoura Rd., Suite 102	Agoura Hills	CA	91301	877-GOINVEST	www.goinvest.com

Market	Hosted Service	Company Name	Address	City	State	Zip Code	Phone	URL
Finance	Hosts investment management services for institutional investors worldwide.	Princeton Financial Systems, Inc.	600 College Rd. East	Princeton	NJ	08540	609-987-2400	www.pfs.com
Finance	Aggregates pricing, news, research, analysis, portfolio tools, and data into a hub for trade execution.	Tradebonds.com	4100 MacArthur Blvd., Suite 315	Newport Beach	CA	92660	949-852-6561	www.tradebonds.co
Finance	Hosts B2B buying, selling, and shopping environments for insurance and financial services organizations.	ChannelPoint	10155 Westmore Dr., Suite 210	Westminster	CO	80021	888-454-CHPT	www.channelpoint.com/
Finance	Hosts Quicken, ExpensAble, and other expense management applications.	Managemark Inc.	2 Corporate Plaza,Suite 275	Newport Beach	CA	92660	949-640-0701	www.managemark.com

Selected ASPs Offering Major Types of Hosted Applications

Type of Hosted Application	Hosted Service Description	Company Name	Address	City	State	Zip Code	Phone	URL
ERP	As part of Oracle Business Online E Business Suite	Oracle Corp.	500 Oracle Pkwy.	Redwood Shores	CA	94065	650-506-7000	www.oracle.com/online_services/components/index.html?content.html
ERP	As part of eCenter Application Hosting Solutions	PeopleSoft	4460 Hacienda Dr.	Pleasanton	CA	94588	925-225-3000	www.peoplesoft.com/en/us/products/eCenter.html
ERP	As part of Lawson Tone ASP Solutions	Lawson Software	380 St. Peter St.	St. Paul	MN	55102	651-767-7000	www.lawson.com/asppartners/index.html
ERP	Hosts SAP, Lawson, Oracle, Peoplesoft, etc.	Agilera (merged with Applicast)	9780 Mt. Pyramid Ct., Suite 300	Englewood	CO	80112	888-878-9828	www.agilera.com
ERP	As part of mySAP Hosted Solutions	SAP	SAP AG Walldorf Neurostrass 16	Walldorf	Germany	—	49-6227-7-47474	www.sap.com/solutions/hostsolutions/
CRM	As part of Intelligent Enterprise e-business suite	Corio, Inc.	959 Skyway Rd., Suite 100	San Carlos	CA	94070	650-232-3000	www.corio.com
CRM	FSP that hosts Siebel CRM	USInternet working	One USi Plaza	Annapolis	MD	21401-7478	800-839-4USI	www.usi.net
CRM	FSP that hosts Clarify CRM	Breakaway Solutions	100 River Rd. Suite 400, 4th Floor	Consho-hocken	PA	19428	800-925-7100	www.breakaway.com
CRM	Hosts CRM for small and mid-size financial services companies.	SEDONA Corp.	455 South Gulf Rd., Suite 300	King of Prussia	PA	19406	484-679-2200	www.sedonacorp.com

Type of Hosted Application	Hosted Service Description	Company Name	Address	City	State	Zip Code	Phone	URL
CRM	FSP that hosts its own INIT CRM.	Interliant Inc.	12 Gill St.	Woburn	MA	01801	781-756-3700	www.interliant.com
Content management	Hosts its own i-DOX services.	CyLex Systems Inc.	5201 Congress Ave., Suite 232	Boca Raton	FL	33487	561-998-7175	www.cylex.com
Content management	Hosts document management and does document conversion and storage.	DocMan Technologies	31300 Bainbridge Rd.	Cleveland	OH	44139	888-6DOCMAN	www.docmantech.com
Content management	Hosts its own iD solutions.	CinAPPS (ASP of CinCOM)	55 Merchant St.	Cincinnati	OH	45246	513-612-2769	info@cincom.com
Content management	Hosts document management and does conversion, storage.	Micro Media Imaging Systems	1979 Marcus Ave.	Lake Success	NY	11042	516-355-0300	www.dochost.com
Content management	Hosts document management and does conversion, storage	FilesOnThe Net (ASP of Critical Technologies)	100 Park Ave., Suite 500	Oklahoma City	OK	73102	405-235-8400	www.filesonthenet.com
e-commerce	Hosts horizontal e-procurement.	Integris	300 Concord Rd.	Billerica	MA	01821	800-789-1188	www.integers.com/managed.html
e-commerce	Builds and hosts applications based on Microsoft Site Server, Commerce Edition platform.	Imago ASP Systems	15550 W. 109th St.	Lenexa	KS	66219	913-888-8882	www.imagoasp.com
e-commerce	Hosts Commerce Edge e-commerce management application.	Ecommerce Systems Inc.	2005 Hamilton Ave., Suite 200	San Jose	CA	95125	888-995-3274	www.ecommercesys.com

Type of Hosted Application	Hosted Service Description	Company Name	Address	City	State	Zip Code	Phone	URL
e-commerce	Hosts value chain management, e-procurement, B2B network.	Ariba Inc.	1565 Charleston Rd.	Mountain View	CA	94043	650-930-6200	www.ariba.com
e-commerce	Offers end-to-end e-commerce through its ASP channel.	Open Market, Inc.	1 Wayside Rd.	Burlington	MA	01803	781-359-3000	www.openmarket.com
e-commerce	Hosts total e-commerce solution	Nexternal	785 Grand Ave., Suite 216	Carlsbad	CA	92008	800-914-6161	www.nexternal.com
e-commerce	Hosts marketing, electronic catalog, shopping cart, on-line payment and transaction support, order fulfillment, content management.	Agiliti	3025 Harbor Ln., Suite 400	Plymouth	MN	55447	612-918-2000	www.agiliti.com
e-commerce	Hosts Vation Integrated Platform, managed services, and professional e-marketing services. Includes e-commerce, personalization, e-CRM, customer interaction, content management.	Vation	111 West Monroe St., 23rd Floor, East Bldg.	Chicago	IL	60603	312-601-2100	www.vation.com
e-commerce	Hosts B2B e-procurement	Tradec	84 W. Santa Clara St., Suite 500	San Jose	CA	95113	408-291-2565	www.tradec.com

Type of Hosted Application	Hosted Service Description	Company Name	Address	City	State	Zip Code	Phone	URL
e-commerce	Hosts B2B procurement software and trading services for digital marketplaces.	Clarus Corp.	3970 Johns Creek Ct.	Suwanee	GA	30024	770-291-3900	www.claruscorp.com
e-commerce	FSP that hosts e-commerce, CRM, ERP, etc.	Surebridge	10 Maguire Rd., Suite 332	Lexington	MA	02421	781-372-3222	www.surebridge.com
e-commerce	Hosts revenue chain management to mobile devices.	Daleen Technolo-gies, Inc.	1750 Clint Moore Rd.	Boca Raton	FL	33487	561-999-8000	www.daleen.com
e-commerce	Hosts e-business platform and modules for accounting, CRM, etc.	Maestro Commerce, Inc.	800 Quail Ridge Dr.	Westmont	IL	60559	630-455-6300	www.maestrocommerce.com
e-commerce	Hosts Vignette e-business application.	Interpath Communi-cations	PO Box 13961	Research Triangle Park	NC	27709-3961	919-253-6000	www.interpath.net
Sales automation	Hosts Act! 2000 from Interact Commerce Corp.	EServer, Inc.	1081 Camino del Rio South, Suite 212	San Diego	CA		619-294-5903	www.eserver.com
Sales automation	Infrastructure service provider that hosts Goldmine and Symantec ACT 2000 through ASP partners.	Crossrun (was thinter.net)	3031 Tisch Way, Floor M	San Jose	CA	92108	408-248-2500	www.crossrun.com
Sales automation	Hosts own sales force automation application.	Khameleon Software	13830 58th St. North, Suite 401	Clearwater	FL	33760	727-539-1077	www.khameleonsoftware.com

Type of Hosted Application	Hosted Service Description	Company Name	Address	City	State	Zip Code	Phone	URL
Sales automation	Hosts own sales automation application with contact management, CRM, wireless, etc.	XSellsys	31831 Camino Capistrano, Suite 100	San Juan Capistrano	GA	92675	949-47-9648	www.xsellsys.com
Office productivity	Hosts Microsoft Office 2000 Developers Edition.	Hostwindows	1011 Brookside Rd.	Allentown	PA	18106	888-299-4552	www.hostwindow.com
Office productivity	Hosts Lotus Smartsuite Millenium 9.5.	ASP Computer Systems Corp.	3516 Cadieux	Detroit	MI	48224	313-884-8444	www.ASPComputer Systems.com
Office productivity	Hosts Sun MicroSystems' StarOffice Application Suite	InsynQ	1101 Broadway Plaza	Tacoma	WA	98402	253-284-2000	www.insynq.com
Office productivity	Hosts WordPerfect Office 2000 from Corel	Network Technology Group	4041 Essen Ln., Suite 100	Baton Rouge	LA	70809	225-214-3800	www.ntg.com
Data warehousing	Hosts enterprise business intelligence with ASP partner, PlanetEBI, to complement existing ERP systems.	erp.com	4909 Murphy Canyon Rd., Suite 120	San Diego	CA	92123	858-707-7522	www.erp.com
Data warehousing	Hosts WebIntelligence from Business Objects.	Pasporte Limited (European ASP)	ESPS House London Rd.	Bagshot	Surrey United Kingdom	—	00-44-1276-450-455	www.pasporte.com
Collaboration	Hosts collaboration technology for teams and organizations of all types and sizes.	eProject. com	100 West Harrison North Tower, Suite 400	Seattle	WA	98119	206-341-9117	www.eproject.com

Type of Hosted Application	Hosted Service Description	Company Name	Address	City	State	Zip Code	Phone	URL
Collaboration	Lotus Business Partner hosting workflow.	Business Oriented Software Solutions Inc. (BOSS Inc.)	3040 Holcomb Bridge Rd., Suite D2	Norcross	GA	30071	770-447-4787	www.boss-solutions.com
Collaboration	Hosts collaboration and ad hoc workflow.	B2Bscene (ASP of Open Text, Inc.)	175 Columbia St., Suite 109	West Waterloo	Ontario, Canada	—	519-888-7111	www.b2bscene.com
Collaboration	UK ASP hosts that knowledge management and workflow for financial services.	IntelliFlo, PLC	First Floor, Tuition House	Wimbledon	London SW19 4DS United Kingdom	—	44-020-8971-0350	www.intelliflo.com
Collaboration	Hosts workflow and imaging for financial services.	Bridium	154 Technology Pkwy., Suite 100	Norcross	GA	30092	866-448-1776	www.bridium.com
Messaging	Hosts e-mail to corporate clients and ASPs, ISPs, and others.	Global Messaging Solutions Inc. (GMSI)	10801 Mastin, Suite 610	Overland Park	KS	66210-1658	913-338-3000	www.gmsi1.com
Messaging	Hosts Microsoft Exchange and Novell Groupwise.	EasyLink Services Corp.	399 Thornall St.	Edison	NJ	08837	732-906-1113	www.easylink.com

Defining Your Low-Level ASP Requirements

To define what they require from an ASP, technical personnel on your buying team should ask themselves the following questions regarding each chapter:

Chapter Two
The ASP Coalition—No Single Vendor Can Do It All

1. Does the ASP's hardware support *massive* scaling?
2. Does the ASP's network have sufficient capacity?
3. Is the ASP's network scalable enough for your requirements?
4. Are you paying for network capacity you don't need?
5. Do you need an expensive, high-end ASP with multiple data centers and multiple major network carriers?
6. Do you need a less-expensive mid-range ASP with mid-size network carriers and a regional focus?
7. Do you need an even less-expensive small ASP with smaller networks and a very defined target customer?
8. Do you need thin or thick client software?
9. Are the ASP's enterprise applications scalable enough for your requirements?
10. Do you prefer dealing with a TBA that knows you and your market, and offers hosted services using ASP partners "under the covers"?
11. Do you need a hosted application that is customized to your unique business processes?
12. Should you use an ASP that can customize the hosted application later because your business processes will change as you grow rapidly or merge with other companies?

13. Should you use an ASP that can convert the hosted application to an installed solution later on?
14. Do you need an ASP that can perform accelerated deployment?
15. Do you need to outsource IT or executive personnel from your ASP?
16. Do you need an ASP that can provide bonus functionality like leased storage or especially high data security?

Chapter Three
The ASP Hardware Platform

17. Have you visited the ASP's data center and inspected how the hardware for your hosted solution is provisioned, managed, and maintained?
18. Is the hardware sufficiently overprovisioned to support your requirements?
19. Do you prefer that ASP use dedicated server provisioning?
20. Can you afford the increasing equipment and management costs of dedicated provisioning as the ASP scales your servers over time?
21. Do you prefer that ASP use shared provisioning?
22. With shared provisioning, can you live with the trade-off between lower price and possible risks like compromised data availability?
23. Are stand-alone servers at the ASP sufficient for your data access requirements?
24. Do you need the faster and more flexible data access of clustered servers?
25. Do you need intelligent load balancing by the ASP to distribute user requests more efficiently to appropriate servers?
26. Do you need Web server caching from the ASP so your users can access certain Web content faster?
27. Do you need "capacity-on-demand" server deployment strategies so the ASP can provision servers especially fast for new users?
28. What "capacity-on-demand" strategies are best for your requirements? Redundant chips? Servers in waiting? Anything else?
29. Will the ASP need to upgrade servers by expanding I/O and memory after installation?
30. Can the ASP upgrade the servers without interrupting system operations?
31. With which of your legacy components (such as different clients, operating systems, databases, storage devices, and wireless devices) will the ASP's servers need to interoperate?

32. Can the ASP's servers accommodate all your interoperability requirements?

33. Will your ASP need to deploy different and isolated server configurations, for instance, to keep less-stable applications from corrupting mission-critical ones?

Chapter Four
The Data Center

34. Have you visited the ASP's data center?

35. In general, are you comfortable with the ASP's approach to major data center issues like backup, disasterproofing, and security?

36. With what practices at the data center are you not comfortable?

37. Will the ASP modify them to suit your needs?

38. What hours of live data center staff "availability" will you require from the ASP?

39. What level of data center staff "responsiveness" (interval between customer query and provider response) will you require from the ASP?

40. Does the ASP need to field your user queries in "real time" by dedicating staff to take your phone calls?

41. Can the ASP field your user queries in "nonreal time"? You'll leave inquiries in staff's voice mailboxes, contact them by e-mail, and so on.

42. If you require real-time support, do you need it for all your applications and components, or can you support just mission-critical ones to save money?

43. Is the ASP's standard backup and recovery plan (list of backup procedures and time intervals) sufficient for your requirements?

44. Does the ASP back up all customer data to an independent storage site at least daily?

45. If you need real-time backup (mirroring) for some applications and less-frequent backup for others, can the ASP meet your requirements?

46. Can the ASP meet your RTOs for recovering your various applications and data?

47. If the ASP can't meet your RTOs, will you have to pay the ASP extra to have them met?

48. Does the ASP keep backed-up data on-site in a fireproof vault?

49. Does the ASP have to store backed-up data manually at an alternate data center that's off the primary data center's power grid? Can you tolerate the delay in manually transferring data such a distance?

50. Does the ASP have to use electronic vaulting to back up data to an off-site facility? Can you afford the higher cost of this faster data transfer?

51. If the ASP provides electronic vaulting services, does it maintain a log of that backup activity?

52. Does the ASP's disaster recovery plan document standard policies and each employee's specific responsibilities in the backup and recovery procedure?

53. Does the ASP's disaster recovery plan indicate how often the ASP trains its employees in disaster recovery procedures?

54. Does the ASP update its disaster recovery plans at least twice a year after each disaster recovery testing phase?

55. Does the ASP update its disaster recovery plans when it loses, gains, or changes personnel within its operation?

56. Does the ASP update its disaster recovery plans when it adds new hosted applications?

57. Does the ASP update its disaster recovery plans when it changes corporate locations?

58. Does the ASP update its disaster recovery plans when it makes a major hardware or software purchase such as a SAN?

59. Do you require that the ASP make monthly or quarterly disaster recovery plan updates?

60. Does the ASP adhere to best practices by performing three types of disaster recovery plan testing—at least alternate site, automated, and tabletop or walkthrough tests?

61. Will you accept less than three types of disaster recovery tests from the ASP for less cost? For example, only one or two disaster recovery tests at least twice a year?

62. Does the ASP let you participate directly in at least one disaster recovery test per year?

63. Do you require simulation disaster recovery testing from the ASP?

64. Is the ASP granting you two eight-hour days of disaster recovery testing per year performed on-site at the ASP?

65. Will the ASP let you purchase more disaster recovery testing time if you request it?

66. How is the ASP affected by the disaster recovery plans of its partners, like its infrastructure service provider? Are you comfortable that the arrangement will not cause service disruption for you?

67. Does the ASP's data center have the HVAC required to support its IT operation?

68. Does the ASP's data center have raised floors for ventilation and wiring security in any room housing IT equipment?

69. Does the ASP use waterless fire suppression and has it constructed separate fire zones and special cabinets to contain fires within a single building unit?

70. Has the ASP hardened and stormproofed the data center facility and installed special cabinets with internal seismic bracing to protect against earthquakes?

71. Does the ASP store your servers and other colocated equipment in the same data center room, cabinets, or racks as other customers' equipment? If so, are unauthorized parties denied unsupervised physical access to those areas?

Chapter Five
The ASP Network

72. Can the ASP provide basic network availability? In other words, is the network susceptible to unscheduled downtimes long enough to jeopardize your business?

73. What are the ASP's standard hours of network service with scheduled down periods for maintenance and other activities?

74. Can the ASP's network accommodate your peak capacity requirements without breaking your budget?

75. How long do you have to wait for the ASP to provide additional network capacity?

76. If you require it, can the ASP provide different qualities of service for varying numbers of users, intensity of use, periods of use, and so on?

77. Is the ASP's data center LAN-to-WAN network infrastructure redundant and robust enough to service you and the ASP's other customers without performance degradation?

78. Does the way the ASP distributes and load balances traffic among the servers within its data centers meet your requirements?

79. Does the way the ASP distributes and load balances traffic among geographically dispersed data centers meet your requirements?

80. If the ASP leases its WAN from a network service provider, who is responsible for network problems that occur from the router nearest the ASP to the ASP's servers?

81. Can the ASP provide the type of secure broadband network that best suits your requirements (leased lines for point-to-point connectivity, privately owned WAN, or a shared, leased VPN for more pervasive connectivity)?

82. If you require, can your ASP provide Frame Relay (which can carry only voice and data, only in WANs, and at speeds from 56 Kbps to 2.048 Mbps)?

83. If you'll use Frame Relay and prefer permanent virtual circuits (which make routing decisions when a connection is created for greater throughput but cannot perform dynamic routing to avoid congestion), can the ASP provide them?

84. If you'll use Frame Relay but prefer switched virtual circuits (which make routing decisions en route and achieve faster throughput with dynamic routing to avoid congestion), can your ASP provide them? And at what additional cost?

85. If you require, can your ASP provide ATM (which transmits voice, data, and video over all network types; offers quality of service; and achieves the fastest data speeds possible)? And at what additional cost?

86. To meet your requirements, how precise and complex does the ASP's traffic management need to be?

87. Will the ASP's ATM/Frame Relay interworking strategy guarantee the throughput you need at the cost you require?

88. In the longer term, if your capacity requirements dictate migrating to a more powerful networking protocol, will the ASP do it? And at what cost?

89. If the density, amount, or dependability of your traffic requires the ASP use WDM or DWDM in its fiber-optic network, will the ASP deploy it? And at what cost?

90. Can the ASP make the WAN-to-LAN network infrastructure nearest you redundant and robust enough to support your needs without performance degradation?

91. Will the ASP WAN link to your on-site LANs require the ASP to upgrade or manage your LANs differently than you have been managing them? At what cost?

92. If the ASP leases its WAN from a network service provider, who is responsible for network problems that occur from the router to the servers nearest you?

93. If you require, will the ASP provide ISDN connections?

94. If you require, will the ASP provide ADSL or ADSL Lite connections?

95. How long will the ASP need to provision ADSL or ADSL Lite?

96 If you require, will the ASP provide cable modem connections?

97. What throughput guarantees will the ASP offer for cable modem connections?

98. If you require wireless network service, will the ASP provide it?

99. By what means will the ASP provide wireless connectivity? A WASP?

100. What service guarantees will the ASP offer to compensate for typical wireless performance problems?

101. Will the ASP's wireless platform be viable through the end of your SLA contract and be interoperable, standardized, and supported by a provider that is still in business?

102. Will the ASP's wireless platform be viable in three to five years?

103. Will the ASP's wireless service require you to dedicate or hire staff to manage wireless users?

104. If you have to switch to another wireless platform at the conclusion of your SLA contract, can you afford the time and money to retrain your administrators and users?

105. Is the ASP's IP network sufficient to support your IP traffic without degradation of performance?

106. Will the ASP's IP network still be sufficient to support your IP traffic without degradation of performance in three to five years?

Chapter Six
Varieties of ASP

107. Will the ASP's pedigree strengthen or weaken the total service package it's able to offer you?

108. Will the ASP's partners strengthen or weaken the total service package it's able to offer you?

109. Will the ASP's unique combination of technology strengthen or weaken the total service package it's able to offer you?

110. Will the way the ASP differentiates itself through aspects of customer service strengthen or weaken the total service package it's able to offer you?

111. Is the ASP's industry acronym, like FSP, consistent with the functional capabilities it can offer?

112. If it isn't, does the ASP understand the ASP market?

113. If the ASP misunderstands the market, will that undermine its services to you?

114. If you choose a pure-play ASP, can it deliver robust enough hosted applications quickly and affordably enough to meet your requirements?

115. If you choose a pure-play ASP, can you do without value-added services?

116. If you choose an FSP instead of a pure-play ASP, which of its value-added services convince you that an FSP-type provider is your best alternative?

117. If you choose an FSP, can you afford the higher total fees?

118. Is the large VAR ASP partnered or competing with its ISVs in the same vertical markets?

119. If it's competing with its ISVs in the same vertical markets, does it have the resources to withstand competition from the ISVs in the long term?

120. Will the fact that the large VAR is competing with its ISVs help or hurt you? Will the VAR offer lower prices? Will it spend too much on marketing and have to raise prices? Will it cut back on customer service to reduce costs?

121. Does the ISV of the large VAR ASP's ISV have a history of selling direct in the VAR's territory without informing the VAR?

122. If so, will this undermine the ISV/VAR relationship later on and cause disruption or termination of your hosted service?

123. Does the small VAR ASP resell its ISVs' hosted services or sell its own?

124. If the small VAR sells its own hosted services, does it have the financial resources to survive competition so as not to disrupt or terminate your service?

125. Is the small VAR ASP selling defensively to keep other ASPs from poaching existing customers? If so, with that defensive strategy is the small VAR ASP paying enough attention to customer service?

126. Who provides the small VAR ASP's customer service and technical support? If it's not the small VAR, then will you have to deal with multiple partners for different services?

127. Is the small VAR ASP's technology current and adequate to support your requirements?

128. Is the large or small VAR ASP trying to induce you to buy other professional services like consulting and integration you don't need?

129. Does the size of your service bureau ASP and its legacy relationship with its ISVs strengthen or weaken its ability to address your service requirements?

130. Does the large service bureau ASP partner or compete with its ISVs?

131. Is the large service bureau leasing hosted services downmarket to SMBs, to its traditional high-end customers, or to both?

132. Does the large service bureau's customer focus help or hurt the type and cost of your hosted services?

133. Is the large service bureau a regional infrastructure service provider for its ISVs?

134. If the large service bureau is a regional infrastructure provider for its ISVs, who provides customer service for the ISVs' hosted services?

135. If your large service bureau ASP is competing with its ISVs for hosting customers, will fallout between the ASP and ISVs disrupt or terminate your hosted services in the future?

136. If you sense your smaller service bureau ASP most desires the recurring revenue streams of hosted services to meet its cash flow requirements, does that help you in negotiating an SLA?

137. If your small service bureau ASP has launched hosted services not provided by an ISV, does it have the financial resources to withstand competition and not disrupt or terminate your hosted services in the future?

138. If your small service bureau ASP has launched hosted services not provided by an ISV, can it offer you adequate customer service?

139 Is your small service bureau ASP trying to lease hosted services upmarket, whereas it sold its traditional installed services to the mid market?

140. If you are a high-end customer, the small service bureau may charge you less than another ASP, but can it fully satisfy your requirements?

141. Can your large SI ASP deliver accelerated deployment for hosted solutions at fixed prices and guaranteed deadlines?

142. Is your large SI ASP's customer service good enough that it outweighs any shortcomings the ASP may have in delivering solutions at fixed prices and guaranteed deadlines?

143. Does your mid-size SI ASP have the technological scale you require?

144. Does your mid-size SI ASP have the financial resources to withstand competition and not disrupt or terminate your service in the future?

145. If a small SI ASP does not resell an ISV's hosted services, does it offer customer service you require?

146. If a small SI ASP does not resell an ISV's hosted services, does it have the financial depth to withstand competition and not disrupt or terminate your services in the future?

147. If your ISV ASP launched its own ASP program, does it help you or hurt you that it is using its best VARs to resell and deploy hosted services?

148. If your ISV ASP launched its own ASP program, does it help you or hurt you that it is trying to win margins from some VARs by offering hosted services directly?

149. If your ISV ASP launched its own ASP program, could you get a better hosting deal on the same application service from one of its VARs?

150. If you lease hosted services within an ASP ecosystem, does it have a critical mass of demographically appropriate participants willing to buy goods and services from vendors virtually advertising them to the community? In other words, does the ecosystem have the customers needed to survive long term?

Chapter Seven
Security Issues for ASPs

151. How much time and money are you willing to invest in the level of security you think you need from an ASP?

152. How do you prioritize these major data security concerns your ASP must address: theft of data, compromises of confidentiality, integrity or availability of data, or interruption of service?

153. If a high priority is guarding against theft of data, how do you want your ASP to do it? Firewalls? Encryption? Anything else?

154. If a high priority is guarding against compromises of confidentiality, how do you want your ASP to do it? Access control and rights and privileges? Encryption? Anything else?

155. If a high priority is preserving data integrity, how do you want your ASP to do it? Checksums? Anything else?

156. If a high priority is ensuring availability of data, how do you want your ASP to do it? Antivirus software? Anything else?

157. If a high priority is preventing interruption or denial of service, how do you want your ASP to do it?

158. How has the ASP demonstrated to you that security is an ongoing process in its operation?

159. How have you performed due diligence on the ASP to guarantee the security of your data?

160. In what situations and for which applications will you need authentication from your ASP? Passwords for users accessing IT resources? Authenticating the peer for applications that interact with each other? Any others?

161. After what time interval does the ASP time out computing sessions for your on-site and remote users?

162. In what situations and for which applications will you need encryption?

163. Do you need highly secure encryption that comes in hardware or less-secure encryption that comes in software?

164. Do you need proprietary or nonproprietary encryption?

165. If nonproprietary, do you need highly secure encryption like TripleDES? Or less-secure encryption like DES?

166. How often does the ASP change encryption keys so hackers have to keep decrypting new keys to break into its systems?

167. Do you send and receive enough e-mail attachments that your ASP should install scanning software in a server located between the ASP firewall and the application to protect against viruses?

168. How will your ASP protect your data against Trojan horses?

169. How will the ASP protect your data against "man-in-the-middle" security breaches? Authenticating the sender and receiver? Using secure network protocols? Anything else?

170. Will the ASP run intrusion detection software to determine whether anyone is trying to gain unauthorized access to your data?

171. What are the ASP's policies governing its use of intrusion detection software? For instance, does it regularly review the logs of system activity generated by the intrusion detection software to spot patterns of sniffing?

172. Does the ASP use nonrepudiation to ensure confidentiality and authentication?

173. Does the ASP use nonrepudiation for per-click price models to prove that your users actually used a service or, if an impersonator uses services for which you will be charged, to substantiate the impersonation?

174. Does the ASP use audit and accounting systems for monitoring its systems and maintaining records of system and user activity?

175. How is the ASP securing your data in places (like dial-up connections) other than the networks that its firewalls screen?

176. Do you need proxy servers to protect the real addresses of your data resources or to cache data that's frequently accessed by your users?

177. Do you prefer the ASP use virtual vaults, virtual drives, or different encryption keys to segment your data from other customers or from users in different departments in your organization?

178. What are the ASP's security policies?

179. Are the ASP's security policies documented?

180. If any policies are not documented, how will the ASP assure you the policies will be enforced?

181. Does the ASP maintain detailed security logs?

182. Has the ASP had background checks performed on its personnel?

183. Does the ASP sufficiently control access to all its facilities, like data centers?

184. Does the ASP staff facility entrances?

185. Does the ASP require anyone entering its facilities to sign in?

186. Does the ASP use a biometric recognition system at its facilities to identify authorized parties?

187. Does the ASP prevent access to or provide escorts through data center areas housing customer servers and other equipment?

188. If not, what precautions does the ASP use to secure these areas from unauthorized personnel?

189. Are the ASP's IT areas separate from lobbies and offices?

190. If the ASP's IT area houses more than one customer's equipment, is each customer's equipment locked in its own cage or other space that's accessible only to designated ASP and customer employees?

191. Does the ASP deploy security personnel on the facility grounds?

192. Does the ASP use automated security devices like motion detectors and video monitors to detect intruders both in the data center and on the surrounding perimeter where it keeps critical contingency equipment like backup generators?

193. Does the ASP store backup copies of your data at least on tape and house it at an off-site location secure from unauthorized personnel?

194. Is that storage location geographically far enough away that the backed-up data won't be affected by a local disaster?

195. Does your ASP need a vulnerability assessment before you do business with it?

196. Do you need to conduct a security audit to ensure that the ASP has taken sufficient steps to correct any vulnerabilities?

197. Do you need to conduct a special security audit to do business in a particular market like health care or for some other reason?

198. Would you prefer that an outside party remotely monitor all the ASPs facilities like data centers and security equipment like firewalls?

199. Would you prefer an outside party perform intrusion detection to alert the ASP if unauthorized parties may be attempting to access its systems?

200. Would you prefer that an outside party perform incident response to security breaches at the ASP?

201. Would you prefer that an outside party also recommend and implement corrective measures for security breaches at the ASP?

202. Would you prefer that an outside party gather and archive evidence associated with security breaches so it can be presented in court as needed for suits, criminal proceedings, and other matters?

203. Would you prefer that an outside party perform background checks on the ASP's personnel?

204. Could any of the tasks mentioned in this section be done better or less expensively if you used an MSecP rather than, or in addition to, an ASP?

Chapter Eight
ASP Service Level Agreements

205. Which ASP partner is responsible for your network SLA?

206. With which supporting providers like MSPs or MSecPs does the ASP have hosting SLAs?

207. Which ASP partner is responsible for you application SLA?

208. What conditions have you requested in your Application SLA to cover poor application performance resulting from poor performance of the hardware, supporting software, or network?

209. Do these "background" SLAs guarantee performance of the ASP's component services well enough for the ASP to make good on the guarantees it's offering you in its "end-to-end" SLA?

210. If you have engaged a third party like an MSP to monitor the ASP's performance or security, how will you negotiate with the ASP if it does not agree with the outside party's findings?

211. Should you try to cover this contingency in the end-to-end SLA with the ASP?

212. What is a percentage of network availability you will need from your ASP?

213. Do you need more availability for particular applications or parts of the network like busy Web sites?

214. What range of network throughput, including burst speeds, do you require from your ASP?

215. What redundant network elements will you require from the ASP?

216. How quickly do you need those backup elements to take over network operation from the primary elements?

217. What network equipment are you specifying the ASP use?

218. Do you require that the ASP upgrade any equipment before the end of your contract? If so, what equipment and by what date?

219. If you expect to add users or applications, or otherwise make greater demands on the ASP's network, how scalable must the ASP's network be to accommodate them?

220. Are the ASP's network peering arrangements sufficient to accommodate greater geographical reach or enough alternate failover transmission routes throughout your contract?

221. What is the maximum network delay you will accept from your ASP?

222. Do you require different levels of delay for real-time and nonreal-time applications?

223. If you do, what are those different levels of delay?

224. By what means will the ASP prove it's met your network service-level guarantees?

225. What specific network performance metrics will you require that the ASP monitor and report?

226. How often will the ASP have to submit network performance reports to you?

227. How long will you allow the ASP for initial network installation and subsequent equipment upgrades?

228. During what time periods during the day and week do you require network technical support from the ASP?

229. How many technical support agents do you require the ASP have on duty at different times?

230. What type of agents do you need at these times? Management? Database experts?

231. What response time for network problem resolution is the ASP guaranteeing you?

232. Can you get by with fewer agents at slow times for a lower fee?

233. What planned outage periods does the ASP guarantee for routine maintenance and periodic upgrades?

234. What network capabilities will the ASP still offer you during the planned outages?

235. What response times is the ASP guaranteeing you for unplanned outages to resolve unforeseen network problems?

236. What percentage of application availability do you require from the ASP?

237. If you are leasing multiple applications, will you require different availability for different applications?

238. What application performance (transactions per second, keystroke response time, database response time, and so on) do you require from your ASP?

239. If you are leasing multiple applications, will you require different performance guarantees for different applications?

240. If so, what are those different performance guarantees?

241. For failover, what redundant application elements are you requiring from your ASP?

242. Do you require that the ASP replicate redundant application elements on servers at different data centers on different geographical power grids?

243. If so, and the ASP does not offer this level of redundancy as standard procedure, will the ASP do it? How much will it cost?

244. What application platform (models and vendors of operating systems, middleware, and so on) do you require that the ASP uses?

245. What value-added components (like CD creation utilities for generation of reports on CD) do you require your ASP to provide?

246. How scalable do you require the ASP's servers to be throughout the length of the contract?

247. To what extent can your administrators and users manage and customize application elements, like graphical user interfaces for different departments?

248. Will the ASP or a supporting provider monitor your application performance?

249. What application performance metrics will they monitor?

250. What performance measurements does the ASP let you view and when?

251. By what means will the ASP prove it's met its application service-level guarantees to you?

252. What application performance parameters will the ASP monitor and report to you?

253. How often will the ASP provide those reports?

254. How long are you allowing the ASP for the initial application installation period?

255. How long are you allowing the ASP for provisioning new users?

256. What is the extent of the ASP's application technical support for you?

257. What are the daily and weekly time periods during which application technical support is available from the ASP?

258. How many agents do you require in the call center at these times?

259. What type of personnel do you require in the call center at these times? Management? Database expert?

260. What are the planned outages the ASP has specified when an application will be down for routine maintenance and periodic upgrades?

261. What application capabilities will the ASP still offer during the planned outages?

262. What is the ASP's response time to resolve unforeseen application problems during unplanned outages?

263. How will the ASP rebate you if it fails to meet any SLA?

264. If you require other penalties than free service for a certain period, have you stated them in the rebate condition of the appropriate SLA?

265. If the ASP rebates you relatively, based on the scale of a system or network that the SLA failure affected, how does the ASP measure it? Is it sufficient for your requirements?

266. Is the length of your SLA contract comfortable for you?

Chapter Nine
ASP Pricing Models

267. If you will do a high volume of activity with your ASP, is a flat/flat rate the best one for you? If not, what type of rate is better for you?

268. If you have many users whose activity varies, is a flat/tiered rate the best one for you? If not, what type of rate is better for you?

269. If your number of users tends to grow, is a flat/tiered rate the best one for you? If not, what type of rate is best for you?

270. If you want discounts for doing more business with the ASP, is a variable/tiered rate the best one for you? If not, what type of rate is best for you?

271. If you are a smaller customer with moderate usage, is a per-click rate the best one for you? If not, what type of rate is best for you?

272. If your usage fluctuates wildly over different billing periods, is a per-click rate the best one for you? If not, what type of rate is best for you?

273. If there is an optimal combination of different ASP pricing models that best suits you, what is it? Can your ASP charge you that way?

274. How does your ASP charge you for storage in addition to the base fees? How much does it cost?

275. How much is the ASP's one-time "setup fee" for preparing its general ASP infrastructure to accommodate your requirements?

276. What services, equipment, and so forth, do you get for the ASP's setup fee?

277. If the ASP can charge tiered fees (such as Silver, Gold, and Platinum) for different levels of security, different guaranteed network throughput, and so on, which tier is appropriate for your budget?

278. If the ASP's pricing model is too different from the way you are used to being charged for software, can you live with it?

279. If the ASP's pricing model is too complex, do you suspect the ASP is hiding fees or trying to make it difficult for you to comparison shop?

280. Is the ASP's pricing model too variable for you to budget for accurately?

281. If you are comparison shopping for hosted and value-added services from different ASPs, do the fees they charge for various services (for example, technical support) cover the same activities (for example, manned 24/7 technical support with an 800 number)?

282. If you are comparison shopping for hosted and value-added services from different ASPs, is it productive to differentiate providers according the total cost of the entire ASP package each is offering?

283. If you are comparison shopping for hosted and value-added services from different ASPs and two or more seem comparable, what intangible factors (like the ASP's approach to customer service) might make you commit to one over the others?

Chapter Ten
ASP Customer Service and Technical Support

284. ASP customer support is complex, but the ASP should not pass on to you the problems that come with complexity. Is it?

285. If your ASP is or was a small service bureau or VAR, is its customer service comparable with another ASP with similar pricing and services?

286. If your ASP is or was a small service bureau or VAR, does its narrow market/application focus satisfactorily preclude complex customer service?

287. Is the ASP's Web site or sales representative clearly conveying information about pricing and deployment time?

288. Is the ASP's standard SLA acceptable to you?

289. Will the ASP let you amend its standard SLA? If so, how much will it charge for the service?

290. What specific functionality, data, and tasks does the ASP include in the "provisioning" phase before deploying the hosted application? Is this satisfactory to you?

291. If the hosted application requires customization, how long does the ASP estimate it will take? What will the ASP charge for it?

292. What is the number, type, and use of computers to be deployed in the system?

293. What will the IT architecture of the hosted solution be? Is it satisfactory to you?

294. How much disk space does the hosted solution require on all involved computers?

295. How much storage capacity does the hosted solution require on all storage devices?

296. How much server and rack "headroom" will you require from the ASP over the life of the contract? Can the ASP provide it?

297. What value-added system architecture (like clustered servers) will you require the ASP to create? Can the ASP create them?

298. What activities does the ASP include in the platform preparation phase? Are they satisfactory to you?

299. What client software does the ASP have to load on your on-site desktops?

300. If you'll use thin clients, what communication protocol does the ASP have to load on your on-site desktops?

301. If you're using a PC software-based VPN, what VPN security software does the ASP have to load on the on-site desktops?

302. If the ASP will remotely manage the application, what software does the ASP have to load on the on-site desktops?

303. If you require the ASP to integrate your legacy applications with the hosted applications, how much time and money does the ASP estimate it will take?

304. How tightly integrated do you want your mission-critical applications with the hosted applications? Can the ASP accomplish it?

305. What input do you require on the ASP's network policies? Will the ASP allow it?

306. What specific policies will the ASP need to create to cover all the rights, resources, and periods of access for the users of your hosted applications? Will the ASP create them?

307. Do you require that the ASP permit your IT staff some administration authority like adding new users? Will the ASP permit it?

308. Will you require data transfer or data conversion between your legacy applications and the hosted application?

309. Who will do the data conversion? What will it cost?

310. Is the ASP's testing platform adequate to configure and customize your hosted application and then run it through various user scenarios to see if it can hold up to the performance guarantees of your SLA? If not, will the ASP upgrade it?

311. Are there specific or unusual user scenarios in which the ASP will have to test your hosted application? Will the ASP run them?

312. Do the ASP's training course materials and presentations cover all functionality, tasks, and policies uniquely created by your hosted application? If not, will the ASP change the materials to cover them?

313. Does the ASP use standard materials from the software vendor of the application to train hosted application users? Is this acceptable to you?

314. Does the ASP use train-the-trainer strategies to cut training costs, shorten its period of involvement with your users, and ensure that ongoing training occurs after the initial sessions?

315. If it does not use train-the-trainer strategies, are you paying too much for training?

316. What staff in your organization will you designate to be trained as trainers by the ASP?

317. Will you be able to conduct all necessary legitimate business when the ASP goes "live" with your hosted application?

318. How much of the cost for maintenance and upgrades does the ASP include in the leasing fee? Is it satisfactory to you?

319. Will the ASP take sufficient change management measures to ensure that upgrades do not unsatisfactorily interrupt your users' work?

320. Does the ASP routinely upgrade client software on-site as well as the operating systems on the servers in the data center? If not, what does the ASP routinely upgrade?

321. Does the ASP locate and install or develop patches for all software bugs in its vendor's software? If not, how does it address these problems?

322. If so, how long do you have to wait for a fix after you request it from the ASP?

323. Does the ASP keep at your reasonable disposal a database administrator certified on the databases used by the hosted application?

324. If not, do you need to request that a database expert be provided?

325. Will the ASP offer less-frequent backup intervals for lower fees?

326. Is the ASP's monitoring and reporting proactive? If not, why not?

327. Will the ASP maintain your own value-added equipment integral to the hosted application's performance? If so, what is the charge?

328. Do the reports that corroborate SLA performance guarantees that the ASP submits to you contain data that's relevant to your typical production work periods?

329. Do those reports analyze all your relevant performance trends?

330. Can you contact the ASP's support call center in multiple ways like phone, fax, and e-mail?

331. Can you only contact the ASP's call center via phone calls to live agents? Is this sufficient for you?

332. Can the ASP's call center agents access your service history, including all services you are leasing, all bills and payments you've made since serv-

ices were turned on, and all previous support interactions? If not, what data can they access? Is the data sufficient?

333. Does the ASP provide call center agents copies of questions that customers commonly ask, and suitable answers and actions for solving common problems?

334. Does the ASP's call center keep logs of how past problems were escalated from agents to experts, and record the actions taken at each stage of escalation?

335. If the ASP uses multiple call centers or subcontracts some of its support to an outside company, can you call one toll-free number and quickly reach the appropriate personnel at all centers?

336. Does the ASP place FAQs and responses, and other information on its Web sites so your users can conduct their own self-service for low-level inquiries?

337. If the ASP lets you add, delete, and change users, and otherwise mutually administer the application, does it offer some method by which you can do so remotely from your premises? If not, do you require one?

338. For rebates and other areas of negotiation, does your ASP assign one representative who acts as the primary liaison between you and the ASP?

339. Does the ASP offer e-business billing practices like electronic bill presentment and payment and electronic funds transfer? If not, do you require them?

340. Will the ASP bill each of your departments using different hosted applications with separate statements?

341. For usage-based billing, does the ASP use monitoring equipment tied to specific pieces of equipment like scanners, databases, and so on?

342. For usage-based billing, can the ASP track multiple usage metrics for multiple pieces of equipment like different types of servers and storage devices?

343. For usage-based billing, can the ASP identify the user or department that initiated an activity?

344. When the hosted application is bundled with other hosted applications or integrated with your legacy applications, can the ASP track the interrelated activities of multiple applications where certain actions initiate other actions for which you're billed?

345. If certain IT personnel worked with your IT staff to customize the hosted application, will the ASP permit one or more of that group to do ongoing troubleshooting for you?

346. Will the ASP designate specific call center agents, customer account managers, and other liaisons to deal consistently with you?

347. Does the ASP use integrated telephony tools to enable customer service personnel to serve you better?

348 Does the ASP quantify its staff's customer service activities?

349. Does it offer bonuses to individuals who excel in customer service, assign them to the busiest shifts in the call center, and use them to train less adept agents?

350. Are there any specific service goals (number of rings before agents answer a call, number of handoffs they make to other experts, number of callbacks they make to customers, and so on) you want entered in the technical support conditions of your SLA?

351. Does the ASP use its best call center agents on its busiest technical support shifts?

352. Does the ASP use more call center agents on its busiest technical support shifts?

353. Does the ASP maintain records of your technical support behavior over time so it can better predict your busy periods and adequately plan for them?

354. Does the ASP offer tiered customer service plans (such as Silver, Gold, and Platinum) so you can purchase different levels of customer service according to your budget?

Chapter Eleven
Enabling Technologies for ASPs

355. Do you need only low-level encryption on your ASP's VPN? Can it be accomplished inexpensively with encryption software on PCs?

356. Will the ASP need to encrypt transmissions from your remote users using encryption software on their laptops or other devices? Is the encryption software on the laptops compatible with the encryption in the routers?

357. If you require router-based encryption on your ASP's VPN, are all involved routers compatible and use the same type of encryption?

358. If you require router-based encryption on your ASP's VPN, is your anticipated network traffic light enough that it will not cause bottlenecks?

359. If you will use encryption located in firewalls, is the encryption on all firewalls compatible and from the same vendor?

360. If you will use encryption located in firewalls and must support remote users, is the remote users' encryption compatible with the encryption used in the firewalls?

361. If you will use encryption located in firewalls, will your anticipated network traffic be light enough that it will not create bottlenecks?

362. Do you need highly secure encryption capable of processing high traffic volumes? If so, can you afford VPN-specific boxes?

363. How will various factors like packet size, compression, complexity of the encryption algorithm, and number of simultaneous network users affect the performance of the ASP's VPN equipment?

364. If any of these factors unacceptably degrade performance, what will the ASP do to meet your VPN performance requirements?

365. Do you need to bypass the ASP's primary telecommunications network to transfer dense data quickly between storage repositories?

366. Do your users need to share storage and servers across LANs and WANs?

367. Do you need 100% data availability?

368. Do you need automatic data redundancy and backups, and easy maintenance of nearby disaster recovery copies?

369. Do you need centralized management of storage?

370. Do you need to consolidate storage in one or a few locations to save labor time and cost, and to ensure the most recent and accurate data is available?

371. Do you need flexible and serviceable storage configurations?

372. Do you need storage that is easy to scale?

373. Do you need automated data monitoring and management tools that track trends, foresee potential problems like a disk failure, and preempt failures or service degradation by automatically, say, "hot switching" to a replacement disk?

374. Do you need affordable deployment of remote mirrored arrays so data can be automatically backed up, transferred, and recovered at both local and remote sites for better disaster recovery?

375. Do you need storage that dynamically switches users and applications to backup servers to improve application availability dramatically?

376. If you require any or all of these storage services from your ASP, can you lease SAN storage from your ASP?

377. If you have a SAN in-house, can your ASP or SSP manage it?

378. Do you need to serve files superefficiently to users?

379. Does your ASP or SSP offer NAS to serve files faster?

380. To cut costs and reduce management, do you need a storage specialist to load your customer data onto an off-site storage platform in a data center, periodically back it up, and create archive copies of data and store them in a secure environment like a fireproof safe?

381. Can such a provider be located within *10 miles* of the site where the data is located?

382. Do you need a storage specialist to manage your in-house storage infrastructures as in a traditional outsourcing arrangement?

383. Do you need outsourced disaster recovery services?

384. Do you need to lease warehouses to store hard-copy documents that legally must be retained for fixed periods?

385. Can you lease any or all of these storage services from an SSP?

386. If you are an SMB or dotcom, does simplified management and cost savings merit outsourcing storage to an SSP?

387. If you are a G2000, can you save money by outsourcing all or part of your storage to an SSP?

388. Do you need access to data, applications, and people in your enterprise from a common interface?

389. Do your users need to "personalize" their own version of that interface to display only the applications, information, and personnel they deal with in their company role?

390. Do your users need to toggle between applications on their desktops without exiting one then opening another, and without having multiple windows open at the same time?

391. Do your users need to access multiple data repositories and collaborative tools like chat rooms located on the public Internet simultaneously?

392. Do your users need a common interface to a shared commerce environment based on a virtual community?

393. Do you need to unite a defined group of suppliers, business partners, and vendors around a common objective or business need in a B2B environment?

394. Would obtaining any of these services merit leasing an enterprise portal from your ASP?

395. Would you prefer to obtain hosted services from an ASP via the ASP's own enterprise portal?

396. Do you need hosted wireless functionality?

397. Are you a software vendor or integrator that needs existing or developing applications to be wireless enabled?

398. Are you a wireless service provider or Internet portal that needs to lease general-purpose wireless applications to resell to consumers?

399. Are you a corporation that needs to lease custom wireless applications to empower your mobile employees?

400. Would obtaining any or all of these wireless services merit using a WASP?

401. Could you get more affordable or value-added wireless service from a WASP or from a small Web integrator that develops its own wireless applications and teams with an infrastructure service provider to host wireless applications?

402. If you are a G2000, could you get more affordable or value-added wireless service from a WASP or from a large SI offering hosted wireless services using its own ASP back end?

403. If you are a large wireless service provider, could you get more affordable or value-added wireless service from a WASP or from a large SI offering hosted wireless services using its own ASP back end?

404. If you are a small wireless service provider, could you get more affordable or value-added wireless service from a WASP or some other provider?

405. With wireless technology changing so fast, would you rather lease hosted wireless services from an ASP whose core competence is not wireless, or from a WASP whose core competence is wireless?

Chapter Twelve
The ASP Channel

406. Are you willing to work hand-in-hand with an SI ASP to develop a hosted solution that exactly meets your unique requirements and helps the SI ASP refine its ASP business and technology model?

407. How much of that solution will you let the SI ASP "productize" and resell to other customers?

408. If the SI ASP has teamed with a TBA to sell hosted services through the TBA, does that help or hurt the value proposition for you?

409. In such a situation, is the SI or TBA responsible for customer service, technical support, and customization of the hosted services?

410. If the TBA provides these services, is it experienced and qualified in doing so?

411. If the ISV ASP sells both installed and hosted applications, is it pitching a hosted solution to get you to commit later to a more expensive, installed solution?

412. If the ISV ASP sells both installed and hosted applications, is the customer service and technical support for the hosted applications adequate for your requirements?

413. If you are considering leasing hosted services from any channel player, is the player offering the services defensively to keep its customers for installed solutions from leasing hosted ones from another provider?

414. If so, even if the channel player understands your business and has an existing relationship with you, is its value proposition better than one from, say, an FSP or some other nonchannel player?

Chapter Thirteen
What's Ahead for ASPs?

415. How will your ASP's behavior, in the context of the industry maturation cycle, affect your business relationship with it? Is it just launched? Trying to go public? Already gone public? Trying to get acquired? Already acquired? One of the few leading—or many lagging—ASPs in its chosen niche?

416. Is your ASP's data center on track to being state-of-the-art in two or three years—with vastly improved reliability, scalability, manageability, security, and interoperability?

417. Is your ASP on track to supplying wide area storage in two or three years? Do you need this type of storage?

418. Is your ASP's network on track to using methods like MPLS in the next two or three years? Do you need such capabilities?

419. Before leasing hosted services, can you afford to wait two to three years for Microsoft to prove the viability of its .NET subscription-based application services?

420. Would you benefit from using an ASP that supports tribal commerce in a conglomerate community?

421. Is your ASP pursuing any of these *losing* ASP strategies: Hosting single, horizontal productivity applications? Hosting common enterprise applications in popular vertical markets without further differentiating

value? Differentiating itself only with soon-to-be commodity offerings like value-added storage? Being a regional ASP without further differentiation? Being an ASP that supports multiple customers at healthy margins with no affinity program to maintain customer loyalty? Supporting one conglomerate community that takes forever to assemble members? How will its strategy impact your business?

422. Is your ASP pursuing any of these winning ASP strategies: ASPs rapidly deploying e-business infrastructures for dotcoms? FSPs offering accelerated e-business applications with integration services at competitive rates to SMBs? Small SI ASPs offering similar services to SMBs? Being a top infrastructure service provider? Being a top MSecP or MSP? Being a conglomerate community ASP that does it right and fast? How will its strategy impact your business?

ASP Organizations and Publications

ASP Industry Consortium

401 Edgewater Place, Suite 500
Wakefield, MA 01880
Phone: 781-246-9321
URL: www.aspindustry.com

The ASP Consortium's mission is to educate the marketplace, develop common definitions for the industry, serve as a forum for discussion about the industry, sponsor research in the industry, foster open standards and guidelines, and promote best practices.

WebHarbor.com —The ASP Industry Portal

573 Maude Court
Sunnyvale, CA 94085-2803
Phone: 408-991-9400
URL: www.webharbor.com

Webharbor.com is an ASP portal with a directory of ASPs, archived articles, discussion forums, and other resources.

ASPIndustryNews.com

4941 S. 78th Street E Avenue
Tulsa, OK 74145
Phone: 877/215-9878
URL: www.editor@aspindustrynews.com

ASPIndustryNews.com is a leading newsletter on ASP trends, products, companies, and other news.

Bibliography

Chapter 1

Harney, John. "The Virtual Dimensions of Hosted Applications." *Intelligent Enterprise* March 1, 2000.

Chapter 2

Harney, John. "Virtual Document Management—Part 1." *inform* June 1999.

Gruhn, Marty. "Application Service Providers Market Pioneers Define Strategies and Business Models." Market strategy report. Boston: Summit Strategies, March 1999 (http://www.summitstrat.com).

Gruhn, Marty. "Internet Applications Hosting Goes to Market." Market strategy report. Boston: Summit Strategies, December 1998 (http://www.summit-strat.com).

Kucharvy, Tom. "Virtual Workplaces as the Future of Business Application Software—Part 2: Building Portals around Hosted Applications." Market strategy report. Boston: Summit Strategies, October 1999 (http://www.summitstrat.com).

Nickolas, Stewart. "IBM Application Framework for e-Business: Application Hosting Services." 2000 (http://www-4.ibm.com/software/developer/library/ahs).

Chapter 3

"Genesys—Sun's Platform Vision for the Networked Data Center." White paper. 2000 (http://www.sun.com).

Ferengul, Corey. "Management Service Provider Benefits." Service Management Strategies research note. Stamford, CT: Meta Group, August 15, 2000.

Kauffman, Jeff. "Management Service Providers Unite." *ASP Industry News.* October 19, 1999 (http://www.webharbor.com).

Chapter 4

Application Service Provider Industry Consortium (ASPIC) Best Practices Committee, *A Guide to the ASP Delivery Model.* Wakefield, MA: ASP Industry April 14, 2000.

Schmidt, Eric O. "Will an ASP Protect Your Business Operations? Questions to Ask Any Potential Provider Before Signing an Agreement—Parts I, II, III." *Alentis Trade Journal* June 28, 2000.

Schmidt, Eric O. "Preparing for Calamity: What Natural Disaster, Staffing and Security Issues Your Company Must Examine Before Contracting with an ASP." *Alentis Trade Journal* August 1, 2000.

Chapter 6

Harney, John. "Lost Among The ASPs." *Intelligent Enterprise* February 9, 2000.

McCabe, Laurie. "Bringing Order to the Chaos: Segmenting Service Providers in the ASP Ecosystem." Market strategy report. Boston: Summit Strategies, May 2000 (http://www.summitstrat.com).

Chapter 7

Phone interview with Charles Kolodgy, Research Manager/Internet Security, International Data Corporation (IDC) consulting, December 3, 2000.

Bolar, Suman. "Ask Your ASP Tough Security Questions." *TechRepublic* IT portal. March 13, 2000 (http://www.techrepublic.com).

Flanagan, Thomas, and Elias Safadie. "Internet Security Primer." Tech Guide series. The Applied Technologies Group, 1997 (http://www .techguide.com).

Lawson, Loraine. "Outsourcing Security: Tips for Finding and Dealing with Vendors." *TechRepublic* IT portal. May 31, 2000 (http://www. techrepublic. com).

Schmidt, Eric O. "Will an ASP Protect Your Business Operations? Questions to Ask Any Potential Provider Before Signing an Agreement—Parts I, II, III." *Alentis Trade Journal* June 28, 2000.

Sheesley, John. "Understanding Firewalls." *The Locksmith* section of the *TechRepublic* IT portal. April 6, 1999 (http://www.techrepublic.com).

van Wyk, Kenneth. "Managed Security: Boom or Bandwagon?" *Information Security* June 2000.

Weeks, Andy. "Devices for Securing Your Corporate Data." *TechRepublic* IT portal. June 16, 1999 (http://www.techrepublic.com).

Chapter 8

Application Service Provider Industry Consortium (ASPIC). *Application Service Provider End-User Guide to Service Level Agreements.* 2000 (http://www.aspindustry.org).

Wilson, Warren. "Promises to Keep: SLAs Become SOP for ASPs." Market strategy report. Boston: Summit Strategies, March 2000 (http://www.summitstrat.com).

"The ABCs of SLAs." *ASP Industry News* section of *Webharbor.com* ASP industry portal. November 6, 2000 (http:www.WebHarbor.com).

Chapter 9

Harney, John. "The Price of ASP Cost Models." *e-Doc* July/August 2000.

Harney, John. "Document Management ASP Cost Models." *e-Doc* January/February 2001.

McCabe, Laurie. "ASP Pricing Strategies: The Push to Profitability." Market strategy report. Boston: Summit Strategies, November 2000 (http://www.summitstrat.com).

Chapter 10

Harney, John. "CRM Workflow: Knowledge Management with a Backbone." *Intelligent Enterprise* September 14, 1999.

McCabe, Laurie. "Enterprise Solution Vendors—Take Two on Internet Applications Hosting." Market strategy report. Summit Strategies, August 1999.

Chapter 11

Barker, Richard. "The Next Step for Distributed Computing: Storage Area Networks." *DM Direct*, DM Review.com's electronic newsletter, February 15, 1999 (http://www.dmreview.com).

DiMarzio, Jennifer, and Tom Kucharvy. "Wireless ASPs (WASPs) Swarm the Scene." Market strategy report. Boston: Summit Strategies, August 2000 (http://www.summitstrat.com).

Egan, B., K. Dulaney, and E. Purchase. *How to Build a Wireless Office: The Next Wireless Revolution.* Strategic analysis report. Stamford, CT: Gartner Group, February 4, 2000.

Harney, John. "Virtual Storage—The New Model for Access to Enterprise Applications." *inform* September/October 1999.

"How Does Wireless Technology Work?" In: Frequently Asked Questions, Cellular Telecommunications Industry Association. 2000 (http://www.wow-com.com).

McIntyre, Scott. "Demystifying SAN and NAS." *DM Review* June 2000 (http://www.dmreview.com).

Peterson, Don. "Getting Ready for SAN: How to Intelligently Begin Implementing a Storage Area Network." *DM Direct* August 15, 1999 (http://www.dmreview.com).

Potts, Gary. "Using SAN to Improve HSM." *DM Direct* March 17, 2000 (http://www.dmreview.com).

Third Generation ('3G') Wireless (http://www.fcc.gov/3G).

"Wireless Internet: What the 3G Challenge Means for U.S. Competitiveness." 2000 (http://www.ntia.doc.gov/ntiahome/threeg/3gintro.htm).

Chapter 12

DiMarzio, Jennifer, and Tom Kucharvy. "Integrators and Outsourcers Chart a Path to IAH Riches, Part One: Systems and Network/Productivity Integrators Take to the IAH Skies." Market strategy report. Boston: Summit Strategies, January 2000 (http://www.summitstrat.com).

DiMarzio, Jennifer, and Tom Kucharvy. "Integrators and Outsourcers Chart a Path to IAH Riches, Part Two: Systems Vendors Juggle Competing Aims." Market strategy report. Boston: Summit Strategies, January 2000 (http://www summitstrat.com).

McCabe, Laurie. "Role of the Reseller in the ASP Ecosystem, Part One: The Service Provider Perspective." Market strategy report. Boston: Summit Strategies, May 2000 (http://www.summitstrat.com).

McCabe, Laurie. "Role of the Reseller in the ASP Ecosystem, Part Two: Reseller Considerations." Market strategy report. Boston: Summit Strategies, June 2000 (http://www.summitstrat.com).

Chapter 13

Bartash, Jeffry. "ISP for the ISPs." *CBS MarketWatch* March 19, 1999 (http://www.cbs.marketwatch.com).

Clark, Charles. "SAN Meets WAN." *Network World* March 19, 2001.

Gruhn, Marty. "MySAP.com—Can SAP Hit a Home Run with a Millennium Triple Play?" Market strategy report. Boston: Summit Strategies, December 1999 (http://www.summitstrat.com).

Guzman, Rodney. "Simple Object Access Protocol." *SQL Magazine* July 11, 2000.

Harney, John. "Internet Promotes Guns for Hire." *Knowledge Management* October 1999.

Harney, John. "Virtual Conglomerate Communities." *Knowledge Management* February 2000.

Jones, Allen. "The Simple Object Access Protocol." *IIS Administrator UPDATE* May 9, 2000.

MPLS FAQ. MPLS Resource Center. 2000 (http://www.mplsrc.com).

Sheldon, William. "Get Ready for SOAP on a ROPE." *SQL Magazine* July 25, 2000.

Smith, Mark. "Delivering on the .NET Vision—What to Expect in the Next 2 Years." Windows 2000 December 2000.

Smith, Mark. "Microsoft.NET—Is This Internet Strategy the Next Big Thing?" Windows 2000 October 2000.

Sosinsky, Barry. "The Data Center of the Next Millennium." *Windows 2000 Magazine Online* March 2000 (http://www.win2000mag.com).

Thurrott, Paul. ".NET: A Strategy, Not a Product." Windows 2000 November 16, 2000.

Glossary

AAA (ASP Application Aggregator)

A type of xSP that bundles diverse applications from multiple ASPs, software vendors, and related providers behind a common interface through which customers can access the applications for one bill per one SLA from the AAA.

ADSL (Asymmetric Digital Subscriber Line)

A type of xDSL suitable for users who access the Internet a lot but send over it a little because it accesses transmissions from a broadband network at 1.5 to 8 Mbps but sends transmissions to that network at 16 to 640 Kbps.

ASP (Application Service Provider)

A partnership among players with expertise in hardware, networking, software applications, and vertical markets for the purpose of leasing hosted applications to remote customers over broadband networks.

ATM (Asynchronous Transfer Mode)

A type of packet switched networking technology called "cell relay" that permits the fastest transmission of voice, data, and multimedia across LANs, CANs, MANs, and WANs, as well as advanced traffic management and different "quality of service" for different customers.

BAM (Brick-and-Mortar)

A traditional company that does business without e-commerce technologies, processes, and practices, and owns much actual business infrastructure like warehouses and IT infrastructure like legacy computing systems that impede its implementation of e-commerce.

B2B (Business-to-Business)

E-commerce usually along a "supply chain," in which vendors and their partners and suppliers buy and sell goods and services prior to the shipment of the end product.

B2C (Business-to-Consumer)

E-Commerce in which consumers usually buy goods and services from a vendor Web site and receive customer service virtually over the Internet.

Cable Modems

Broadband network technology that delivers voice, video, and data over customers' cable links via modems installed at the customer premises and is cheaper and slower than leased lines.

CAN (Campus Area Network)

A telecommunications network that links computers and related devices, is often broadband, and services a campus area like a college campus or business park.

CLEC (Competitive Local Exchange Carrier)

A private telecommunications provider in the United States, created after the Telecommunications Act of 1996 to compete with incumbent telecommunications providers in offering long-distance voice/video/data services.

Client/server

A flexible and scalable computing model in which controlling client computers (usually PCs) access data and applications on controlled server computers (can be PCs but often are minicomputers and mainframes) and in which clients can also function as servers and vice versa.

Coopetition

A business practice in which companies simultaneously cooperate as partners on some projects and compete as adversaries on others.

CRM (Customer Relationship Management)

When a company combines best business practices, optimized work processes, apt technology, and relevant knowledge to better service customers and retain their business.

DASD (Direct Access Storage Device)

Magnetic disk storage devices with high capacity and fast retrieval times that randomly access any data directly and quicker than if they sequentially accessed it—initially used in mainframes and minicomputers but later came to be used in hard disk drives for PCs and RAID.

Dotcom

A largely virtual company that can quickly implement, or currently do business using, e-commerce technologies, processes, and practices because it has little actual business infrastructure like warehouses and IT ones like legacy computing systems.

Downmarket

A sales strategy in which a company that previously sold exclusively to a few large customers for high sales margins starts selling to many smaller customers for lower sales margins.

EDI (Electronic Data Interchange)

Direct computer-to-computer transfer of large volumes of business data often over expensive proprietary networks and most commonly carried out by supply chain members for B2B e-commerce.

ERP (Enterprise Resource Planning)

Complex, expensive software sold in interrelated modules for an extended enterprise's different business processes (such as human resources, financial, engineering, and so forth) that requires much integration effort but dramatically improves intra-company and supply chain efficiency.

Extranet

A company's private network that often exploits Internet infrastructure to securely share, typically along a supply chain, its information or operations with suppliers, vendors, partners, customers, or other businesses and may use different types of secure networks such as VPNs to do so.

Fiber optics

The medium and technology associated with the transmission of data as light impulses along a glass or plastic wire or fiber that allows for much faster transmission speed than the conventional copper wire traditionally used for telephone networks.

Frame Relay

A "fast packet switching" network technology in which transmission data is broken down into uniform packets of content and such "overhead" information as the packet's destination to improve transmission speed by reducing overhead and to allow voice and data to be transmitted over WANs.

FSP (Full Service Provider)

A type of ASP that's flexible but expensive because it offers deep solutions in markets/applications, 50% generic hosted applications, value-added services, and one-stop shopping.

G.Lite

A slower, less expensive version of ADSL with access speeds of 1.5 Mbps and send speeds of 500 Kbps that can accommodate most residential end user applications.

Global 2000

A large international company with revenues among the top 2,000 companies in the world that typically owns expensive, state-of-the-art information technology featuring enterprise software and global broadband networks.

HSM (Hierarchical Storage Management)

A storage strategy that conserves cost by storing frequently retrieved data on faster, more expensive, media and infrequently retrieved data on slower, less expensive media and can migrate data to progressively slower, less expensive media as it is accessed less and less.

Interleaving

To conserve costs when using Frame Relay networks, this technique intersperses voice data within a data stream and data into the pauses in voice transmissions to permit fast data transfer and continuous voice transmission over the same technology.

Interworking

Using protocol translation devices and network engineering to integrate ATM with older networks like Frame Relay so network service providers don't have to build out completely new fiber-optic infrastructures for "pure" ATM.

Intranet

An organization's private network (usually a WAN) that uses Internet protocols and includes firewalls and connections through gateway computers to the public Internet that nonemployees with security clearance can use to access certain company resources and employees can use to access the public Internet.

ISDN (Integrated Services Digital Network)

An inexpensive digital networking technology that carries voice, video, and data over phone lines at either 128Kbps or 1.544Mbps.

IXC (International Exchange Carrier)

A global telecommunications provider, usually called a "long-distance carrier," that controls connections between local exchanges in different geographic areas and competes with other types of carriers in offering long-distance voice/video/data services.

LAN (Local Area Network)

A group of computers, associated devices like printers and the common, usually narrowband, telecommunications line that links them within a small geographic area like an office building.

MAN (Metropolitan Area Network)

A telecommunications network that is usually broadband and links computers and related equipment in a geographic area larger than that covered by a LAN but smaller than that covered by a WAN and usually limited to the vicinity of a city.

MPLS (Multiprotocol Label Switching)

A networking technique that lets routers make routing decisions based on the contents of a simple label that accompanies the data packets instead of performing complex route lookups in routers' tables of destination IP addresses. May compete with ATM by enabling multimode transmission over an all-IP network in the future.

MSecP (Managed Security Providers)

A type of xSP that leases virtual IT security services to multiple ASPs and other service providers.

NAS (Network Attached Storage)

Storage devices that attach to any kind of network, but usually to SANs, to super-efficiently serve files for better storage system performance, reliability, and space management.

PDA (Personal Digital Assistant)

A handheld computer that lets you use a stylus and screen and/or a keyboard to store, access, and organize data like addresses and phone numbers, although more sophisticated PDAs can run word processing and other applications, provide e-mail and Internet access, and exchange data with a desktop or laptop computer.

PVC (Permanent Virtual Circuit)

A network connection between source and destination in which routing decisions are made when the connection is created for greater throughput speed but that is incapable of dynamic routing.

RAID (Redundant Array of Inexpensive Discs)

An arrangement of smaller hard drives that lets the user store the same data on different drives, although the drives appear to the operating system as a single logical hard drive, which results in better storage system performance and fault tolerance.

RBOC (Regional Bell Operating Company)

A regional US telecommunications carrier created as a result of the breakup of AT&T by a 1983 US Federal Court consent decree and given the right to provide local phone service—recently also permitted to offer long-distance voice/video/data service in certain circumstances.

RTO (Recovery Time Objective)

Windows of time, usually measured in hourly increments, in which ASP customers must recover their applications or data after a system failure.

SAN (Storage Area Network)

A robust storage network that operates independently of primary computer networks for better performance and that's comprised primarily of RAID storage devices linked by broadband fiber channel to servers so that any server can access any storage device.

SCSI (Small Computer System Interface)

Standard electronic interfaces that let PCs and laptops communicate with peripheral hardware like printers faster and more flexibly than previous interfaces.

SLA (Service Level Agreement)

A contract specifying the deliverables, terms, and conditions between ASPs, related service providers, and consumers that defines specifics such as services the provider will supply the customer, the provider's reporting requirements to the customer, and penalties to the provider for nonperformance.

SMB (Small- to Medium-Size Business)

A small- to mid-size company that is a good candidate for hosted services because typically its cash flow is so limited that it cannot afford to own state-of-the-art IT systems featuring enterprise software and global broadband networks that would make it competitive with G2000s.

SOAP (Simple Object Access Protocol)

The protocol that enables users to pass data through XML-based messages in a distributed environment among dissimilar networks and operating systems to create a cross-platform e-business environment.

SOHO (Small Office Home Office)

A small or home-based business that is a good candidate for low-end, less-expensive network services like xDSL and cable modems.

SONET (Synchronous Optical Network)

An American telecommunications standard that lets carriers with optical networks transmit multiple signals from different sources at different speeds through a synchronous, optical hierarchy so that older networks can interoperate with newer optical ones.

SSP (Storage Service Provider)

A type of xSP that leases both storage infrastructure and personnel to multiple ASPs and other companies.

SVC (Switched Virtual Circuit)

A network connection between source and destination in which routing decisions are made en route at linking devices so that throughput speed results from dynamic routing, not from less handling.

TBA (Trusted Business Advisor)

A company that intimately understands a particular market or application for which an ASP coalition wants to offer a hosted service and that helps the coalition penetrate the target market, often by promoting sales of the hosted services into its existing customer base.

Token Ring

A LAN cabled in a ring topology that passes a "token" from computer to computer to enable each to send data over the network.

Upmarket

A sales strategy in which a company that previously sold to many small customers for low sales margins starts selling to fewer larger customers for higher sales margins.

UPS (Uninterruptible Power Supply)

A device that provides power independent of the local power grid and, in the event of a power outage, powers all IT equipment in an ASP data center.

VAR (Value-Added Reseller)

A channel player that may offer integration services in addition to reselling software and hardware from original manufacturers to specific vertical or horizontal markets.

VC (Venture Capitalist)

A financial company that invests funds at high risk in start-up IT companies that have high profit potential.

VPN (Virtual Private Network)

High-capacity, secure networks that, often because much of their physical connectivity is already provided by the Internet, are much less expensive to build than private WANs and inherently more pervasive than leased lines.

WAN (Wide Area Network)

A telecommunications network, either narrowband or broadband, that spans a broader geographic area than MANs or CANs and can include public networks.

WASP (Wireless ASPs)

A type of xSP that hosts its own custom wireless applications and wireless-enables existing installed or hosted applications for ASPs, network service providers, and corporations.

WDM (Wave Division Multiplexing)

A networking technology that, in using electronic equipment at either end of a fiber-optic line, generates multiple wavelengths of light over the same cable to carry up to 30 times more data so users get greater bandwidth at much lower costs and providers can more easily increase the capacity of fiber-optic networks.

Workflow

A software application that maps and automates an organization's business processes so workers can process and route work items to other workers for additional processing or to administrators for approval.

WORM (Write Once Read Many)

An optical disc technology that writes data once only to discs that can be read by WORM readers for the purpose of creating and accessing long-term records.

x.25

A networking protocol that lets computers on different public networks communicate through an intermediary computer but handles data packets excessively to achieve acceptable routing accuracy and error detection but that can result in slower transmission speeds.

xDSL (Digital Subscriber Line)

A relatively inexpensive digital networking technology that uses the Local Loop copper infrastructure so users can receive broadband voice, video, and data transmissions over their phone line via an xDSL modem installed at the customer premises.

xSP

A generic term for one of the virtual service providers other than ASPs, like MSPs, SSps, and MsecPs, in the ASP industry.

Index

Credits

Permission was received from the following resources in the preparation of this book. Credit lines are alphabetized according to copyright holder.

1. "eBay Case Study," *2Roam Web site* (www.2Roam.com)

2. "Agiliti Inc: An ISV to ASP Case Study of Achieve Online Services," www.agiliti.com

3. "Preparing for Calamity: What Natural Disaster, Staffing and Security Issues Your Company Must Examine Before Contracting an ASP," by Eric O. Schmidt (August 1, 2000), *Alentis Trade Journal*

4. "Will an ASP Protect Your Business Operations? Questions to Ask Any Potential Provider Before Signing an Agreement—Parts I, II, and III," by Eric O. Schmidt (June 28, 2000), *Alentis Trade Journal*

5. "A Guide to the ASP Delivery Model," by Application Service Provider Industry Consortium (ASPIC) (April 14, 2000), *Best Practices Committee*

6. "Application Service Provider End-User Guide to Service Level Agreements," by Application Service Provider Industry Consortium (ASPIC), ASPIC Web site

7. "Internet Security Primer," (1997) a Technology Guide exclusively found at www.techguide.com, produced by The Applied Technology Group, Inc. (ATG)

8. "ISP for the ISPs," by Jeffry Bartash (March 19, 1999), *CBS.MarketWatch.com*

9. "How Does Wireless Technology Work?" entry in Frequently Asked Questions, *Cellular Telecommunications Industry Association* (CTIA) Web site

10. "Lost Among the ASPs," by John Harney (February 9, 2000) originally appeared in *Intelligent Enterprise magazine,* CMP Media LLC

11. "The Virtual Dimensions of Hosted Applications," by John Harney (March 1, 2000) originally appeared in *Intelligent Enterprise magazine,* CMP Media LLC

12. "CRM Workflow: Knowledge Management with a Backbone," by John Harney (September 14, 1999) originally appeared in *Intelligent Enterprise* magazine, CMP Media LLC

13. "Vertical Networks Case Study," *Corio Web site* (www.corio.com)

14. "The Next Step for Distributed Computing: Storage Area Networks," by Richard Barker (February 15, 1999), *DM Direct,* DMReview's electronic newsletter

15. "Demystifying SAN and NAS," by Scott McIntyre (June 2000), DM Review

16. "Getting Ready for SAN: How to Intelligently Begin Implementing a Storage Area Network," by Don Peterson (August 15, 1999), *DM Direct,* DMReview's electronic newsletter

17. "Using SAN to Improve HSM," by Gary Potts (March 17, 2000), *DM Direct,* DMReview's electronic newsletter

18. "The Price of ASP Cost Models," by John Harney (July/August 2000), *e-Doc Magazine*

19. "Document Management ASP Cost Models," by John Harney (January/February 2001), *e-Doc Magazine* Web site

20. "IBM Applications Framework for e-Business: Application Hosting Services," by Stewart Nickolas, IBM Web site library

21. "Virtual Document Management: Part 1," by John Harney (June 1999), *inform* magazine

22. "Virtual Storage—The New Model for Access to Enterprise Applications," by John Harney (September/October 1999), *inform* magazine

23. "Managed Security: Boom or Bandwagon?" by Andrew Briney (June 2000), Information Security magazine

24. "Interliant's ASP services for DataCert.com," www.interliant.com

25. "Management Service Providers Unite," by Jeff Kauffman (October 19, 1999) *ASP Industry News* section of WebHarbor.com

26. "Internet Promotes Guns for Hire," by John Harney (October 1999), *Knowledge Management* magazine

27. "Virtual Conglomerate Communities," by John Harney (February 2000), *Knowledge Management* magazine

28. Phone interview on security issues for ASPs with Charles Kolodgy (December 3, 2000), Research Manager/Internet Security, International Data Corporation (IDC) consulting

29. "Application Service Providers Market Pioneers Define Strategies and Business Models," by Marty Gruhn (March 1999), *Market Strategy Report,* Summit Strategies

30. "ASP Pricing Strategies: The Push to Profitability," by Laurie McCabe (November 2000), *Market Strategy Report,* Summit Strategies

31. "Bringing Order to the Chaos: Segmenting Service Providers in the ASP Ecosystem," by Laurie McCabe (May 2000), *Market Strategy Report,* Summit Strategies

32. "Enterprise Solution Vendors—Take Two on Internet Applications Hosting," by Laurie McCabe (August 1999), *Market Strategy Report,* Summit Strategies

33. "Integrators and Outsourcers Chart a Path to IAH Riches, Part One: Systems and Network/Productivity Integrators Take to the IAH Skies," by Jennifer DiMarzio and Tom Kucharvy (January 2000), *Market Strategy Report,* Summit Strategies

34. "Integrators and Outsourcers Chart a Path to IAH Riches, Part Two: Systems Vendors Juggle Competing Aims," by Jennifer DiMarzio and Tom Kucharvy (January 2000), *Market Strategy Report,* Summit Strategies

35. "Internet Applications Hosting Goes to Market," by Marty Gruhn (December 1998), *Market Strategy Report,* Summit Strategies

36. "MySAP.com—Can SAP Hit a Home Run with a Millenium Triple Play?" by Marty Gruhn (December 1999), *Market Strategy Report,* Summit Strategies

37. "Promises to Keep: SLAs Become SOP for ASPs," by Warren Wilson (March 2000), *Market Strategy Report,* Summit Strategies

38. "Role of the Reseller in the ASP Ecosystem, Part One: The Service Provider Perspective," by Laurie McCabe (May 2000), *Market Strategy Report,* Summit Strategies

39. "Role of the Reseller in the ASP Ecosystem, Part Two: Reseller Considerations," by Laurie McCabe (June 2000), *Market Strategy Report,* Summit Strategies

40. "Virtual Workplaces as the Future of Business Application Software—Part 2: Building Portals Around Hosted Applications," by Tom Kucharvy (October 1999), *Market Strategy Report,* Summit Strategies

41. "Wireless ASPs (WASPs) Swarm the Scene," by Jennifer DiMarzio and Tom Kucharvy (August 2000), *Market Strategy Report,* Summit Strategies

42. "Corio Case Study," Netegrity Inc. Web site (www.netegrity.com)

43. "SAN meets WAN," by Charles Clark (March 19, 2001), *Network World* magazine

44. "The Simple Object Access Protocol," by Allen Jones (May 9, 2000), *Windows 2000 Magazine's IIS Administrator UPDATE,* Penton Media Inc.

45. "Genesys—Sun's Platform Vision for the Networked Data Center," by Sun Microsystems, white paper, Sun Microsystems Web site

46. "Ask Your ASP Tough Security Questions," by Suman Bolar (March 13, 2000), *TechRepublic* IT portal

47. "Devices for Securing Your Corporate Data," by Andy Weeks (June 16, 1999), *TechRepublic* IT portal

48. "Outsourcing security: Tips for finding and dealing with vendors," by Loraine Lawson (May 31, 2000), *TechRepublic* IT portal

49. "Understanding Firewalls," by John Sheesley (April 6, 1999), *TechRepublic* IT portal

50. "The Data Center of the Next Millennium," by Barrie Sosinsky (March 2000), *Windows 2000 Magazine Online*

51. "How to Build a Wireless Office: The Next Wireless Revolution," by B. Egan, K. Dulaney, and E. Purchase (February 4, 2000), *Strategic Analysis Report,* Gartner Group

52. "Wireless Internet Today," (June 2000), Wireless Application Protocol white paper, *WAP Forum* Web site

53. "The ABCs of SLAs" (November 6, 2000) ASP *Industry News* section of WebHarbor. com

54. "JR Abbott Construction ASP Case Study" (copyright 1999-2001), *World Technology Services (WTS)*—the first J.D. Edwards Application Service Provider (ASP)

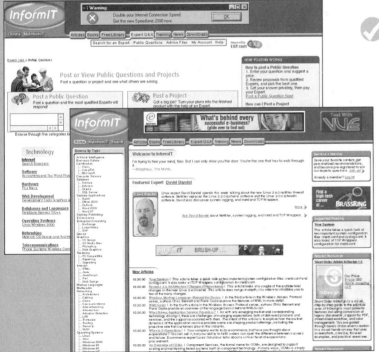

Register
Your Book

at www.aw.com/cseng/register

You may be eligible to receive:

- Advance notice of forthcoming editions of the book
- Related book recommendations
- Chapter excerpts and supplements of forthcoming titles
- Information about special contests and promotions throughout the year
- Notices and reminders about author appearances, tradeshows, and online chats with special guests

Contact us

If you are interested in writing a book or reviewing manuscripts prior to publication, please write to us at:

Editorial Department
Addison-Wesley Professional
75 Arlington Street, Suite 300
Boston, MA 02116 USA
Email: AWPro@aw.com

Addison-Wesley

Visit us on the Web: http://www.aw.com/cseng